Abstractions

Leou

Abstractions 3

ISBN : 9781088707470

nicolaslehoux.com

Abstractions

tome 3

art
Leou

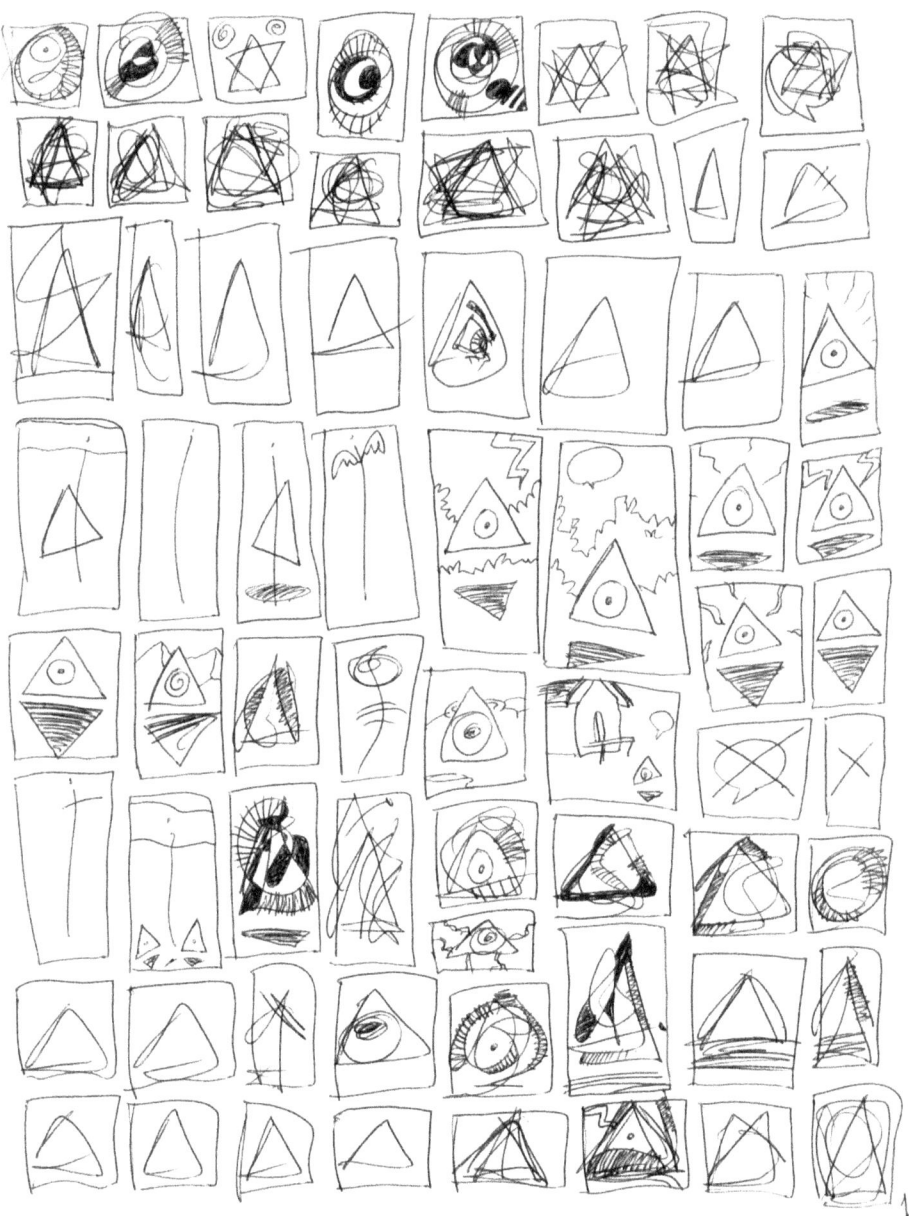

7

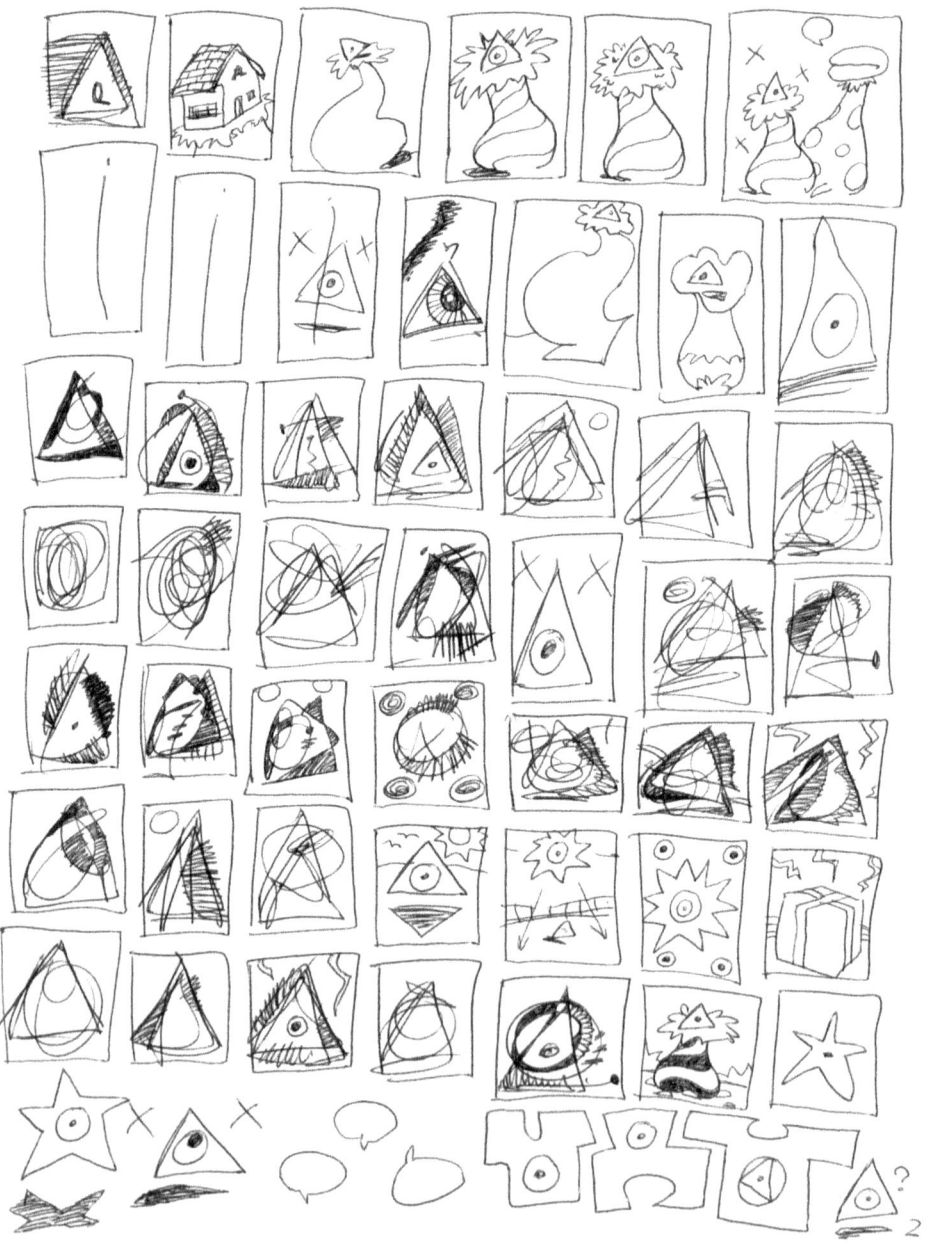

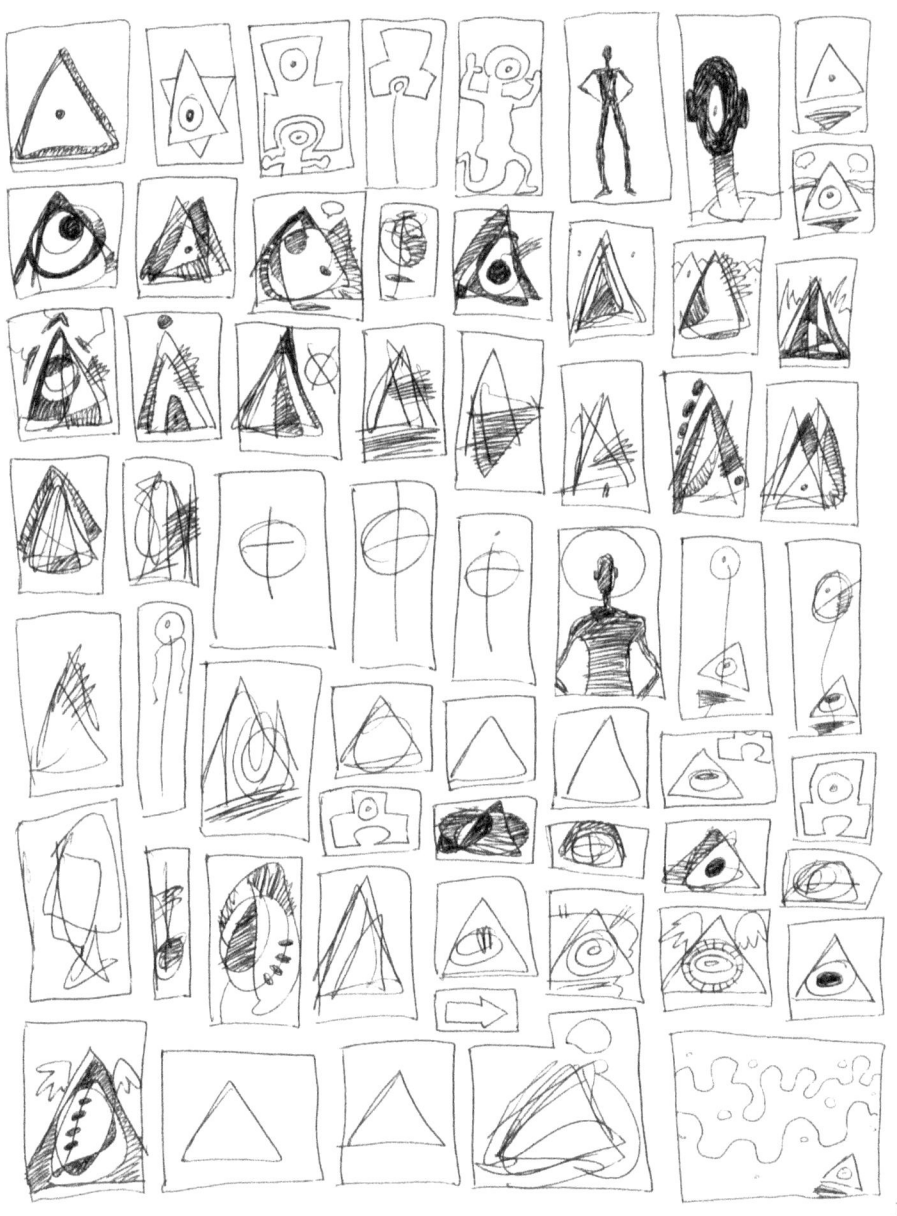

3

9

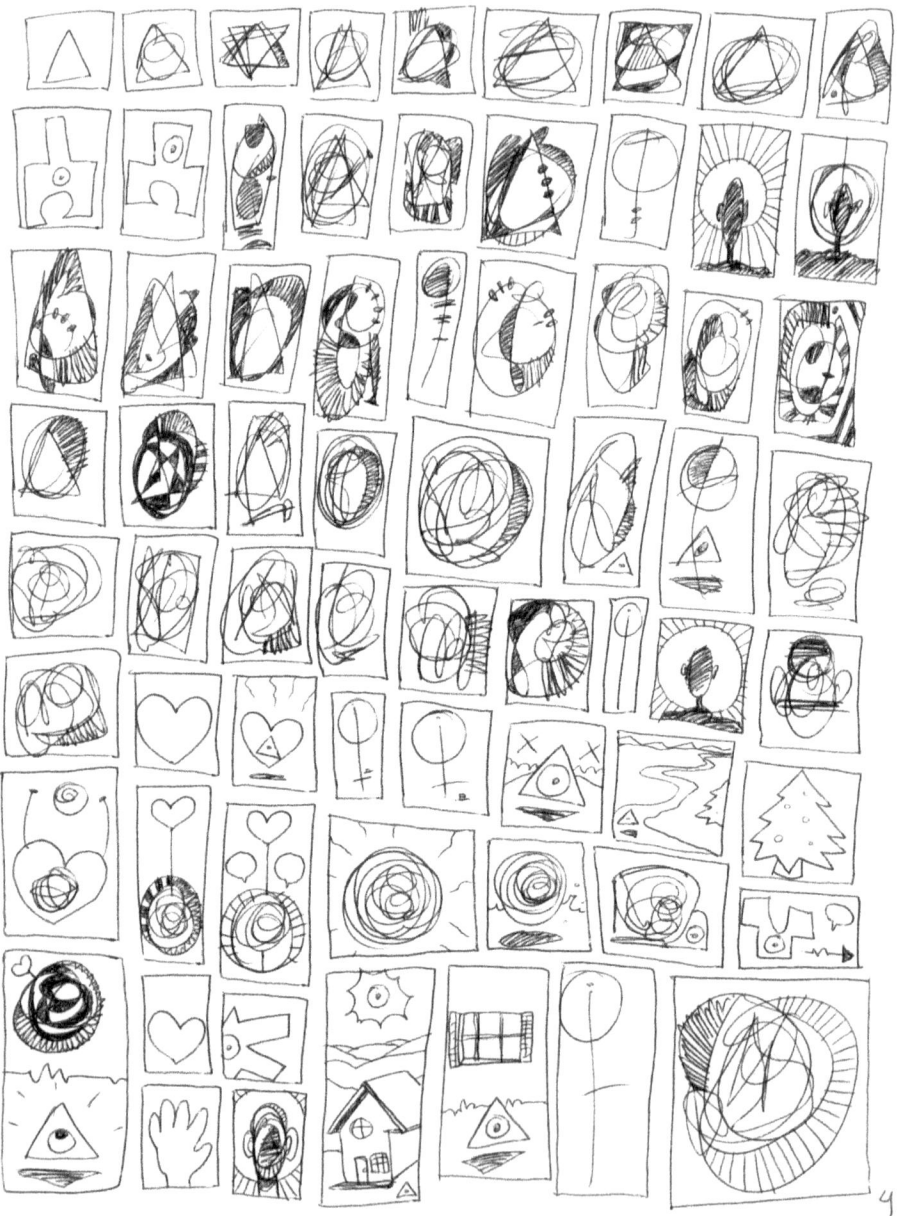

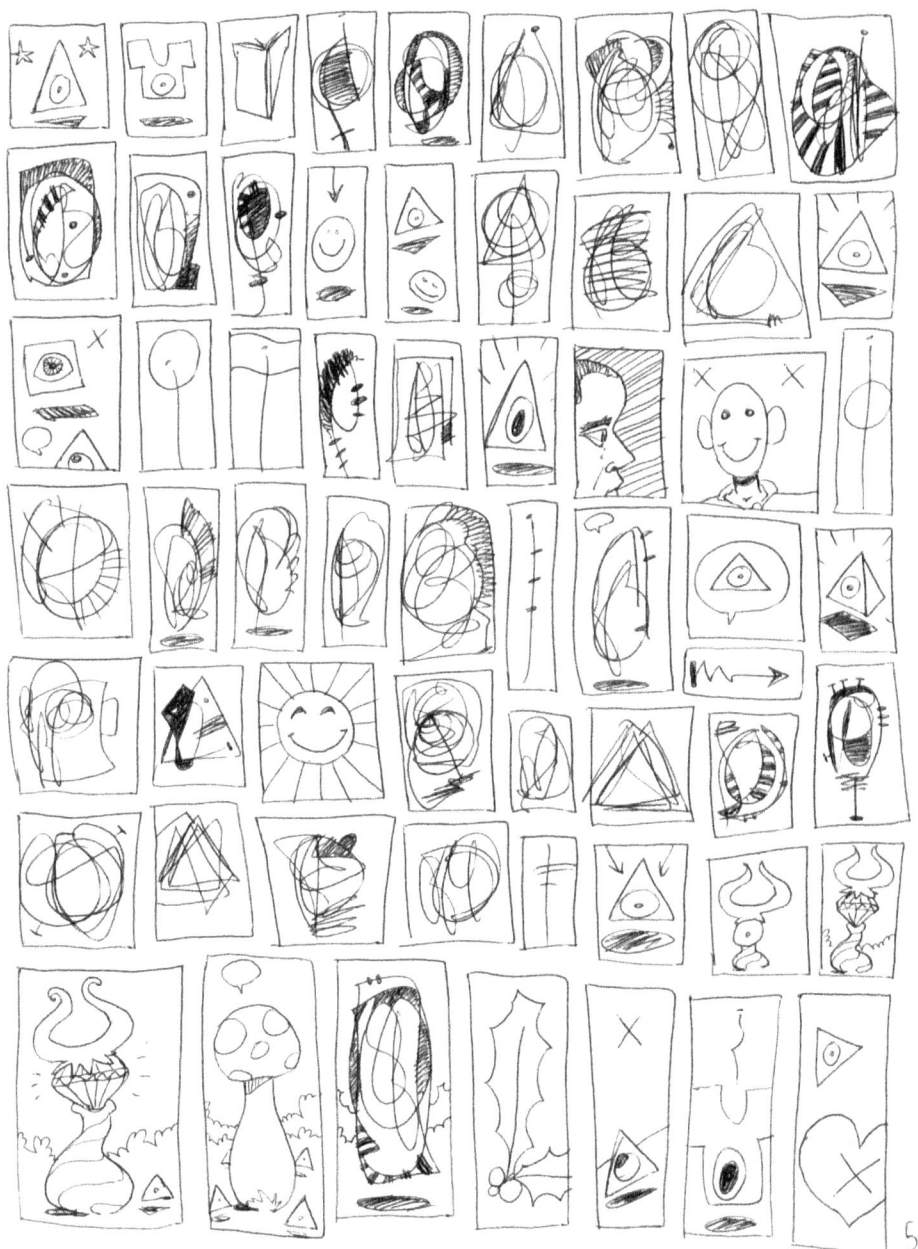

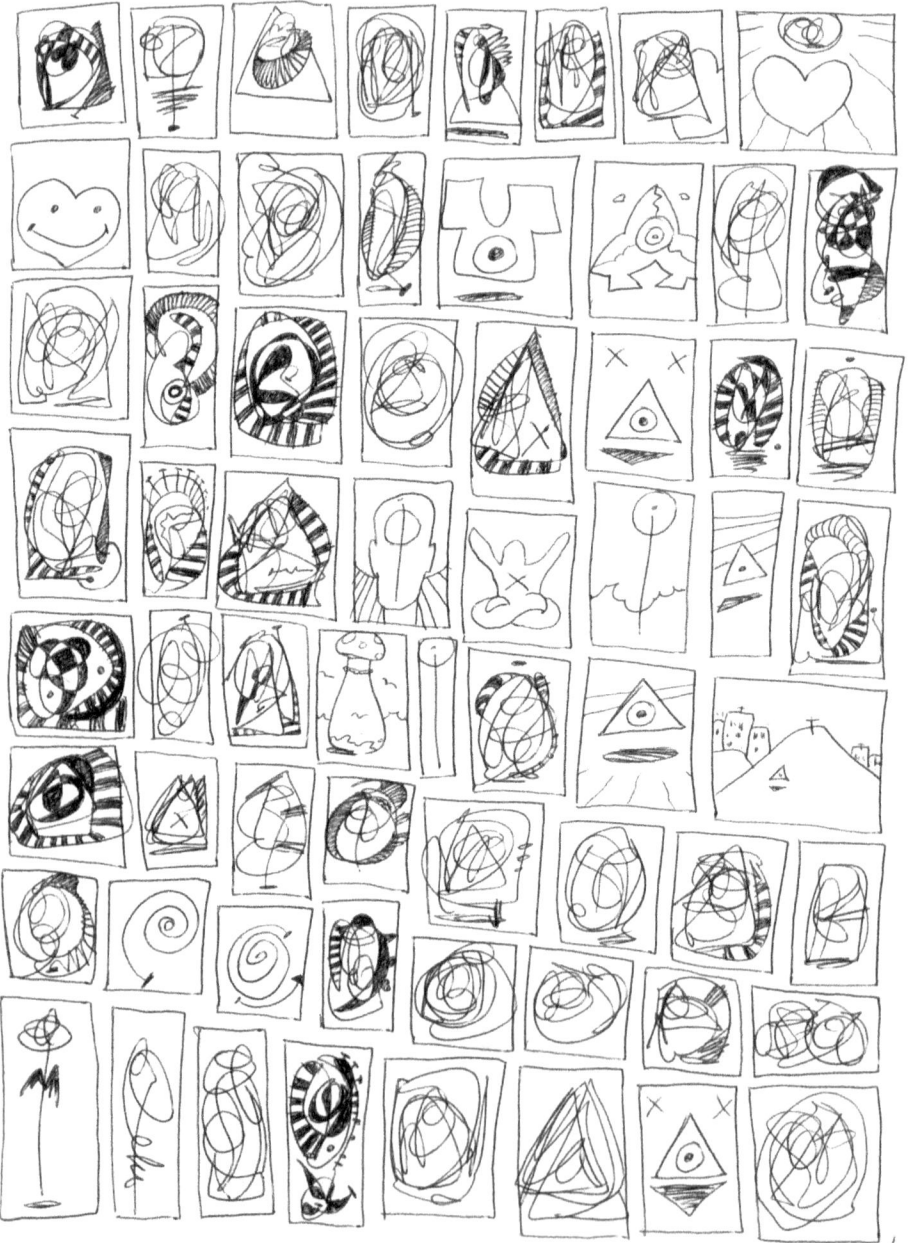

6

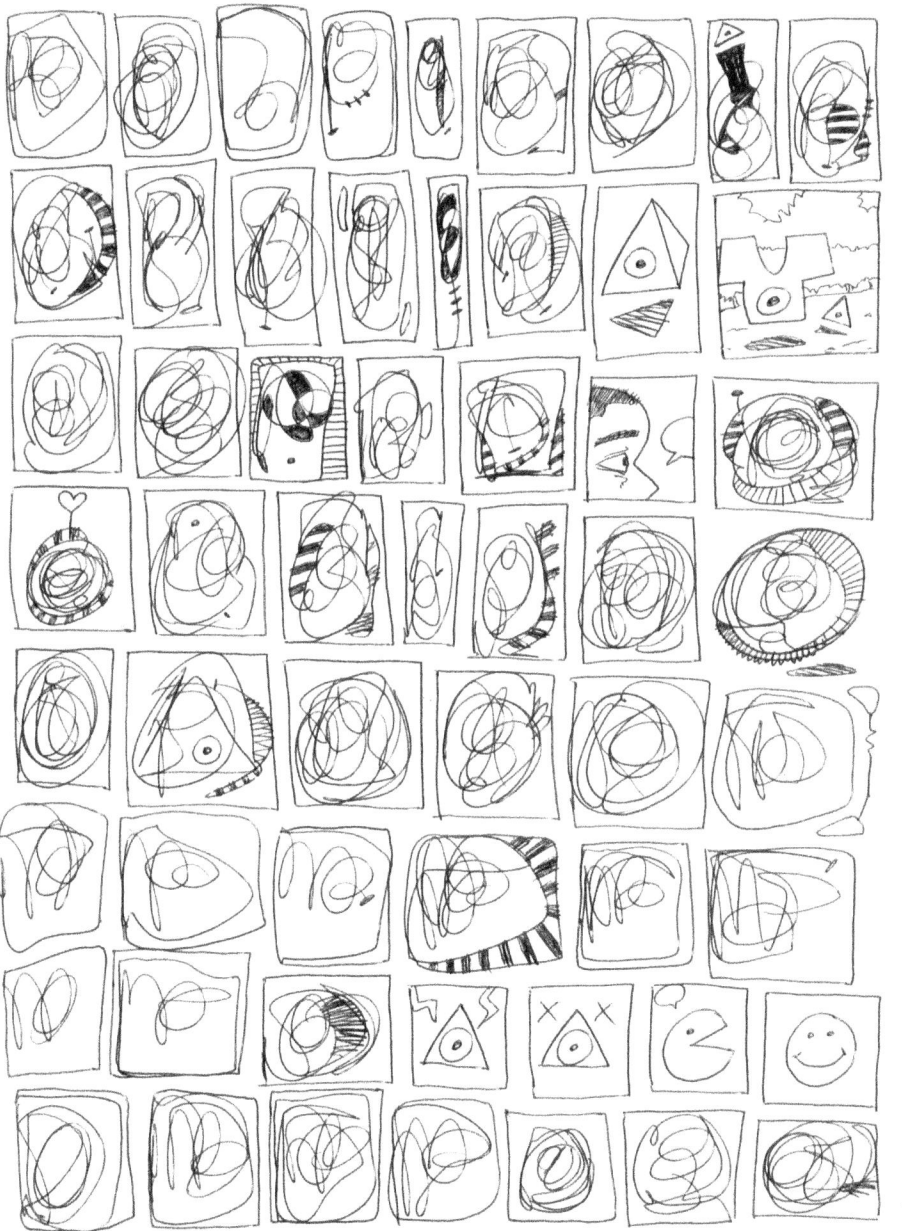

7

13

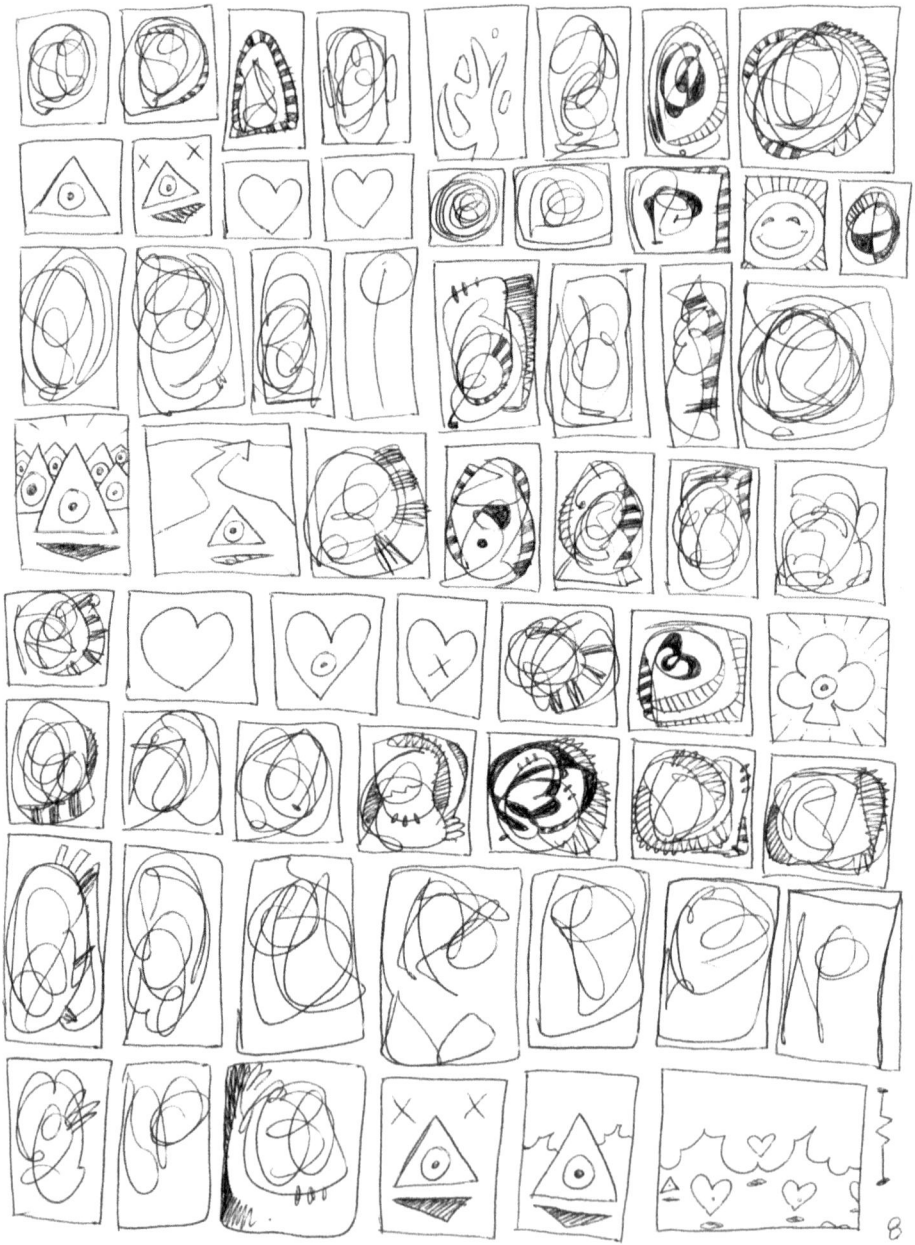

14

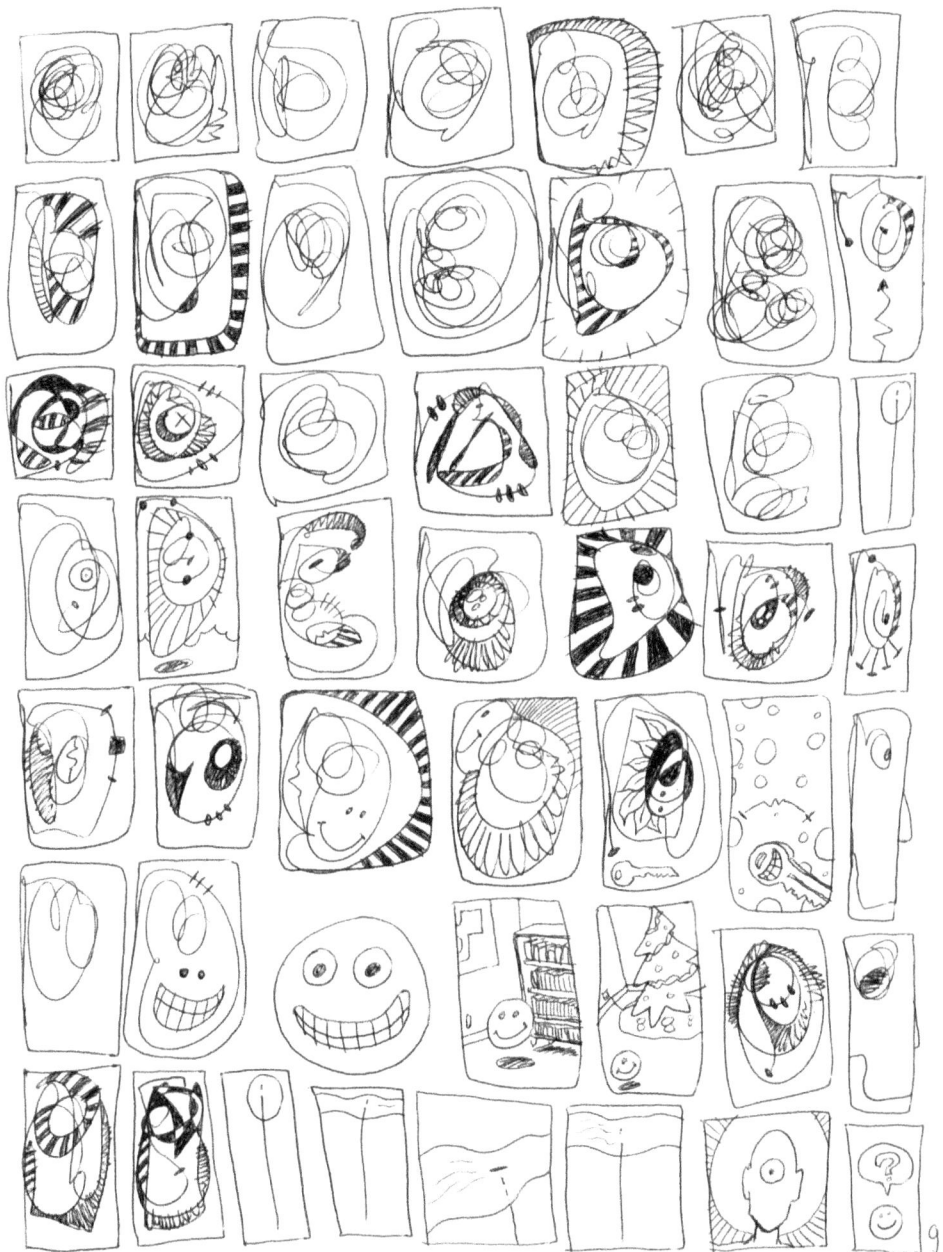

15

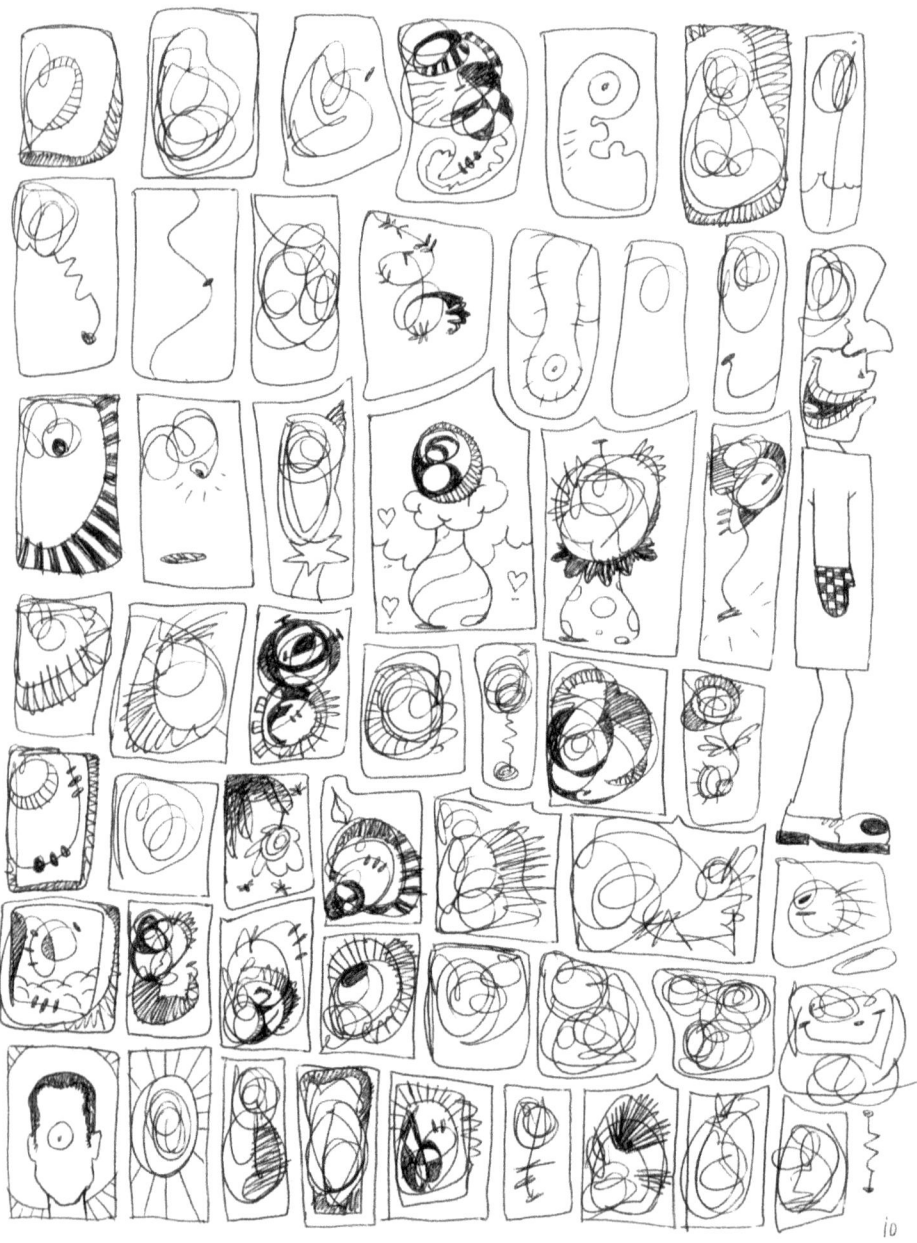

16

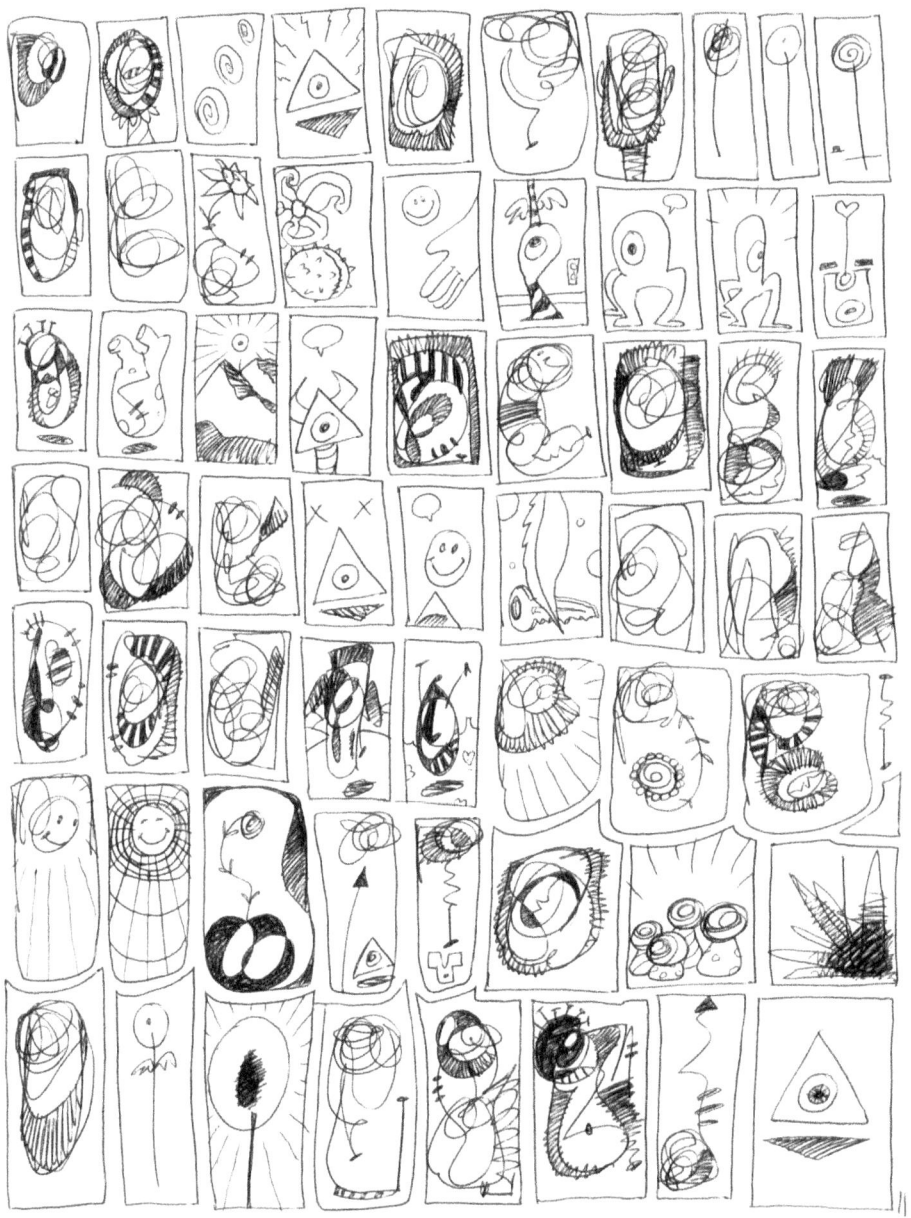

17

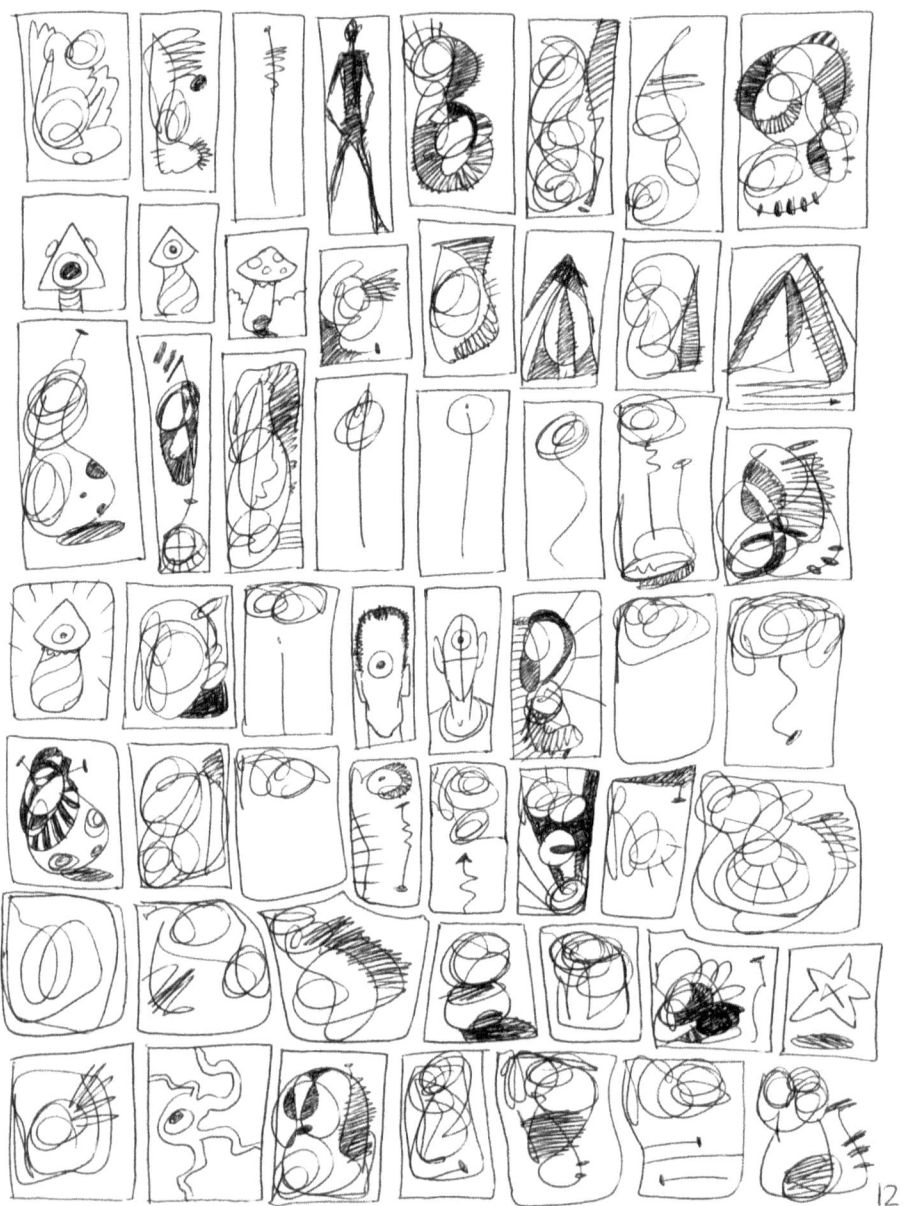

12

18

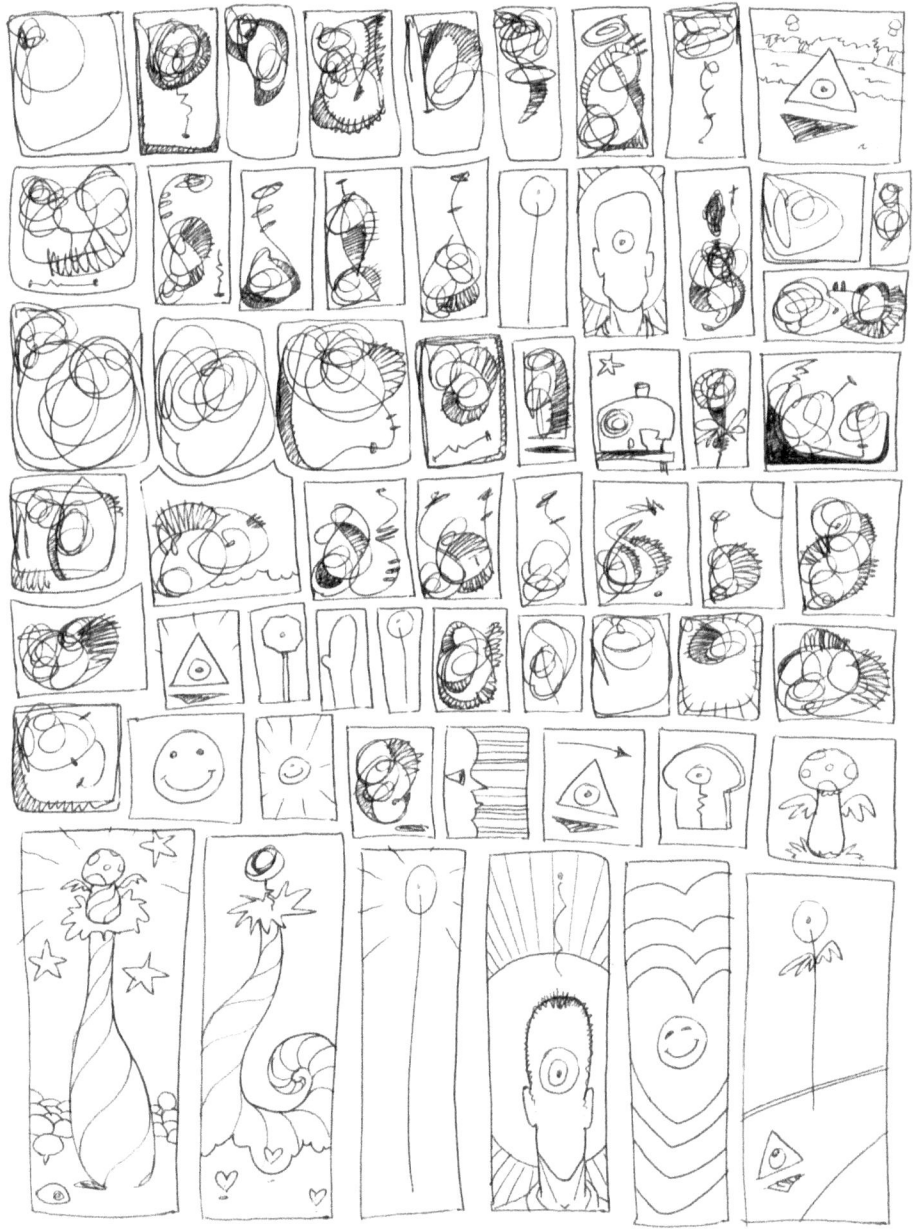

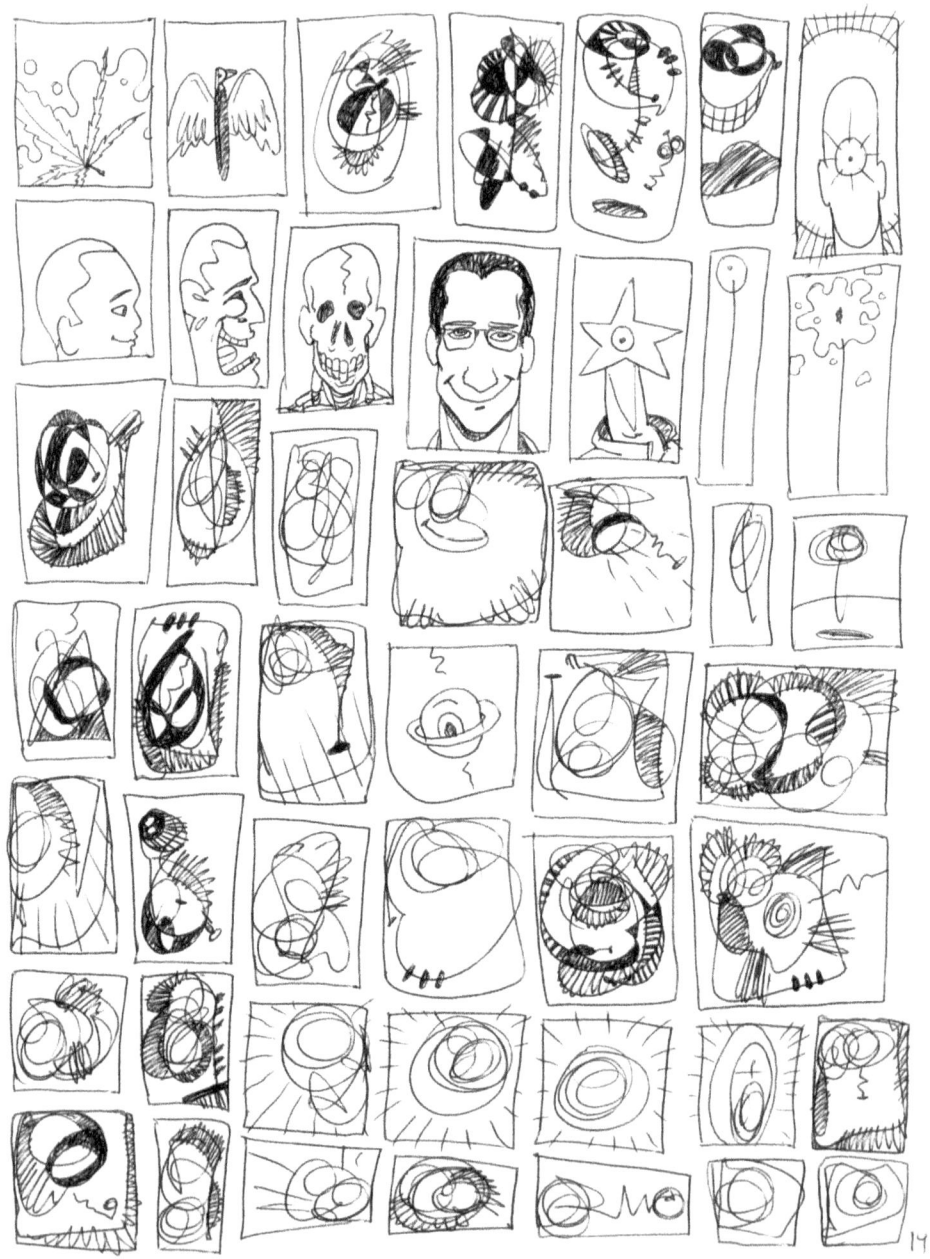

14

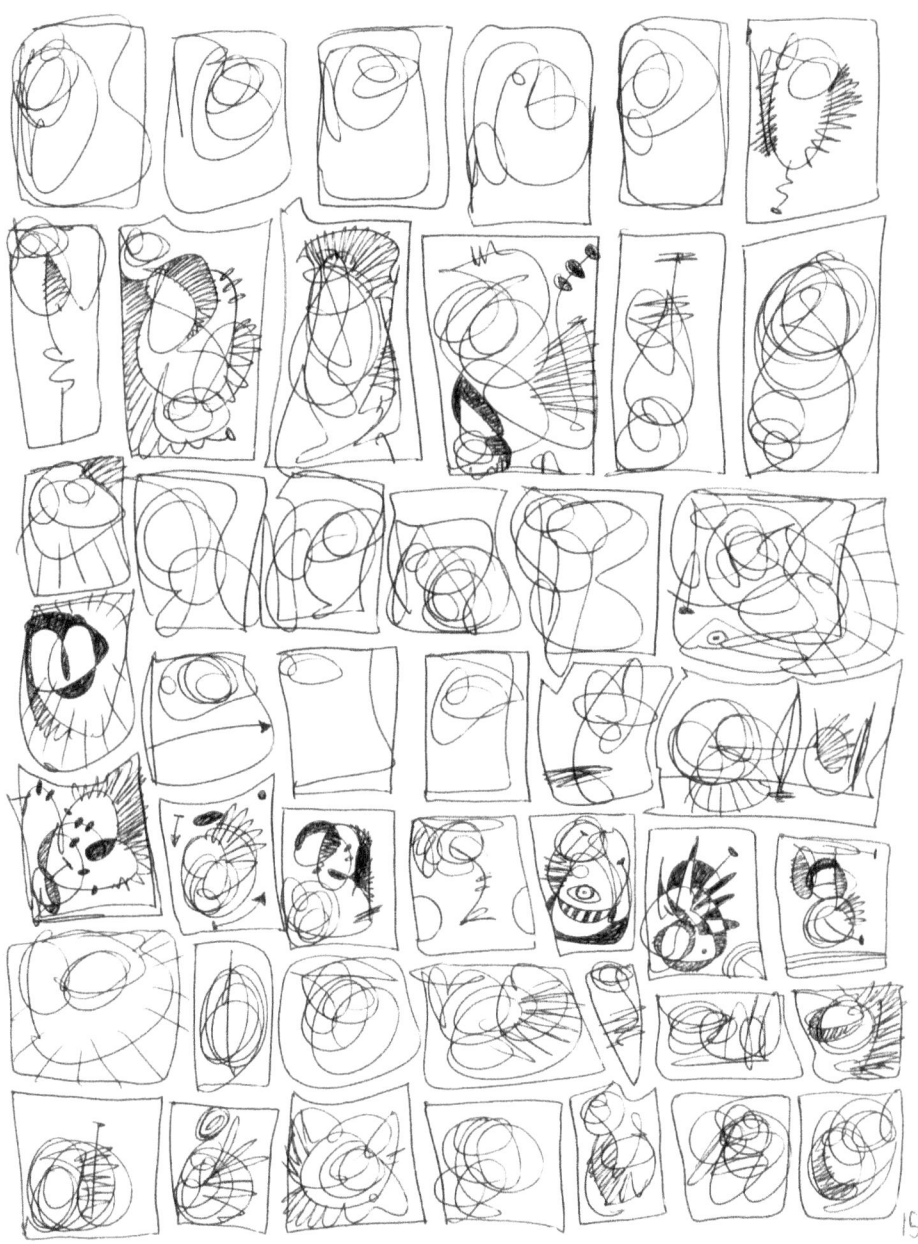

15

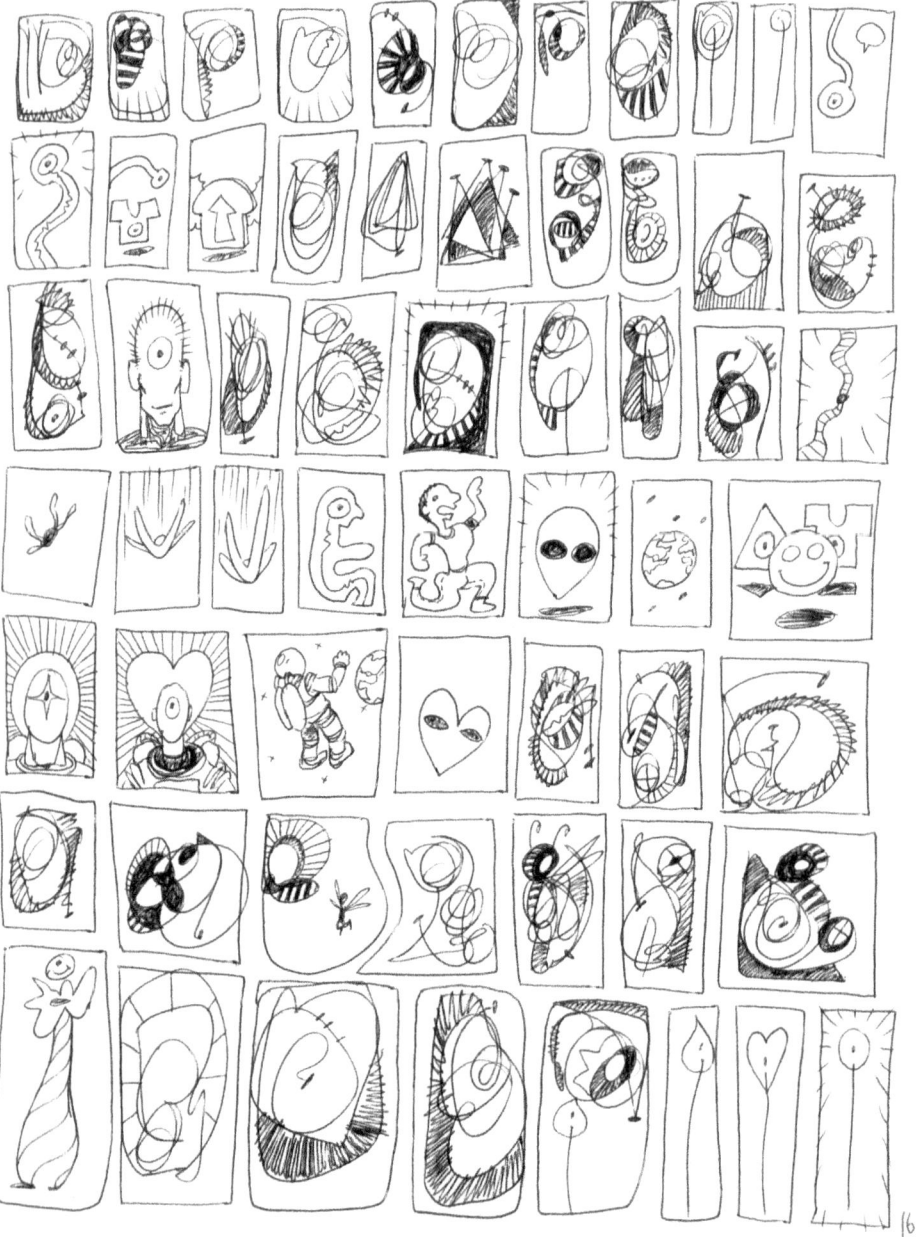

16

22

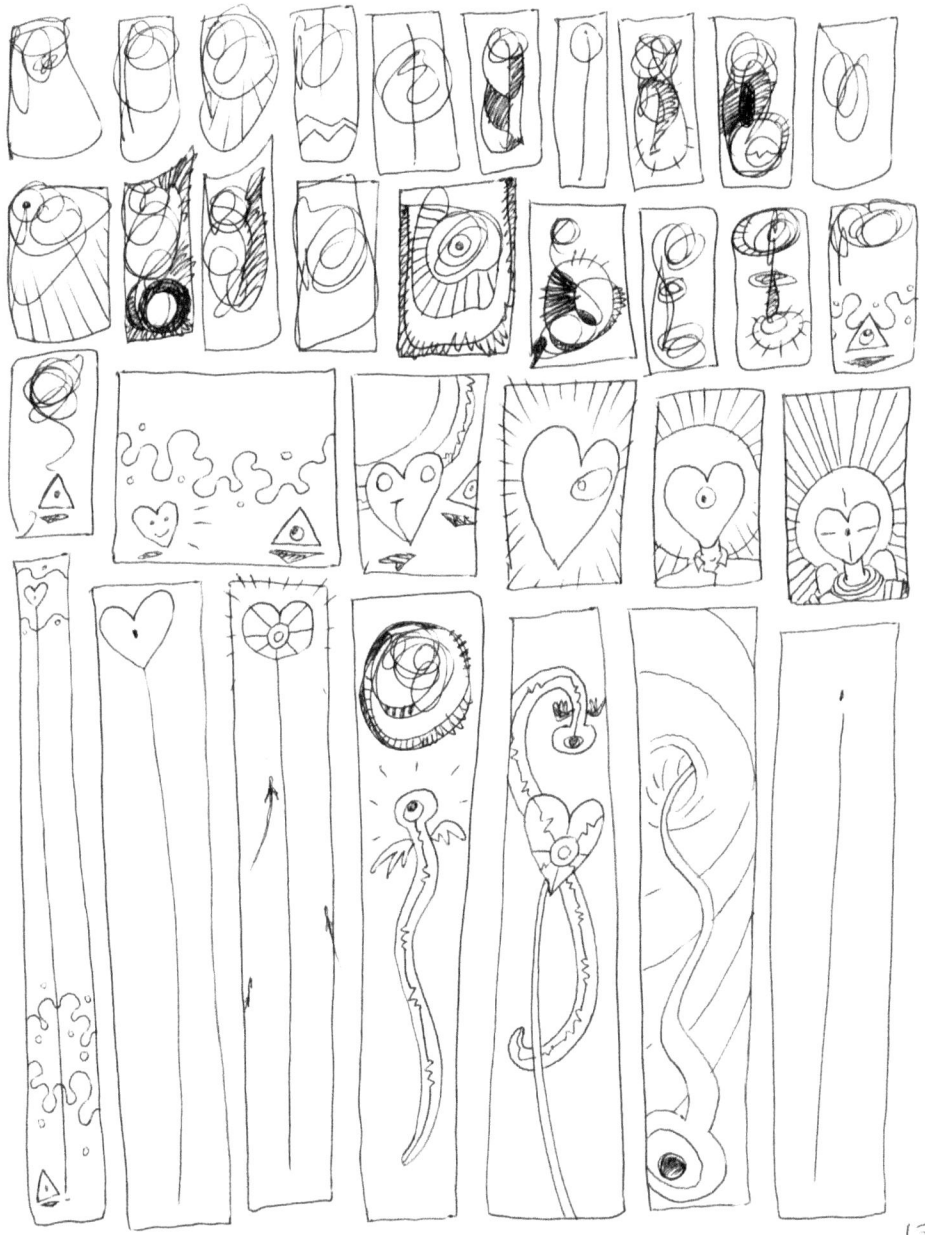

17

23

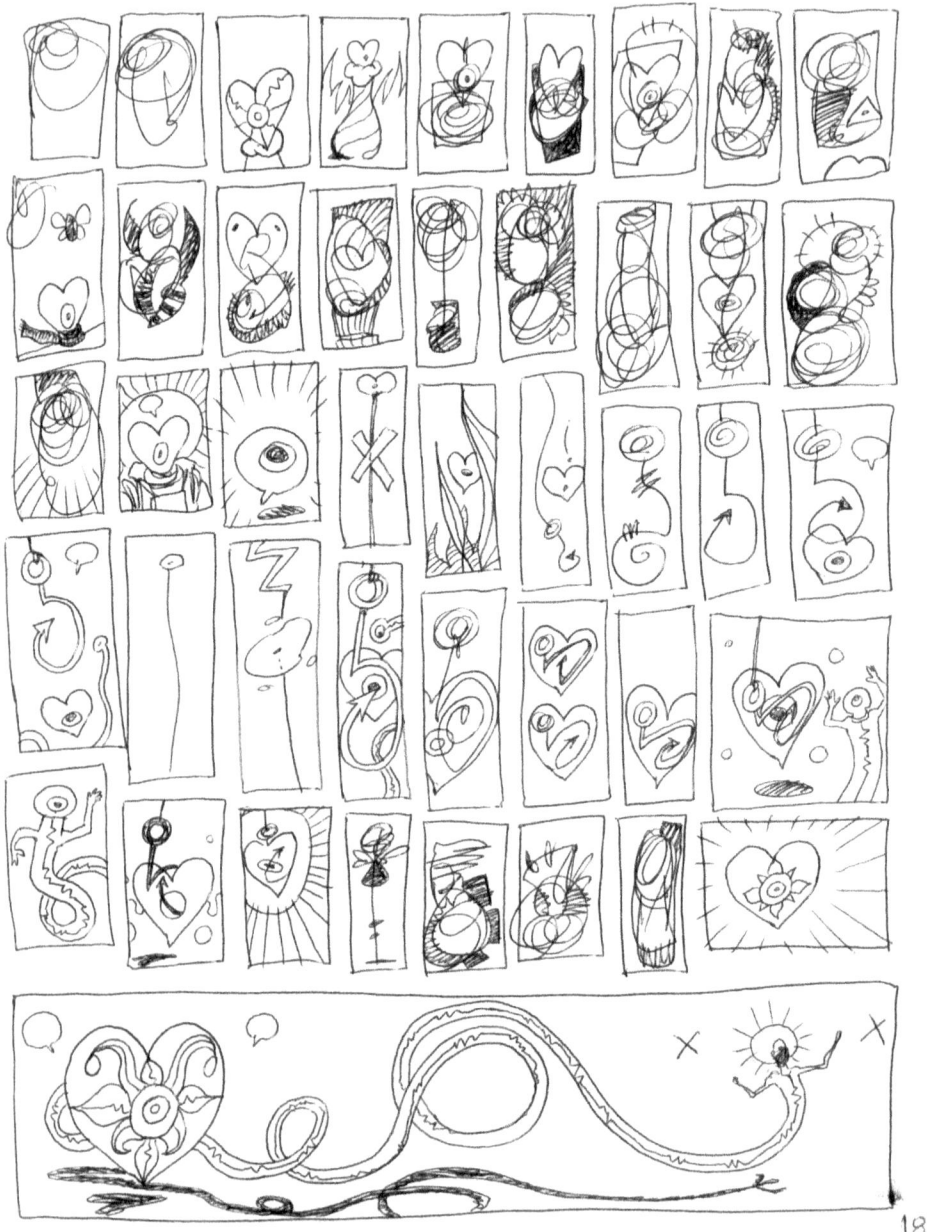

18

24

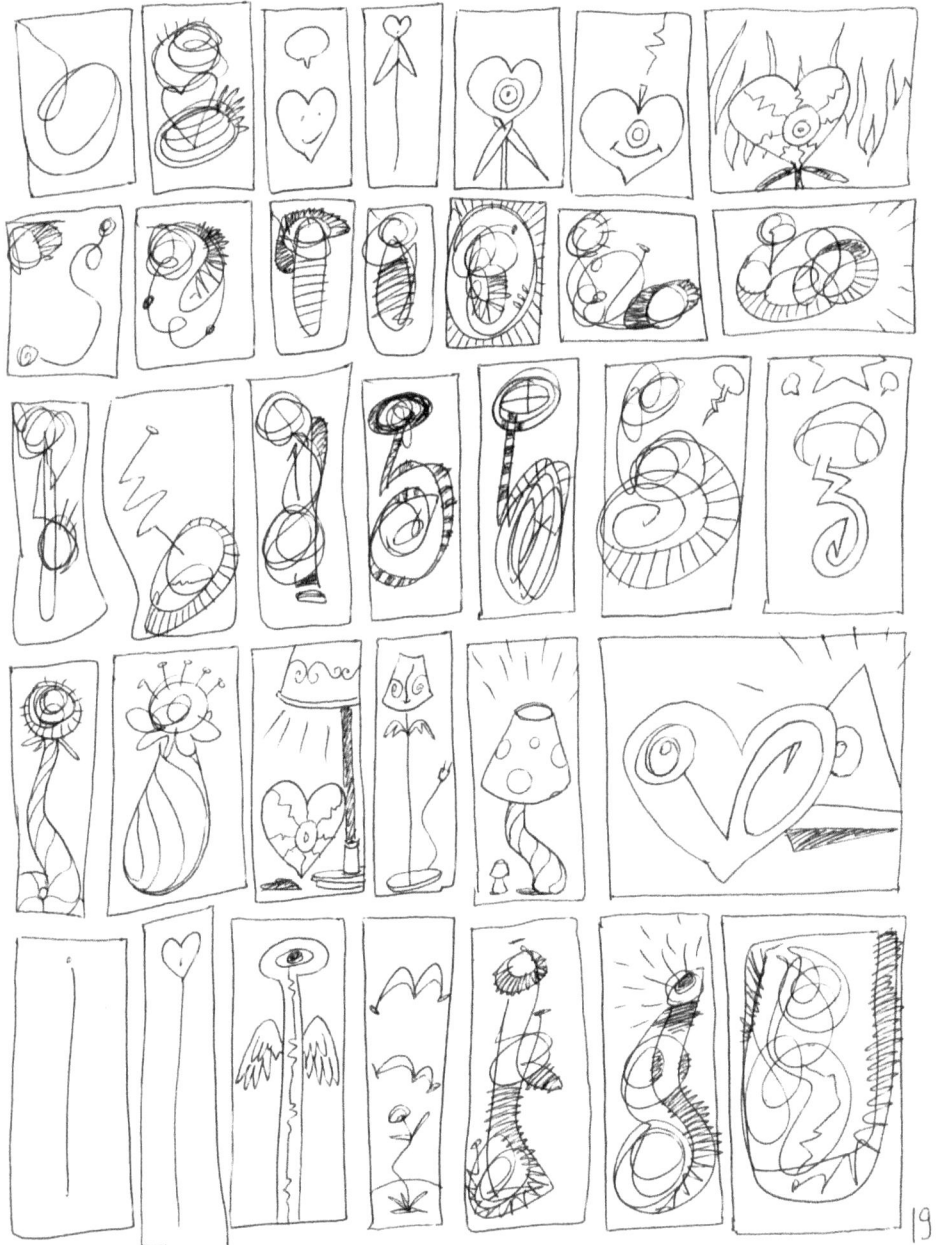

25

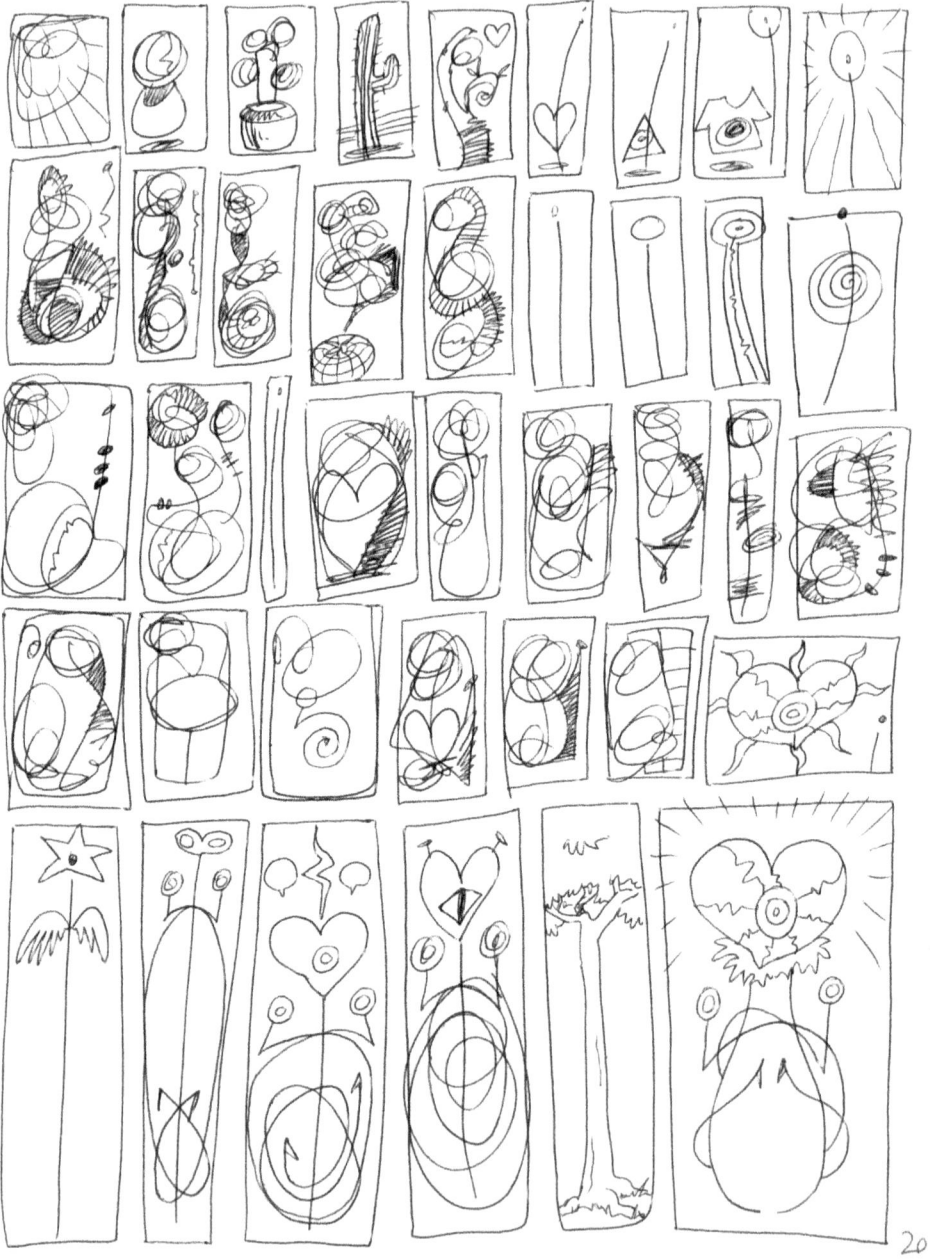

20

26

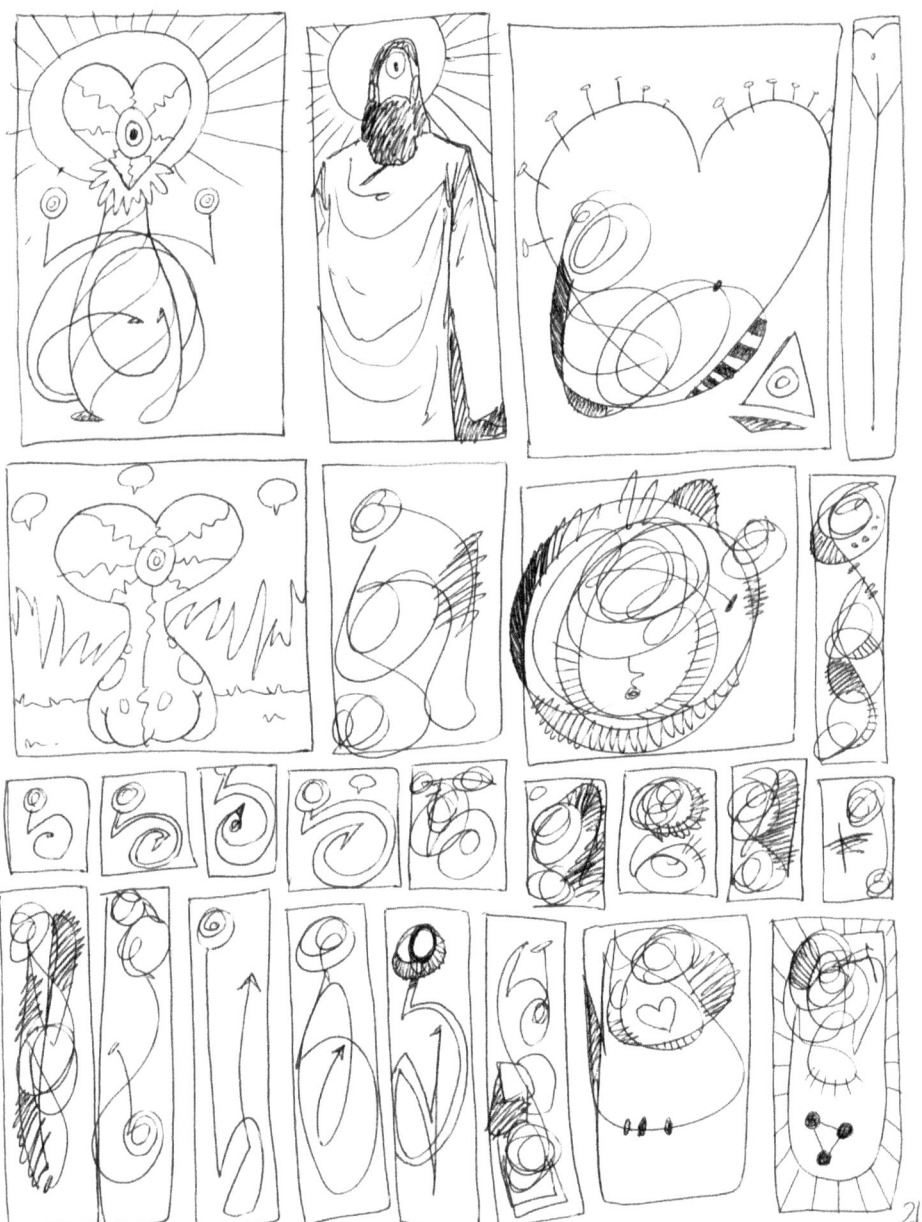

21

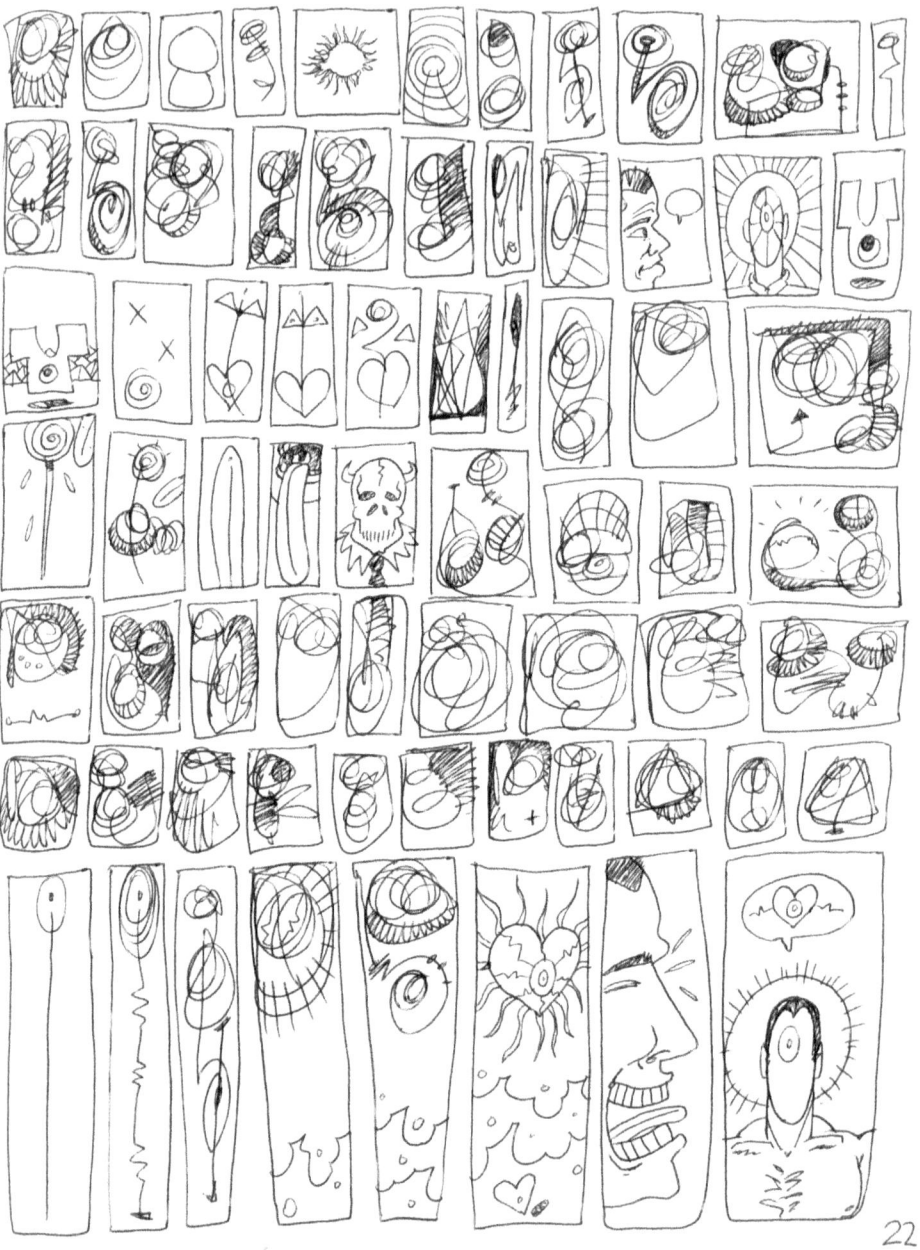

22

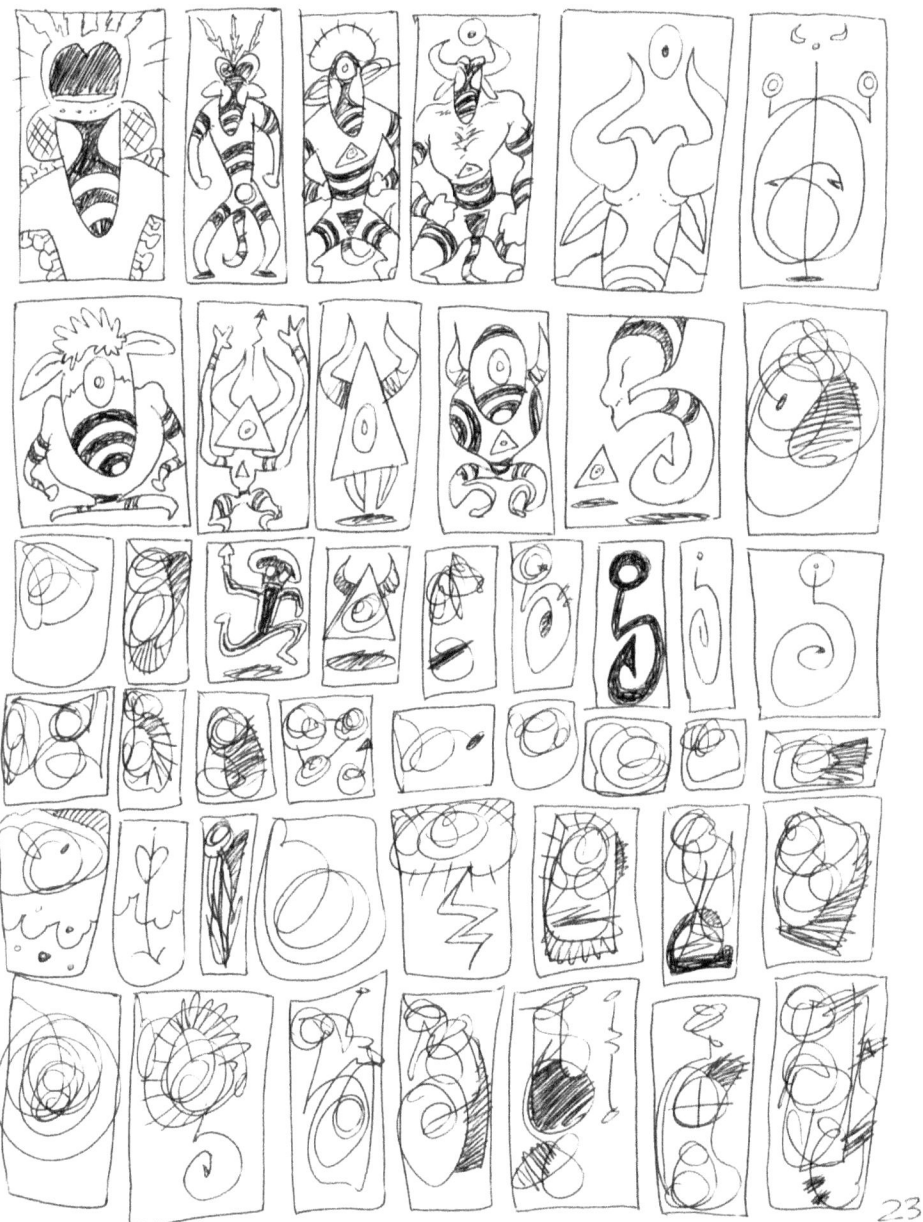

29

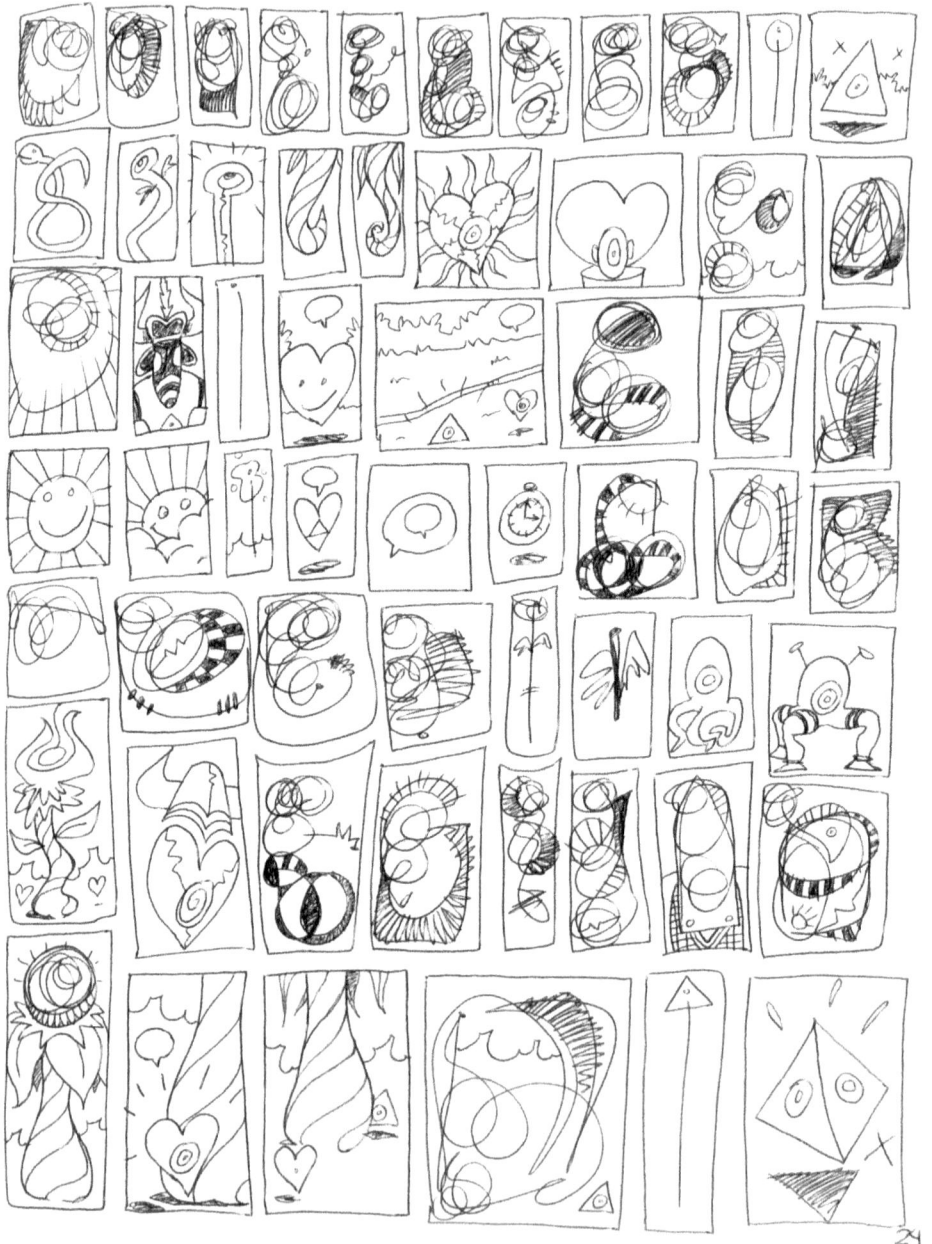

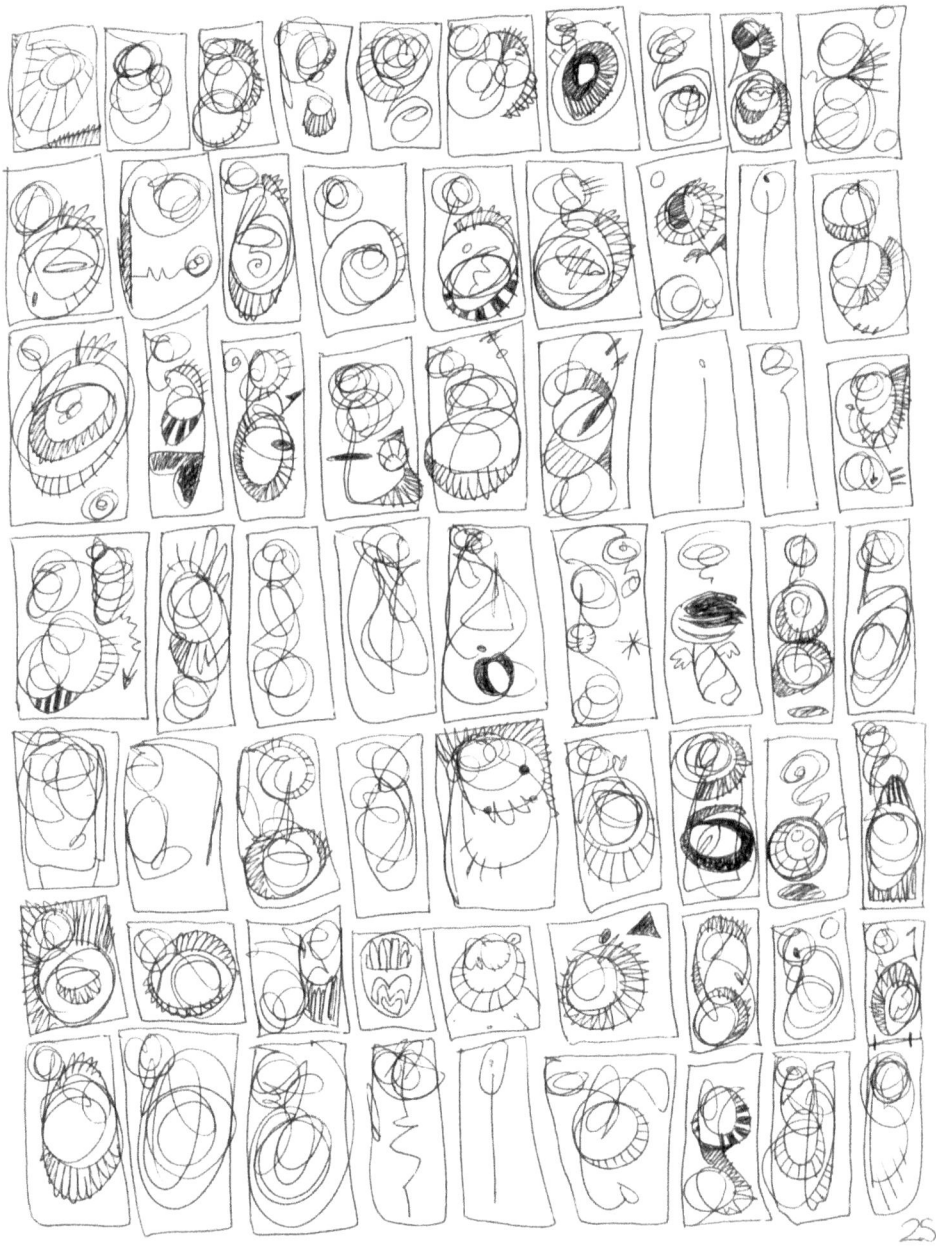

31

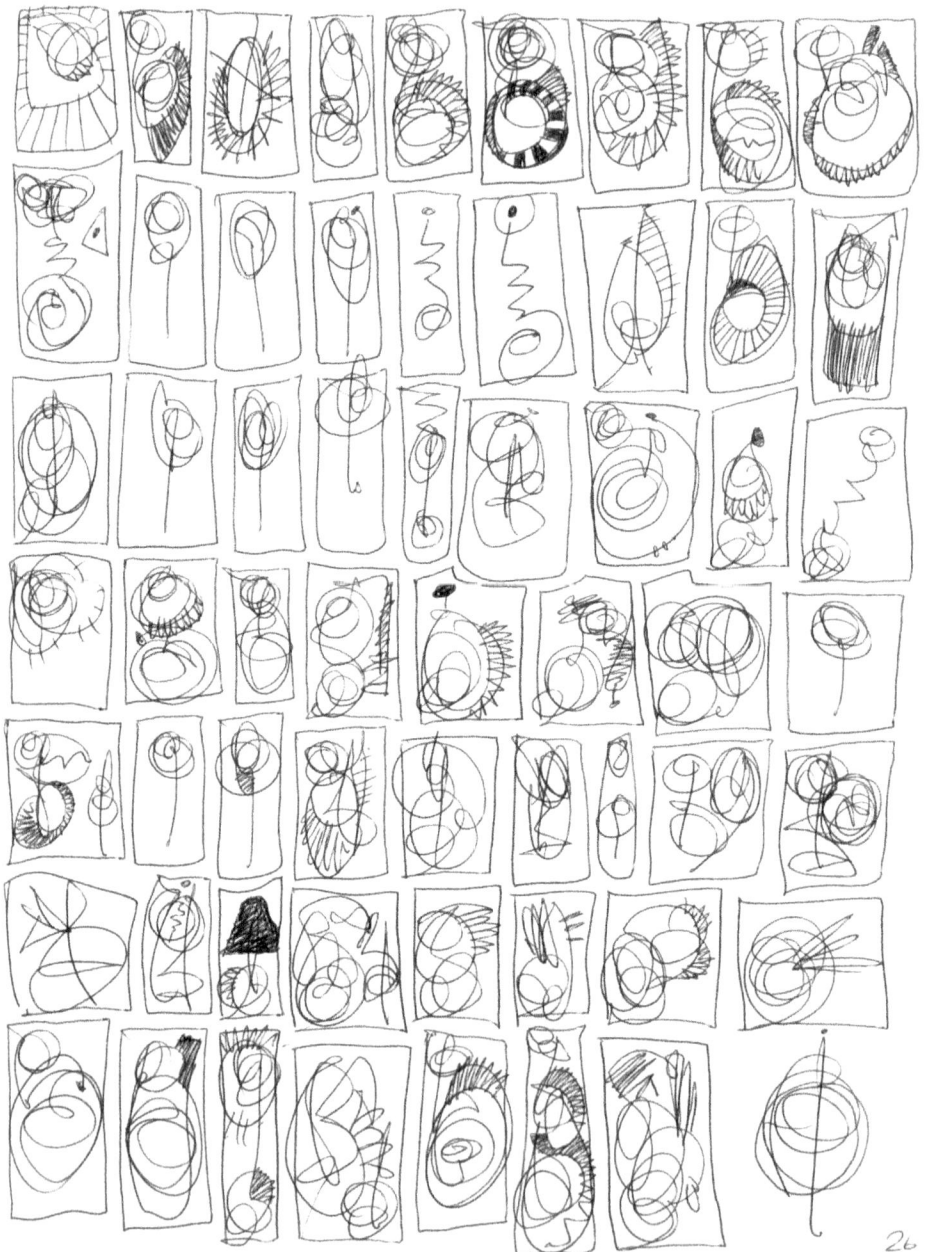

26

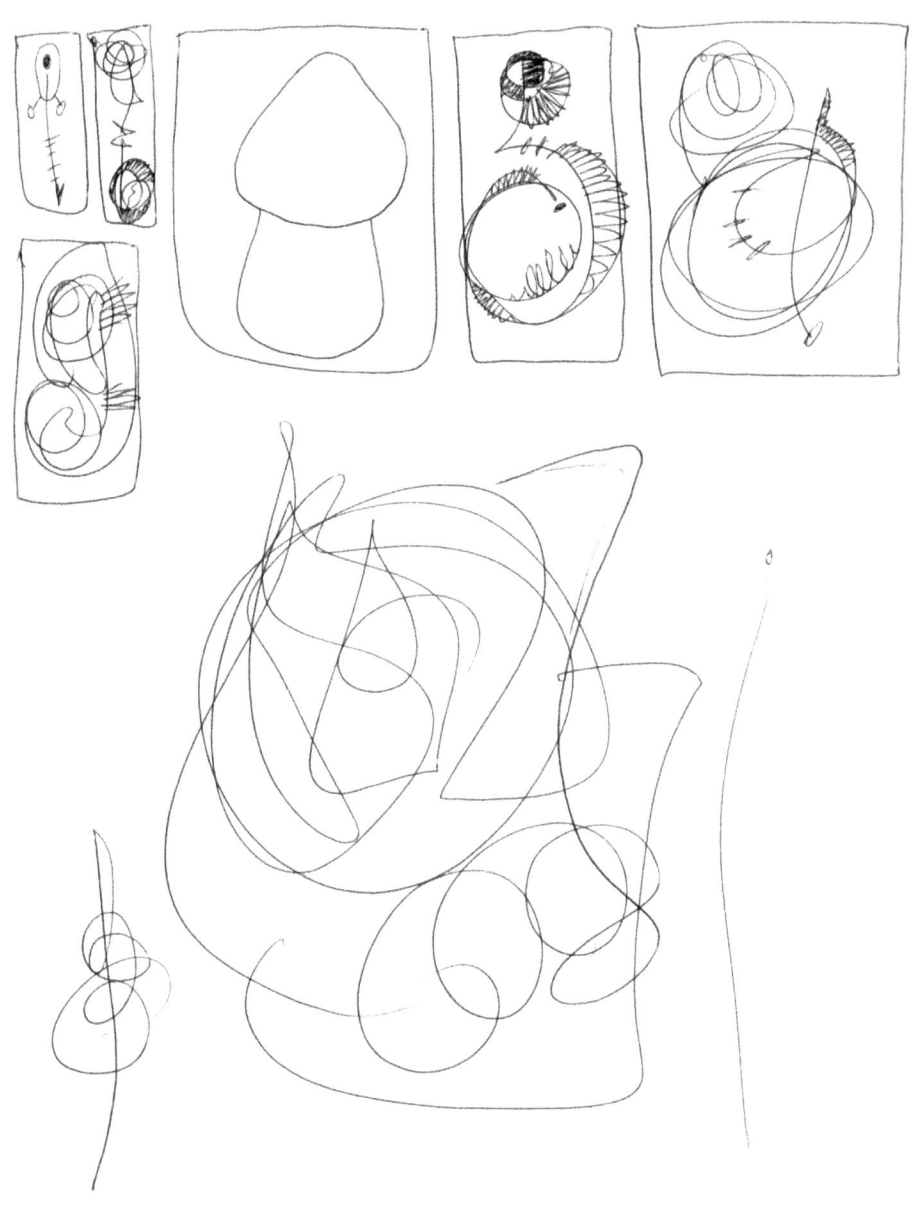

27

33

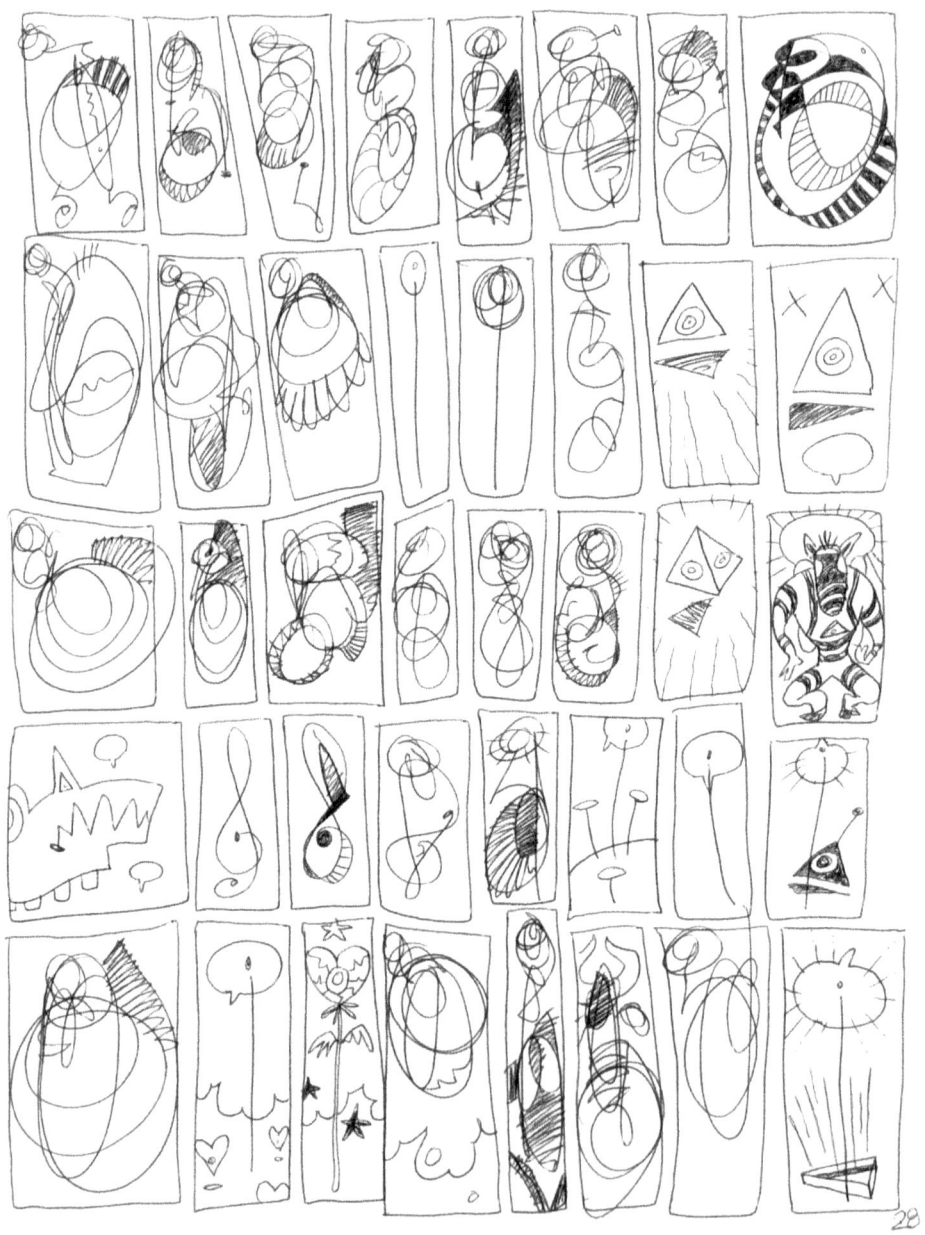

28

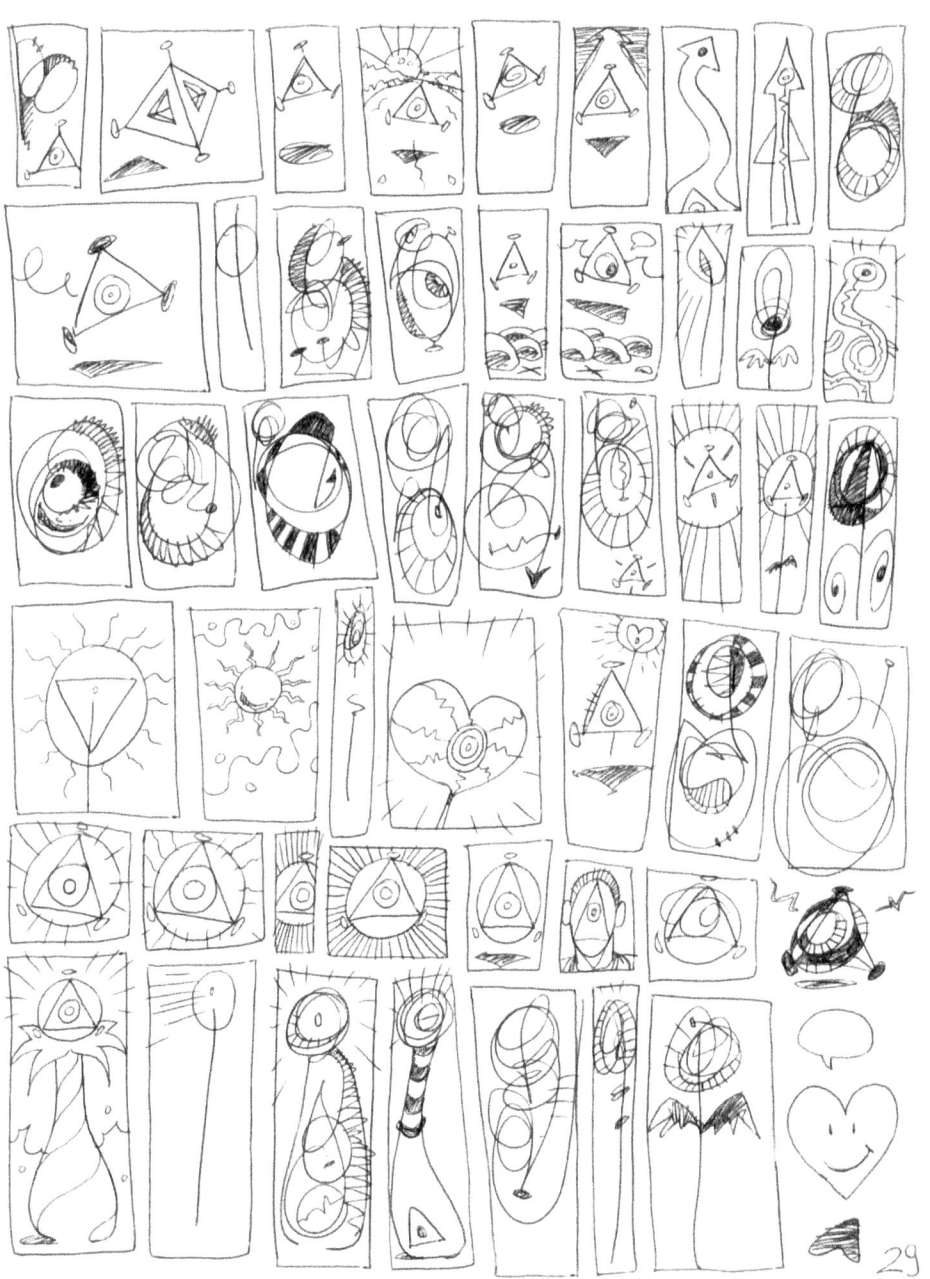

35

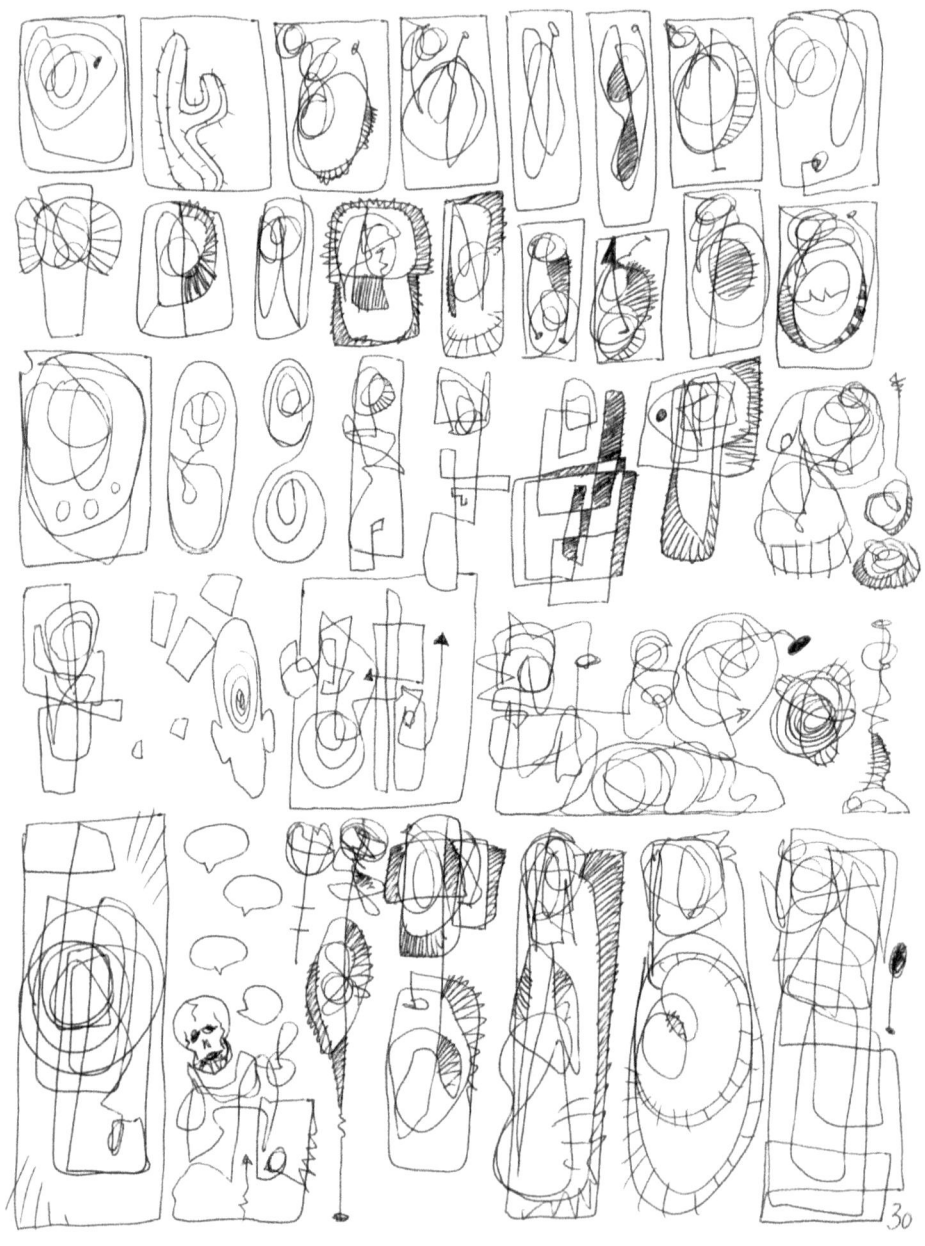

30

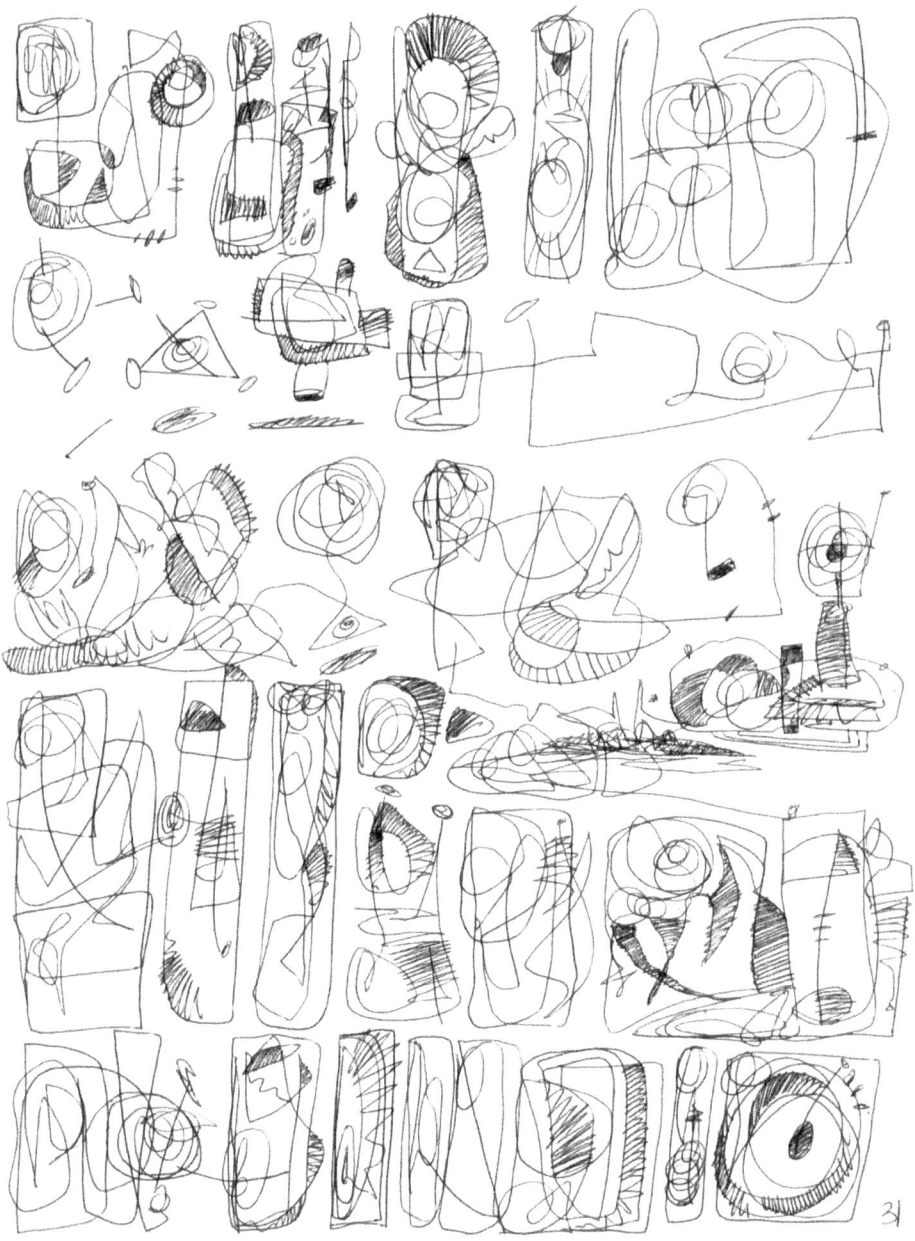

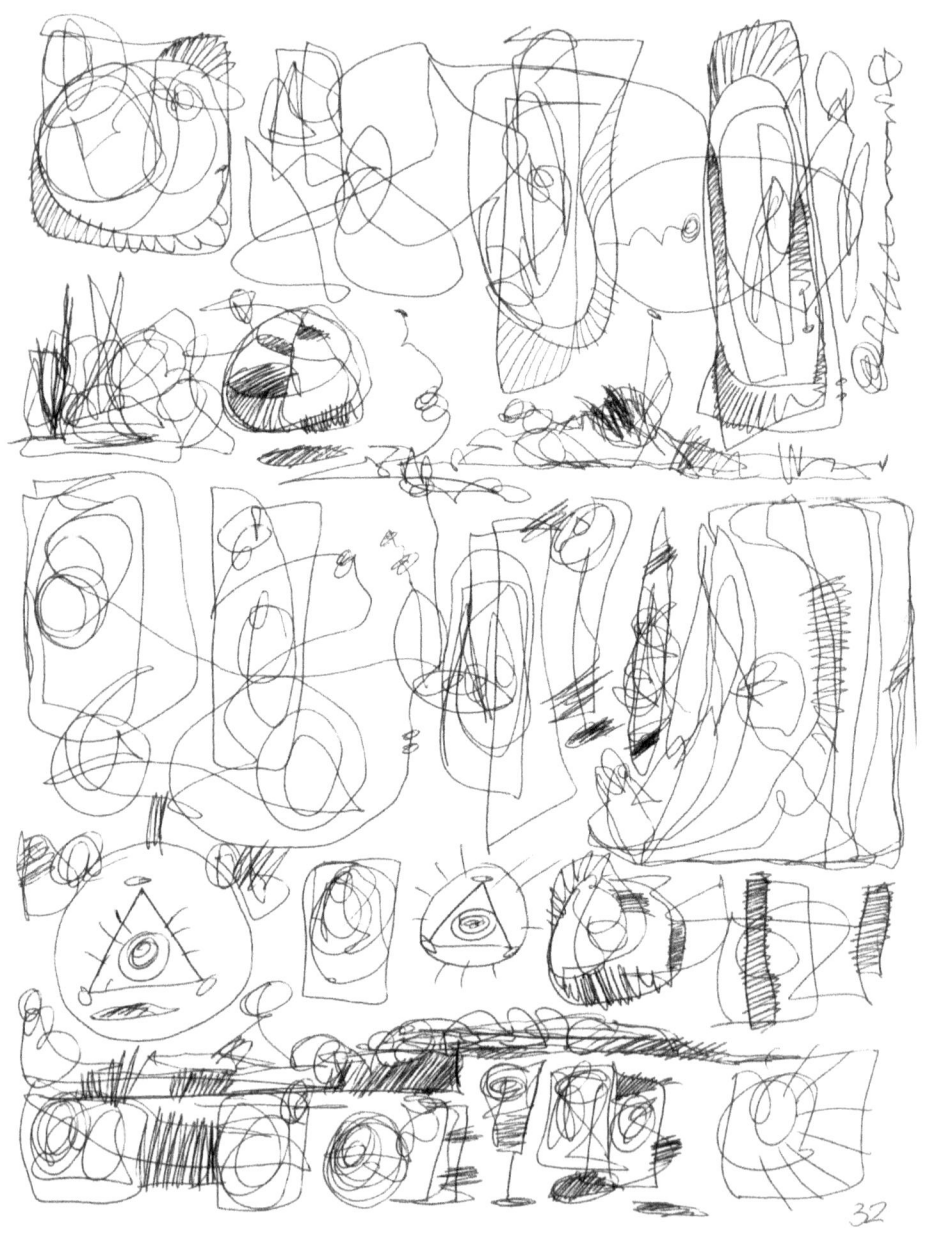

38

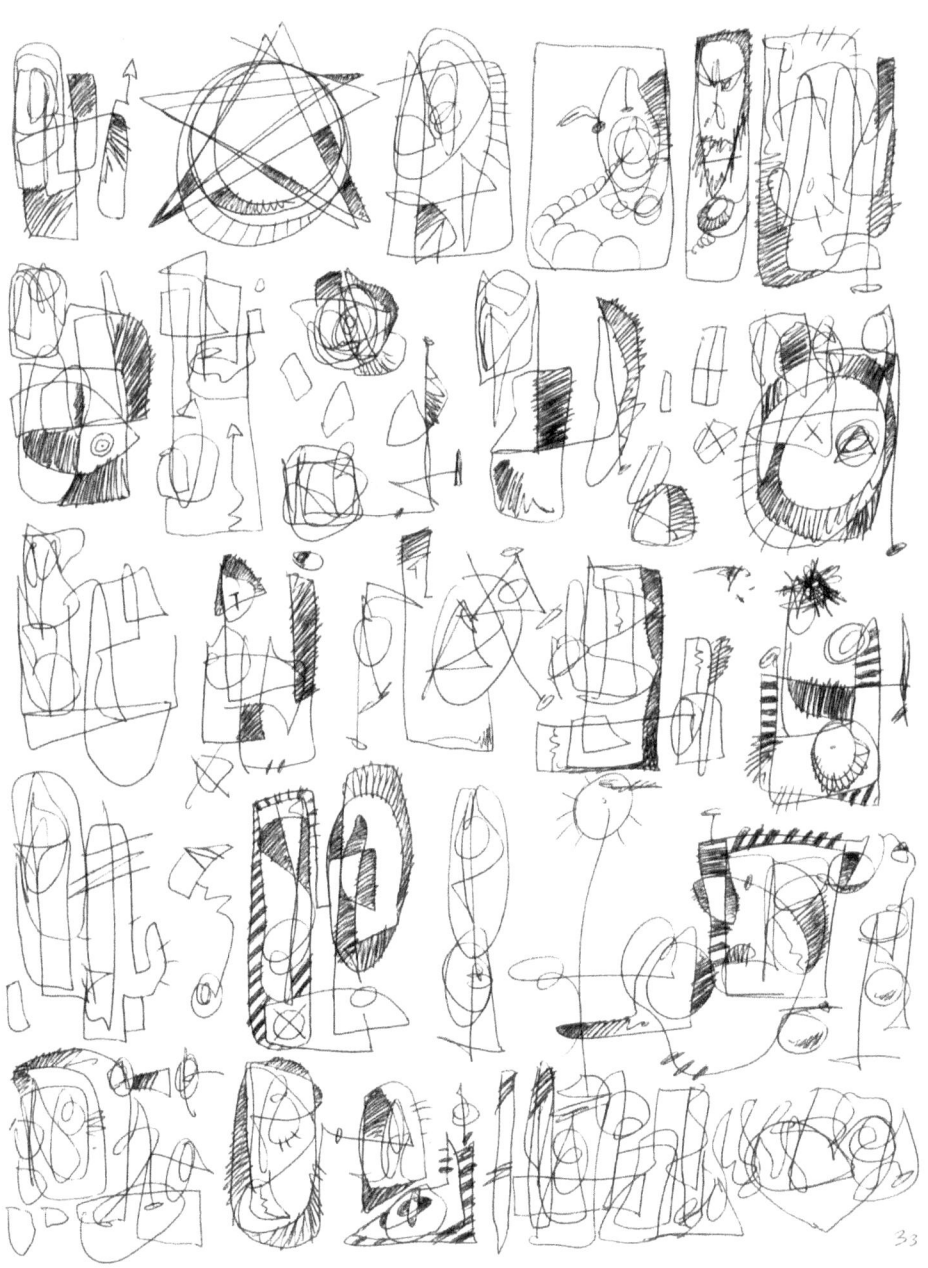

33

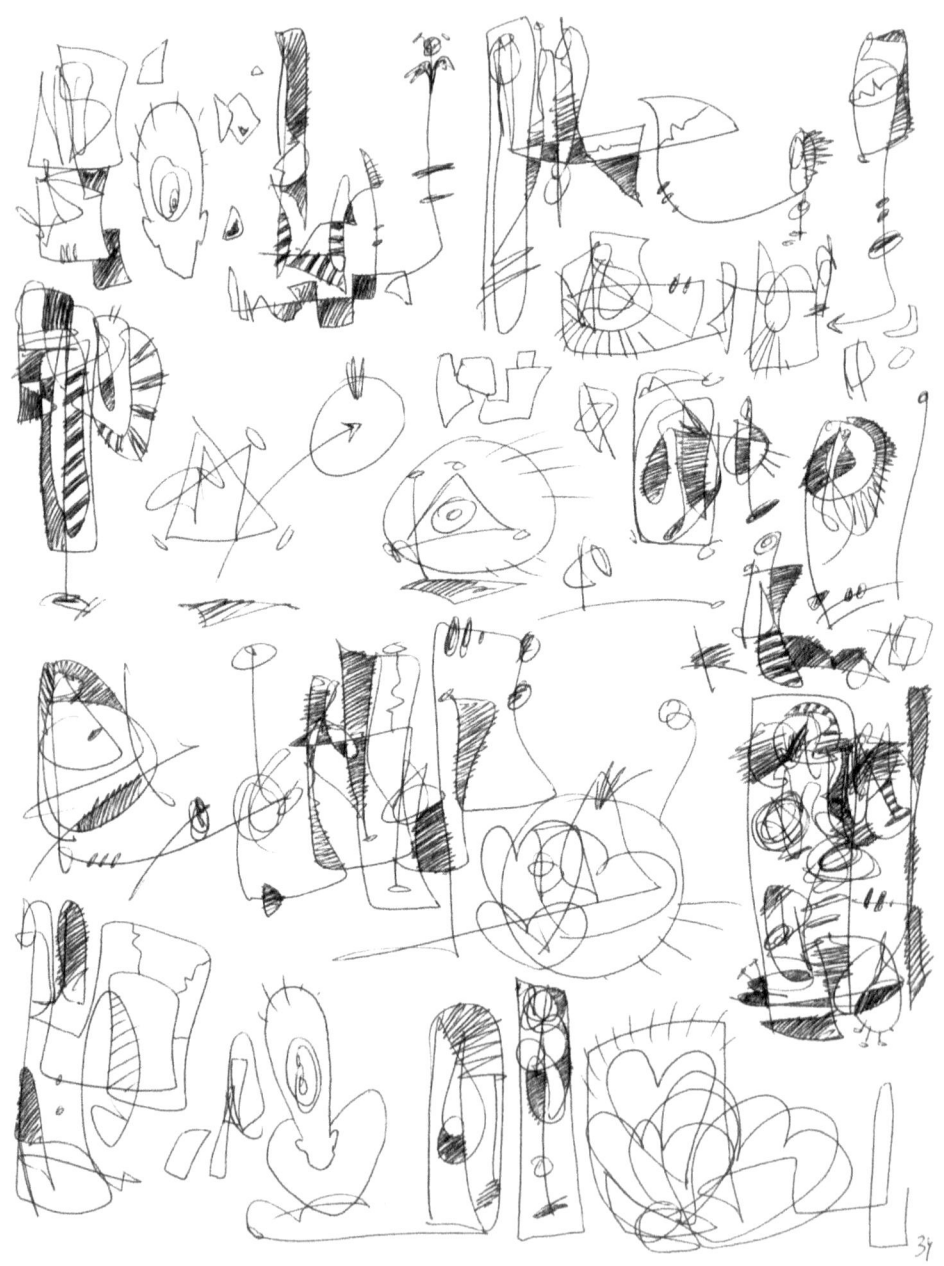

34

40

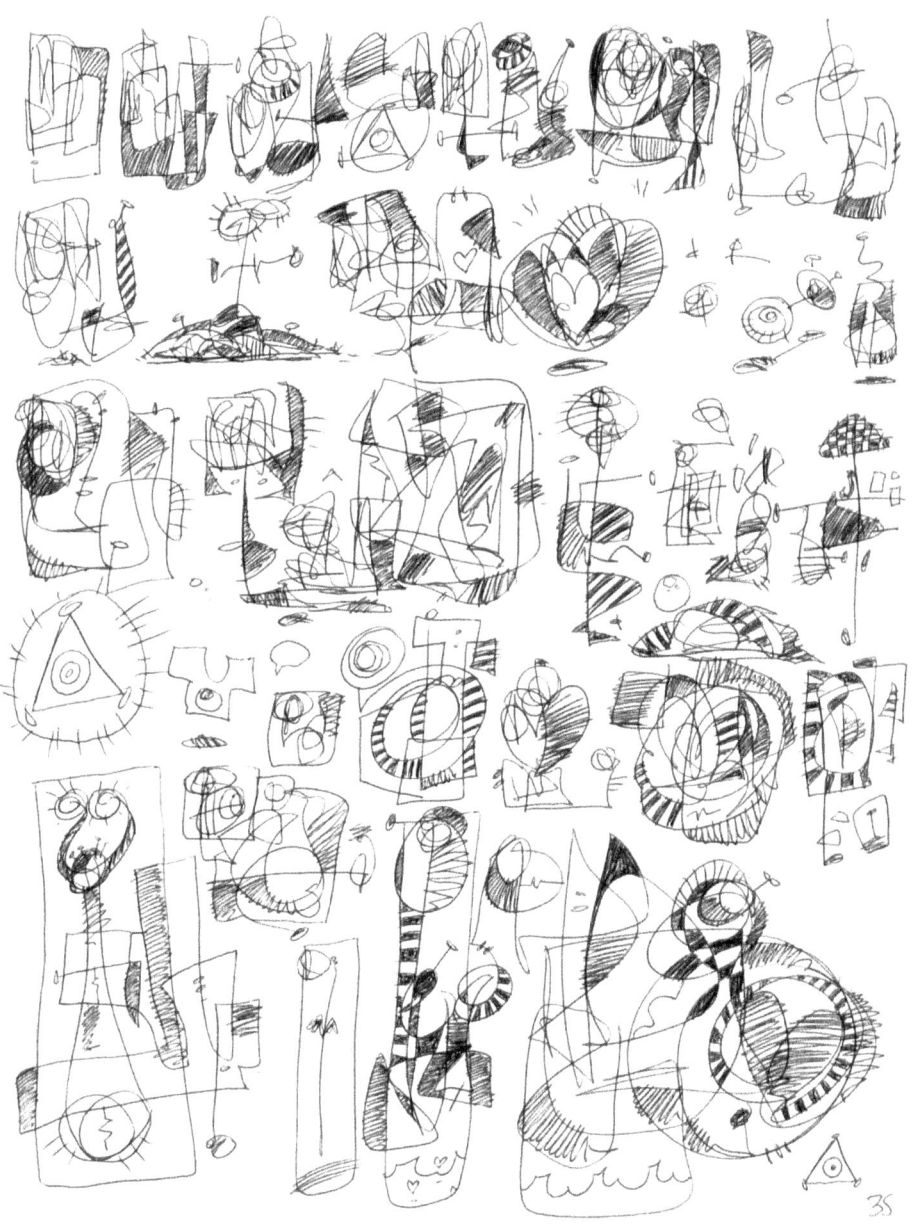

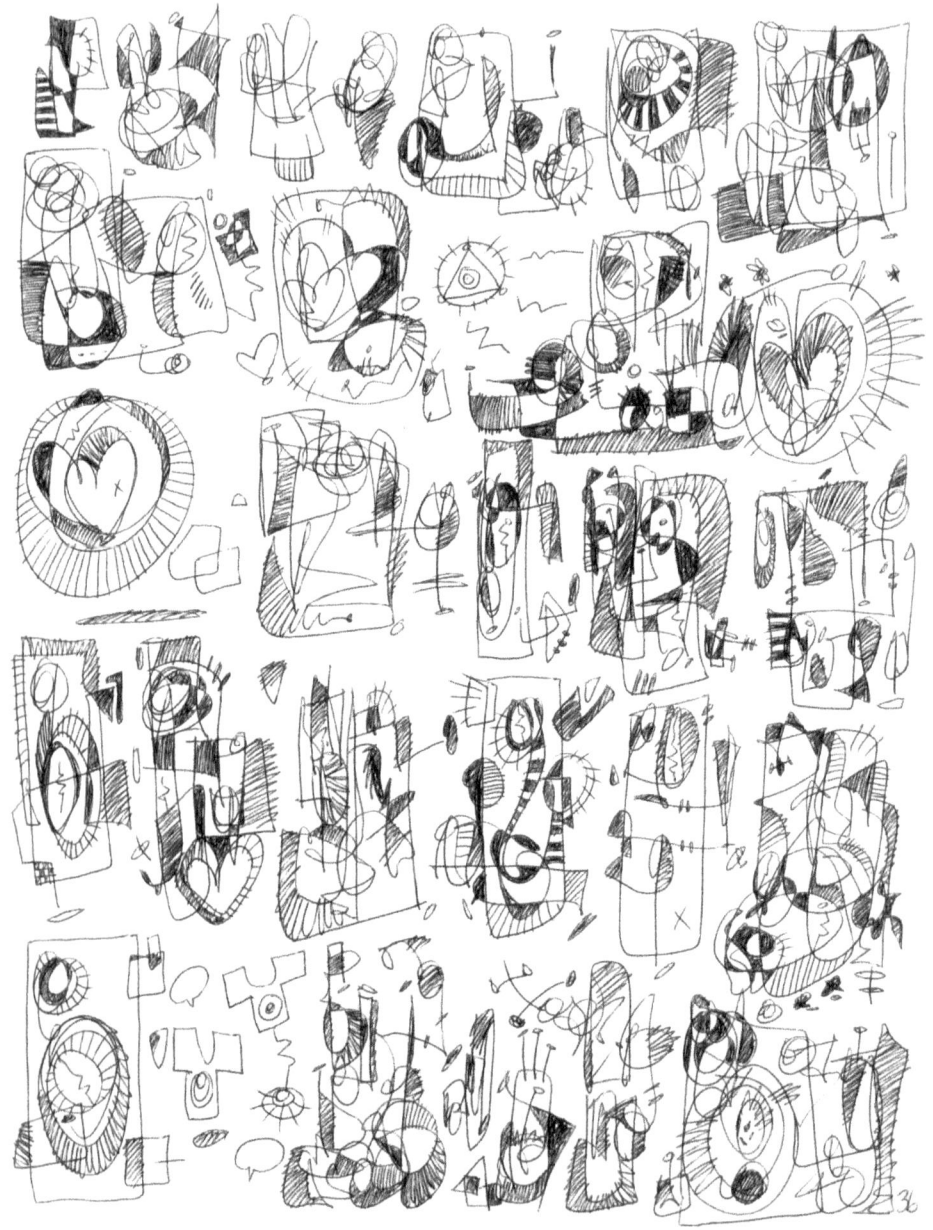

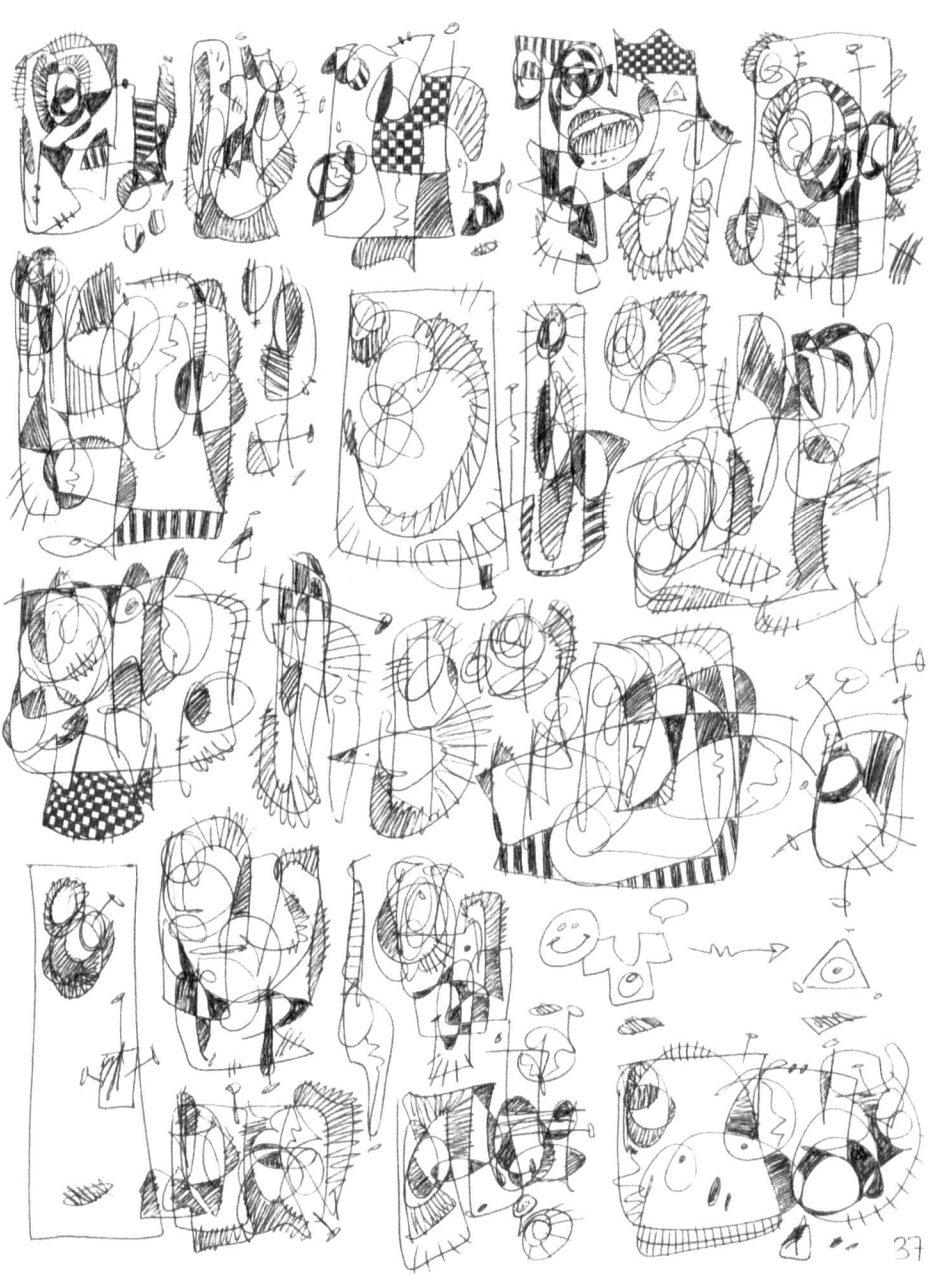

43

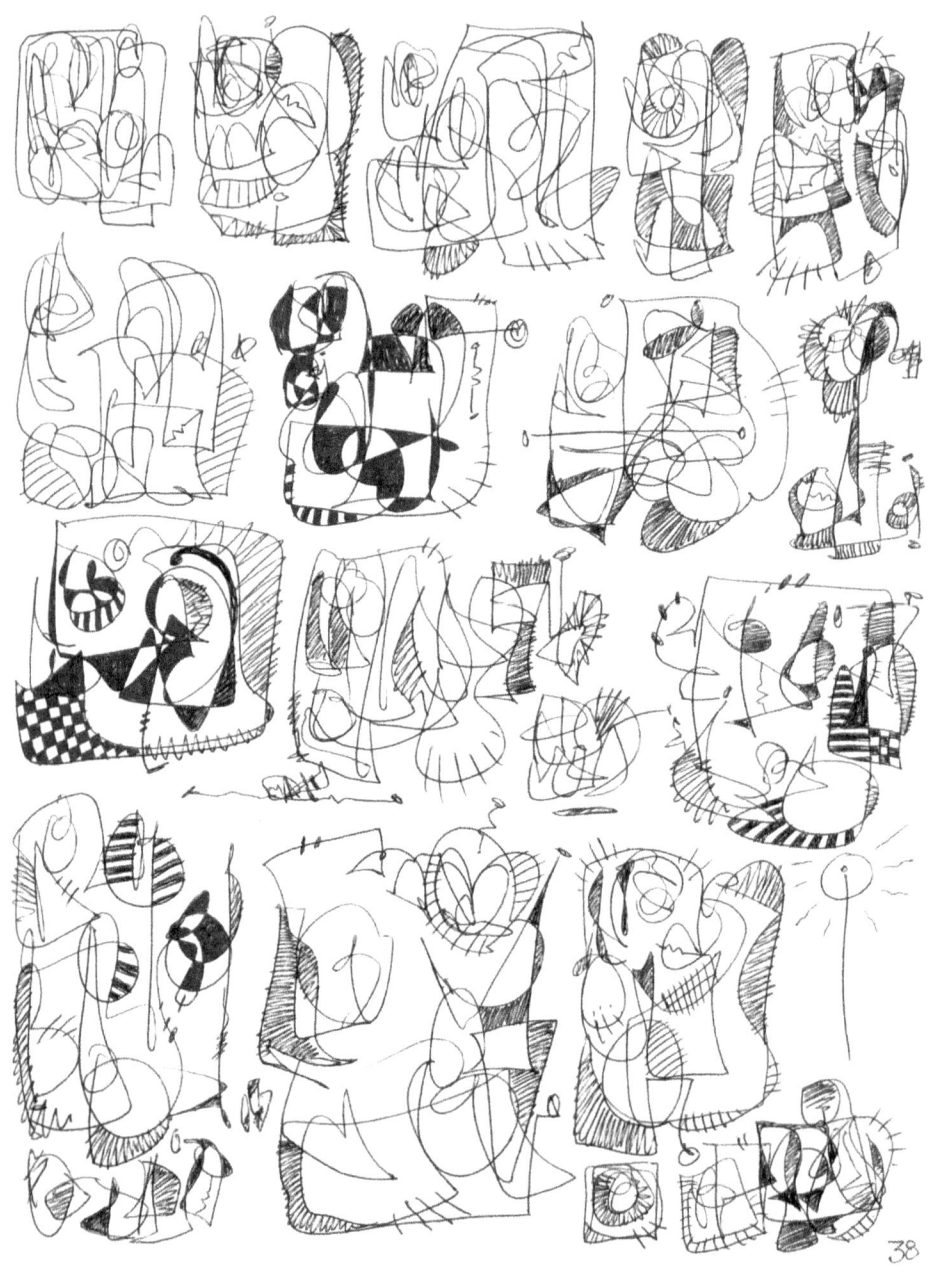

38

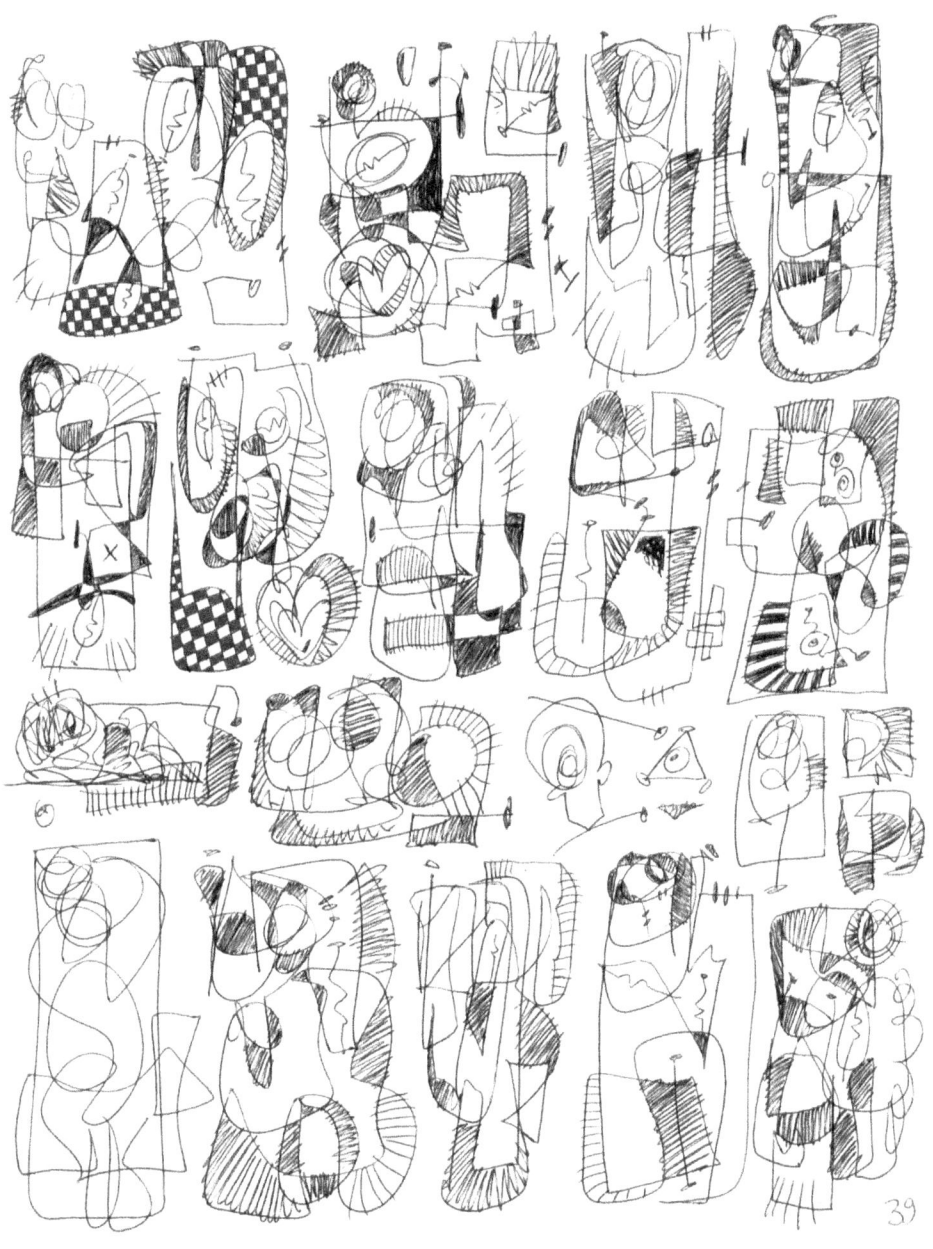

39

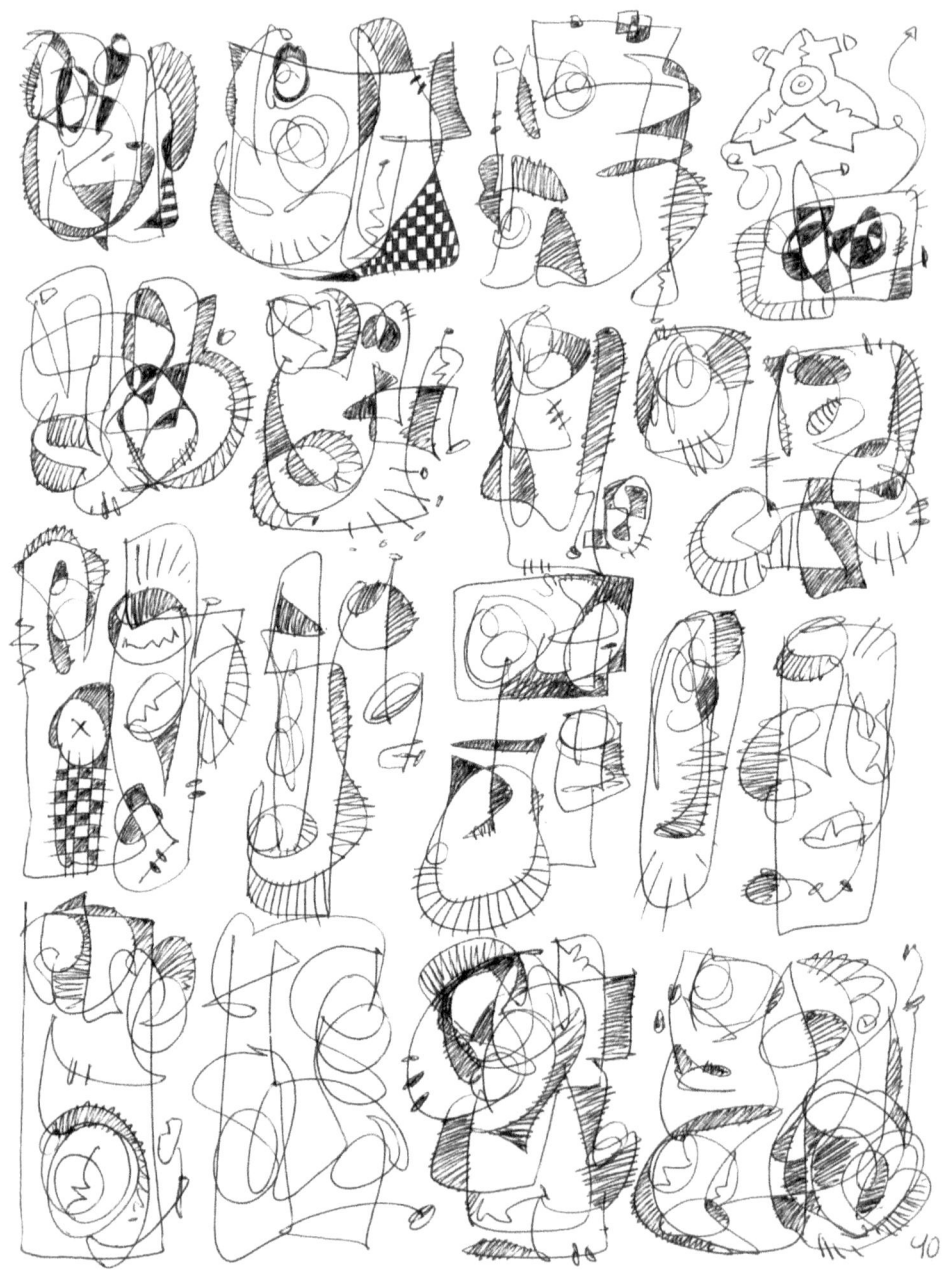

46

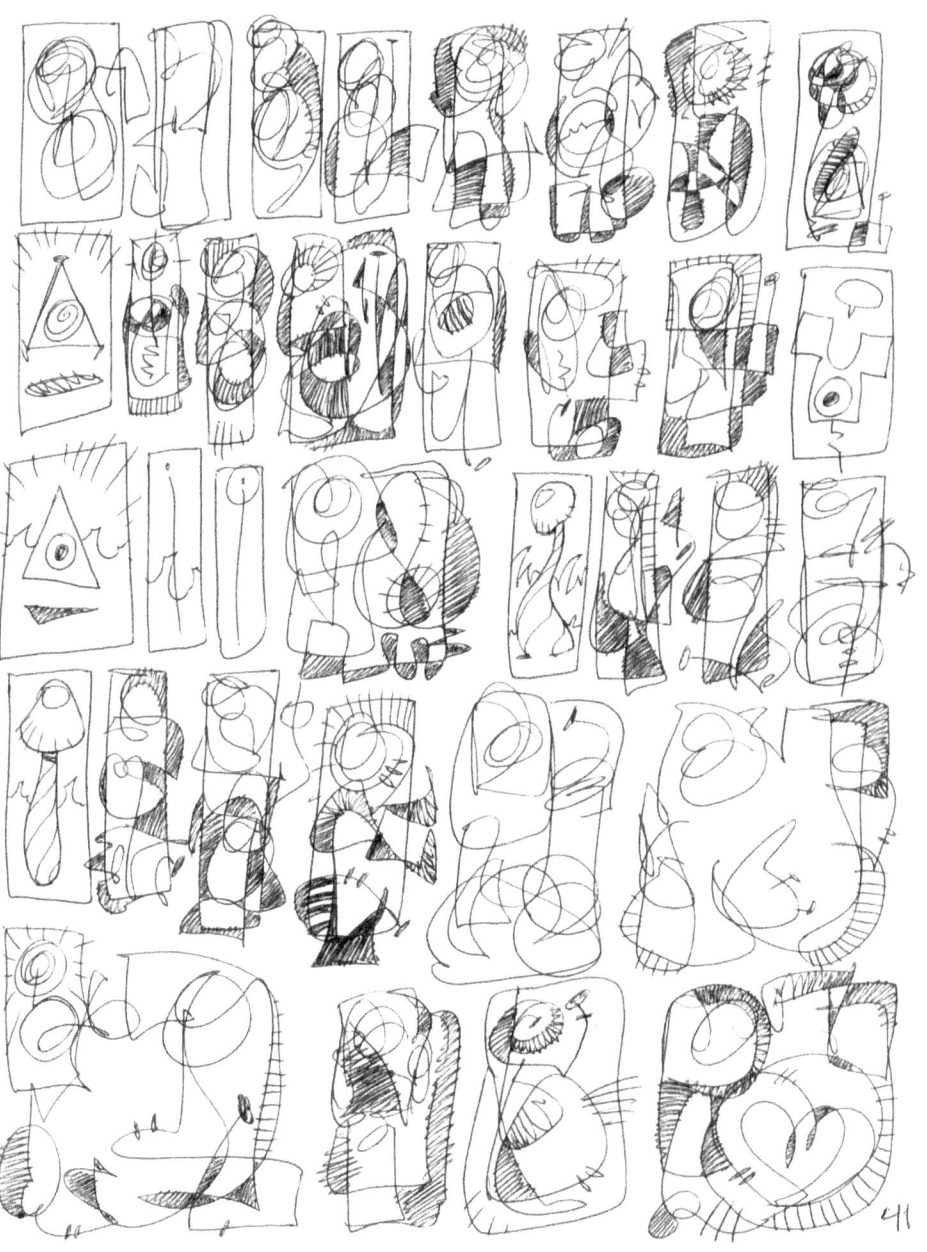

41

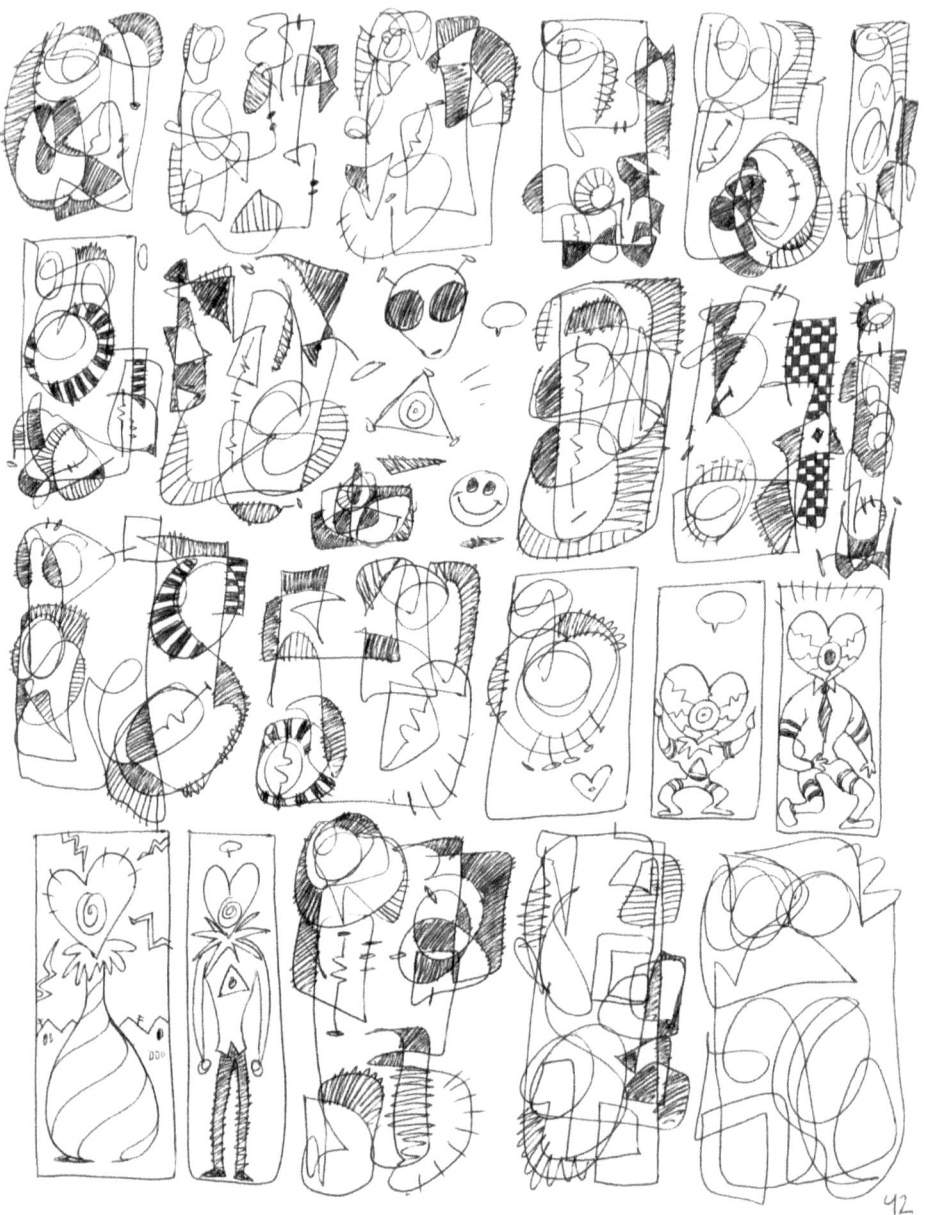

42

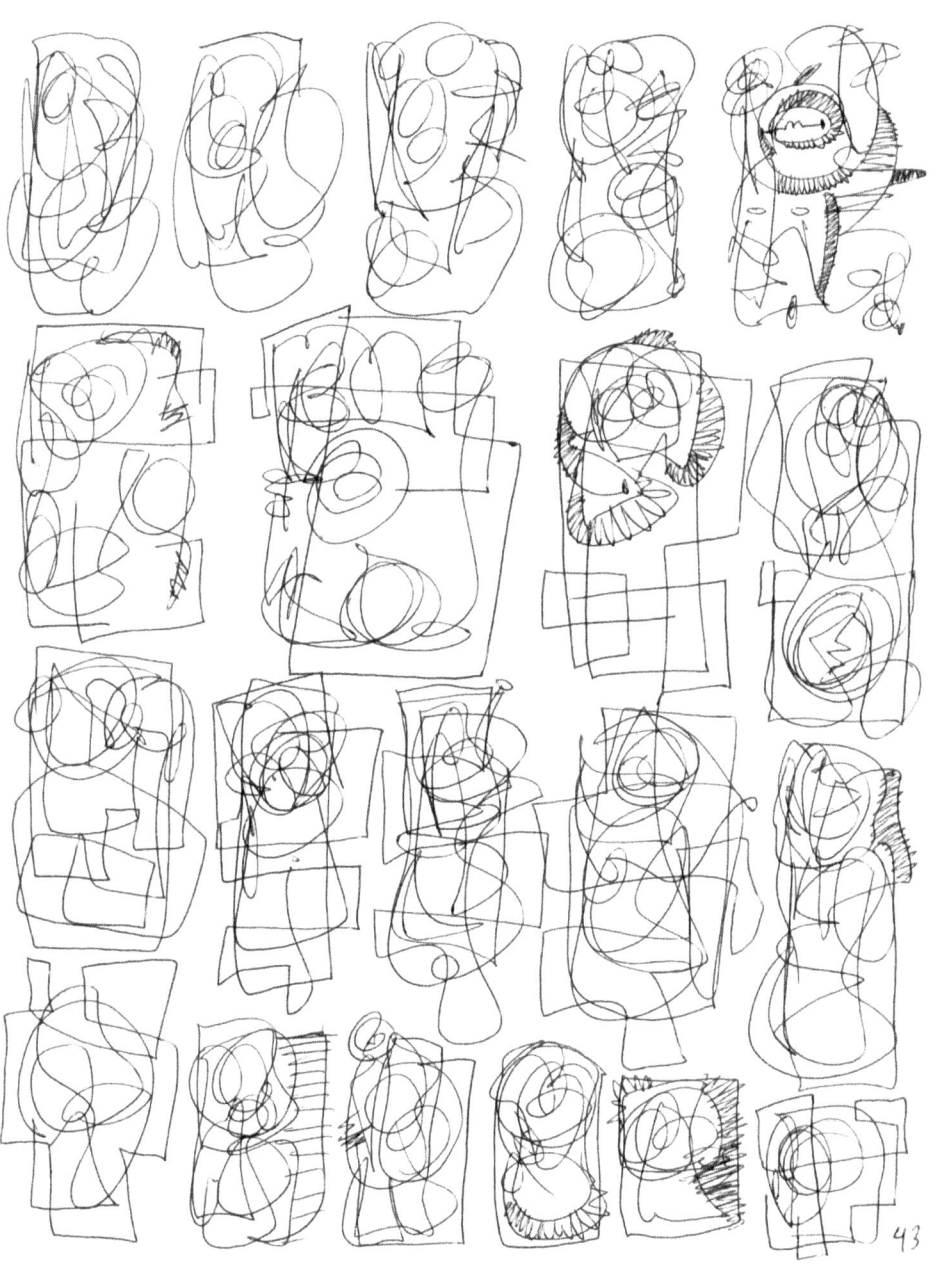

43

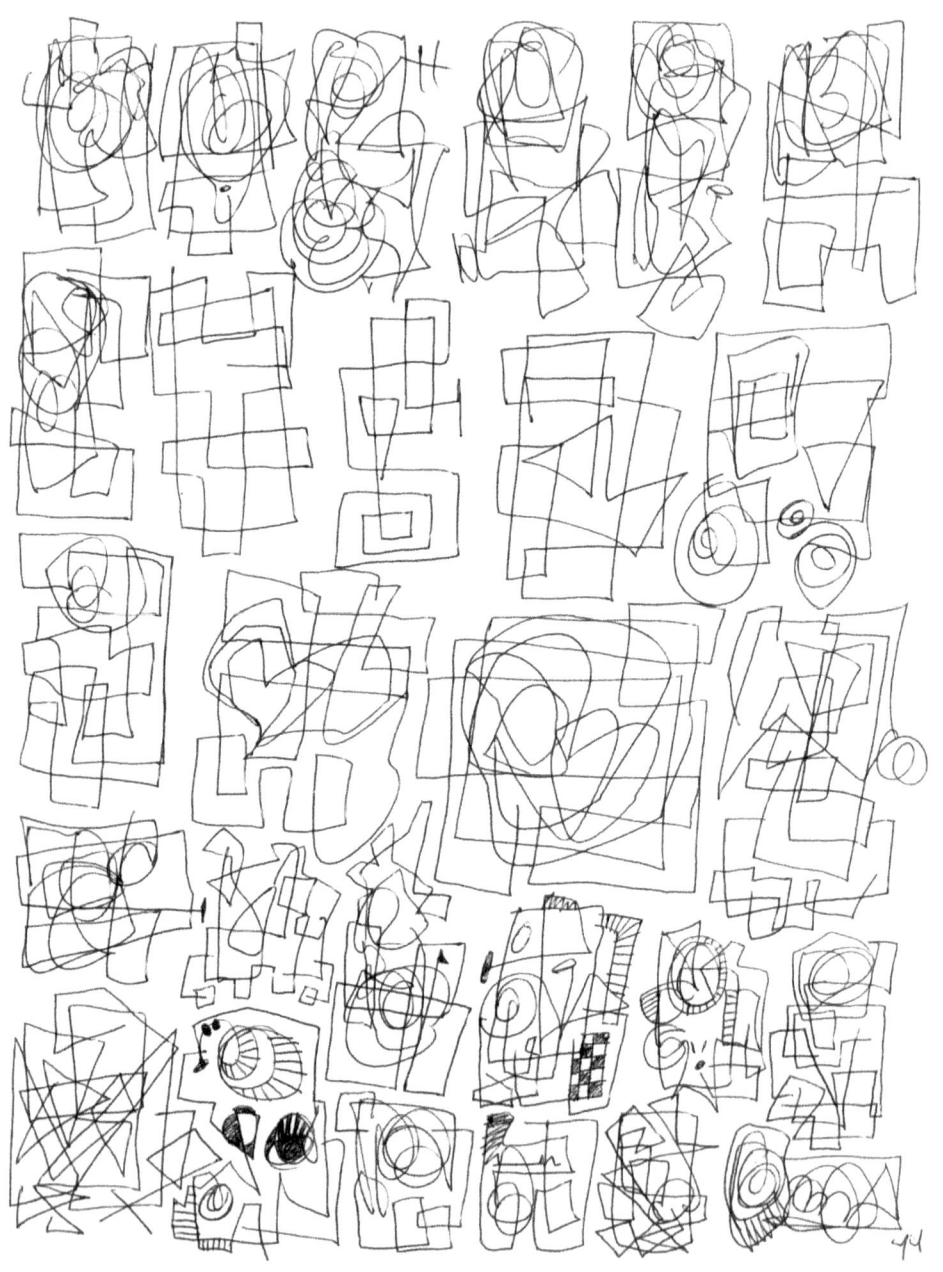

50

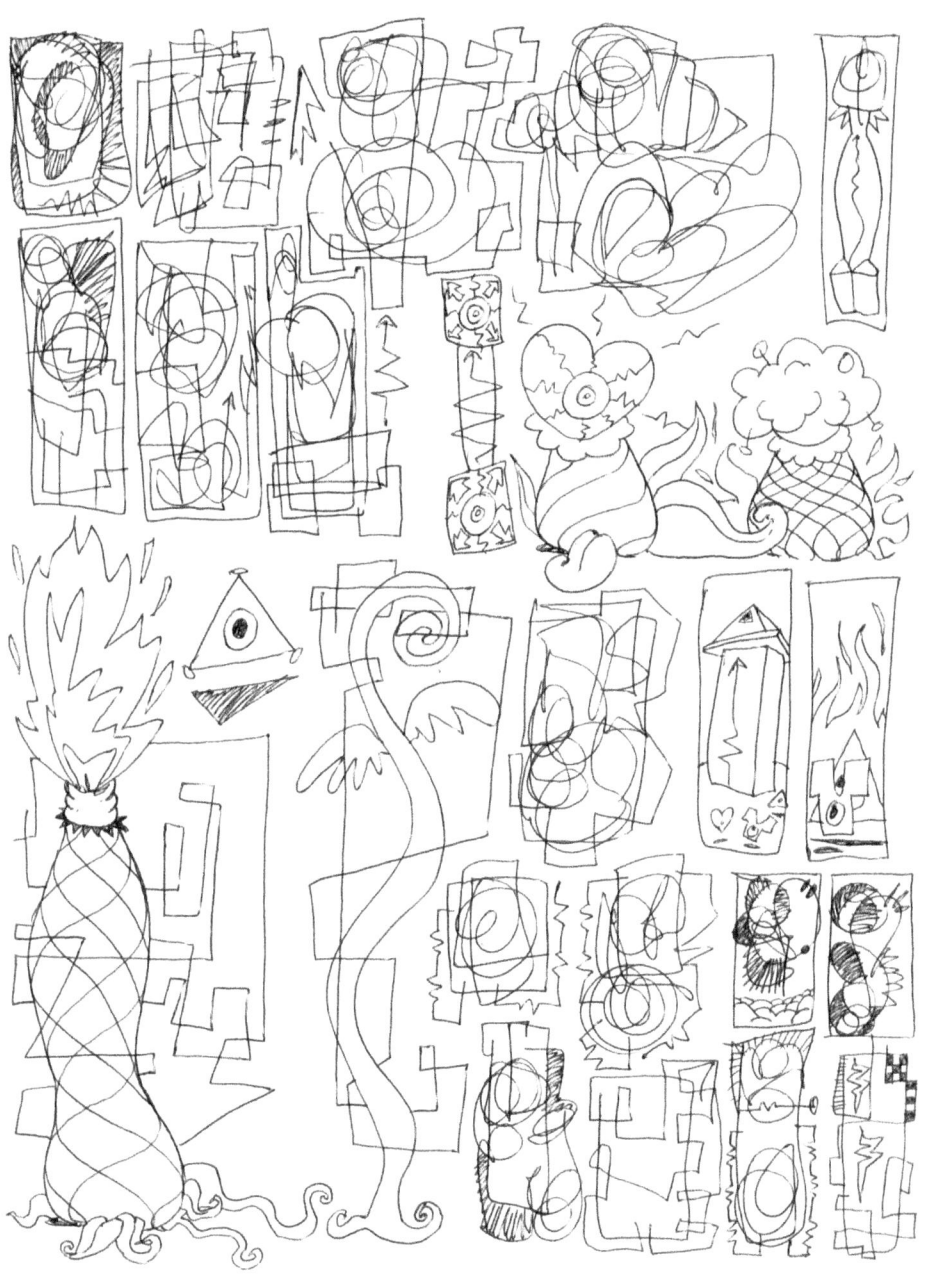

52

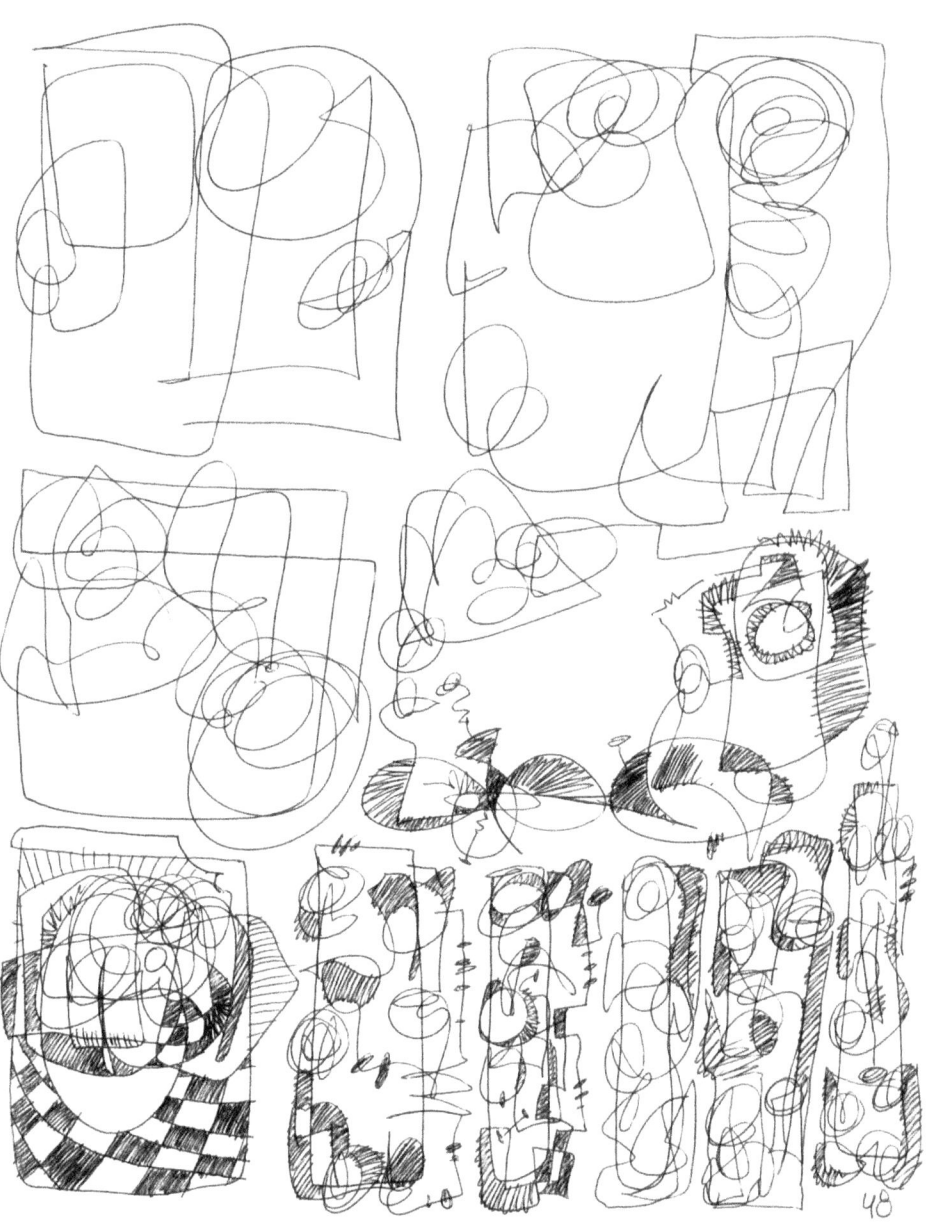

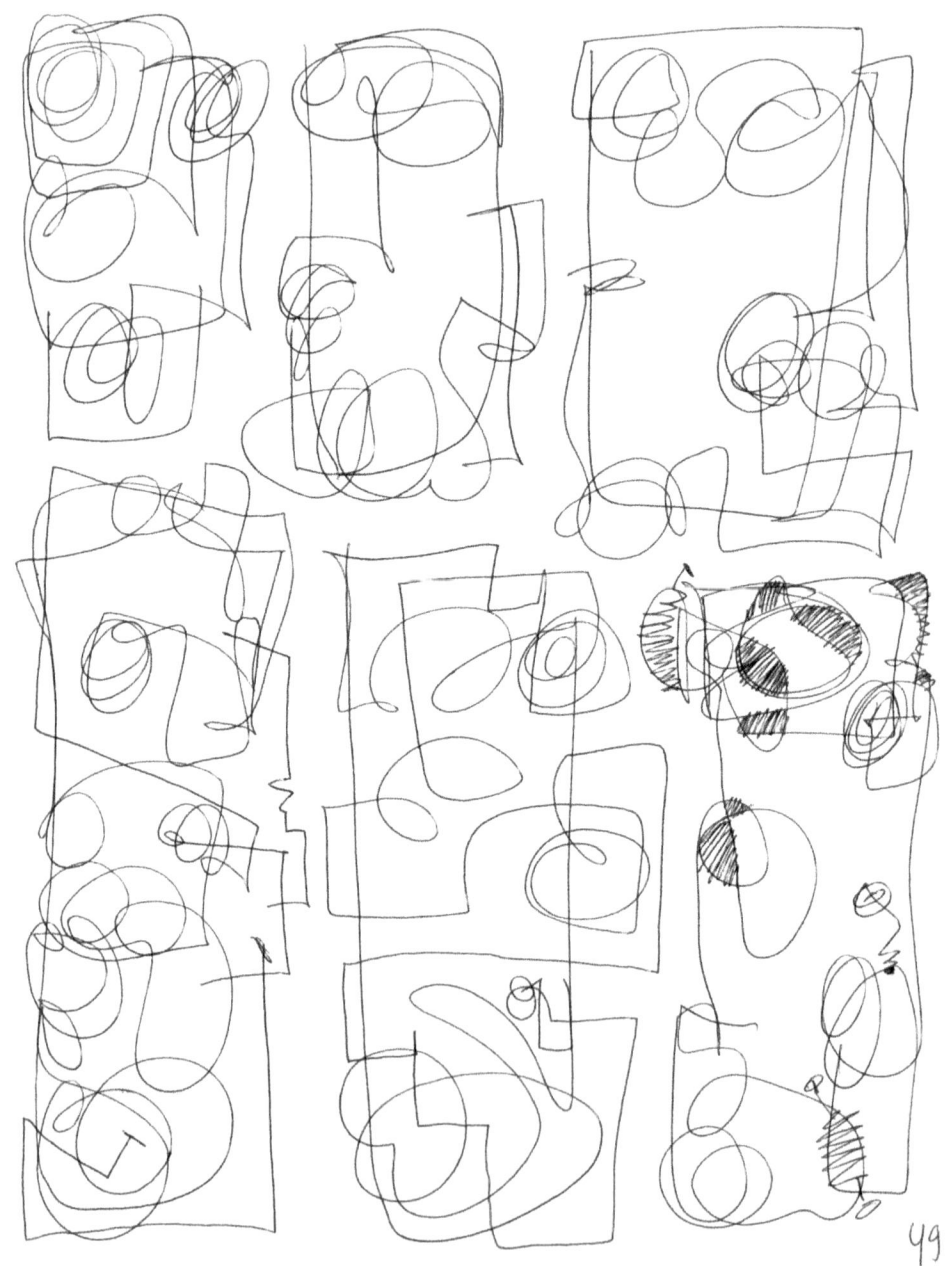

49

55

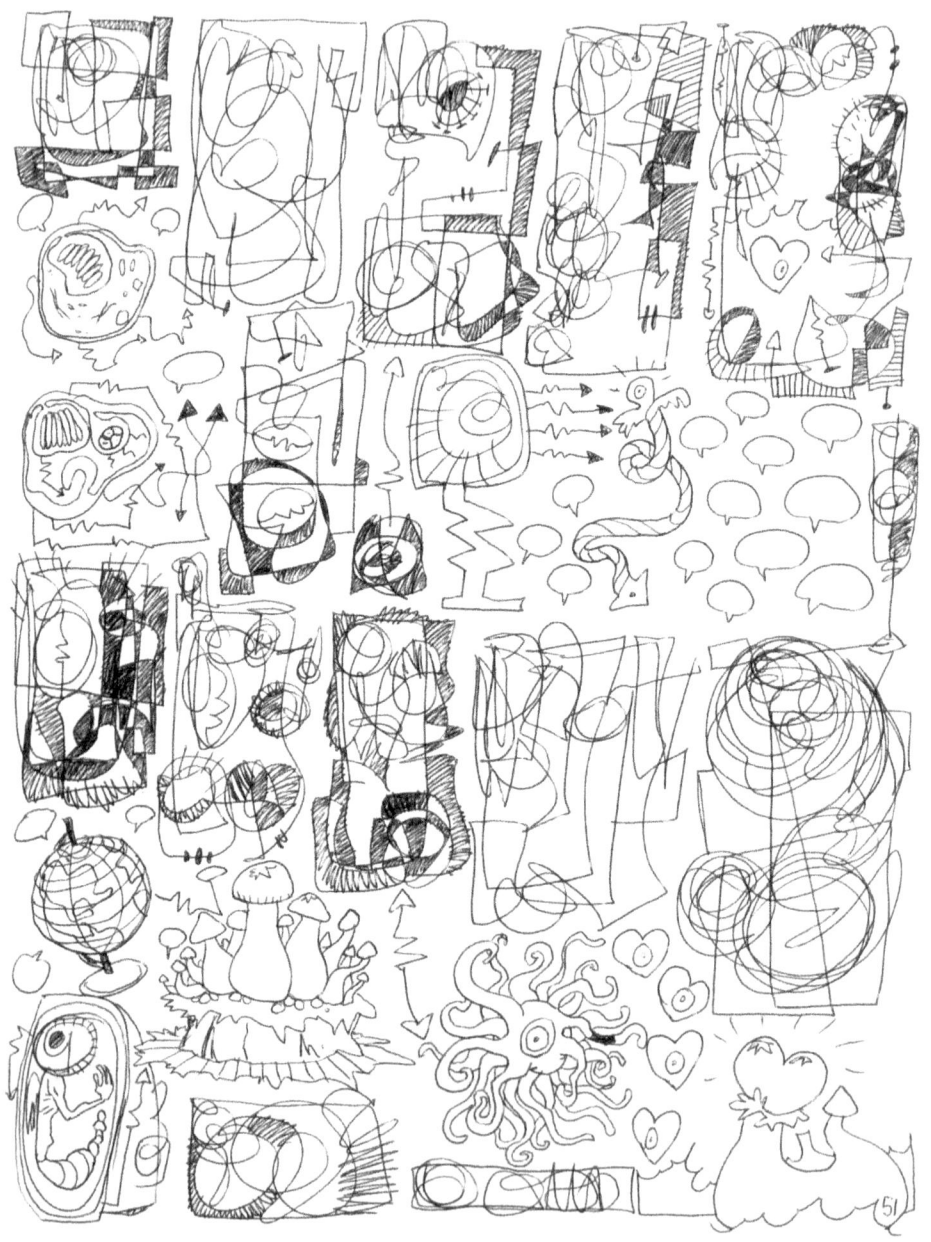

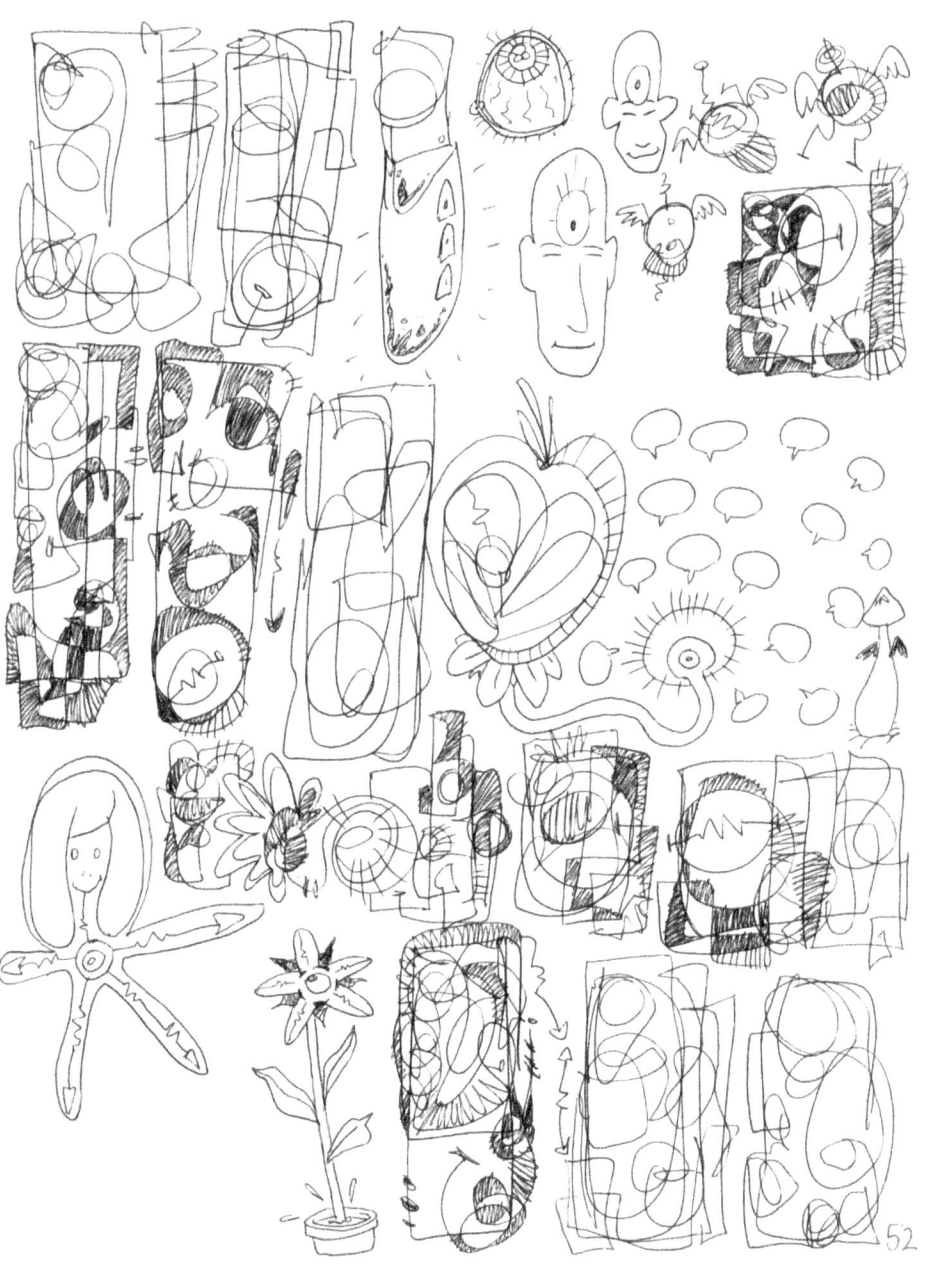

57

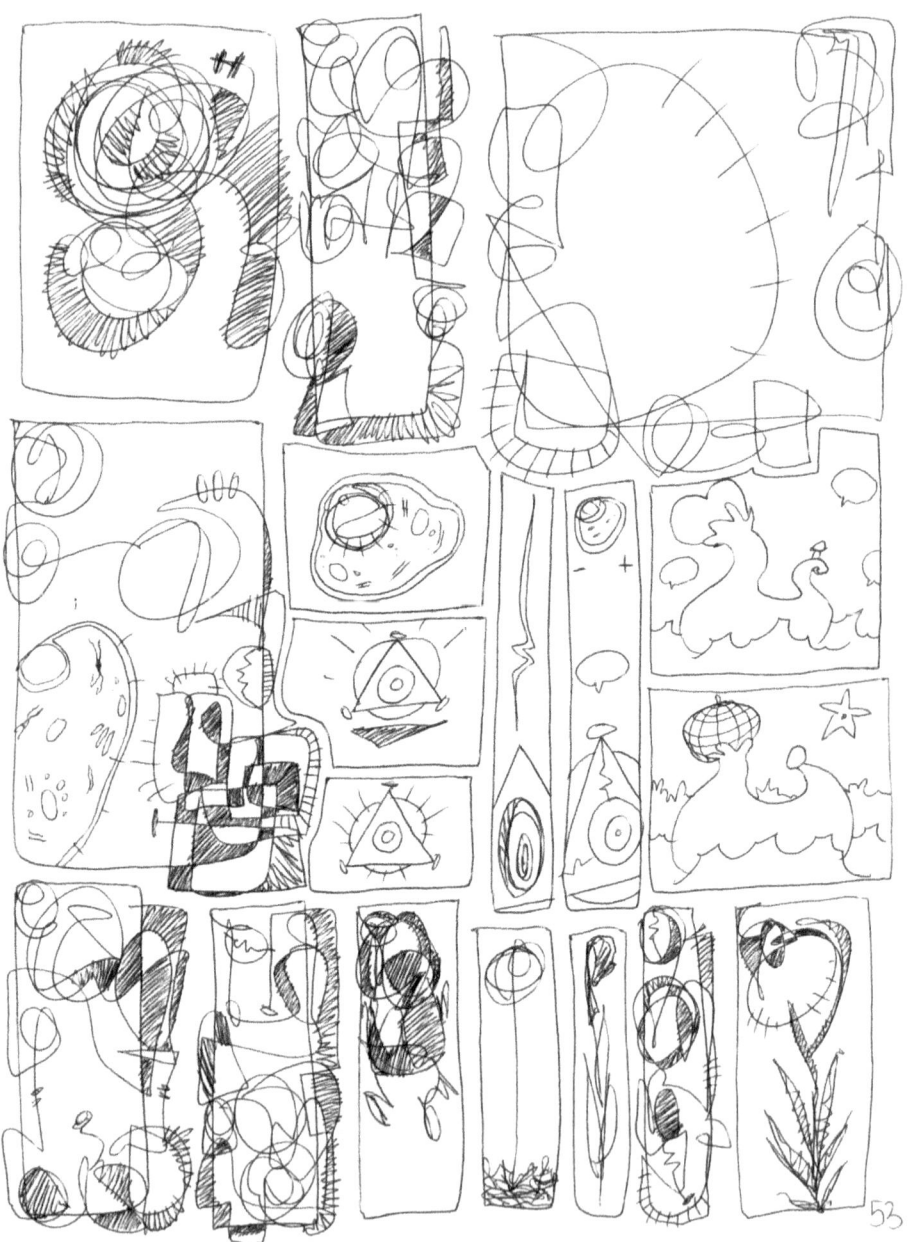

53

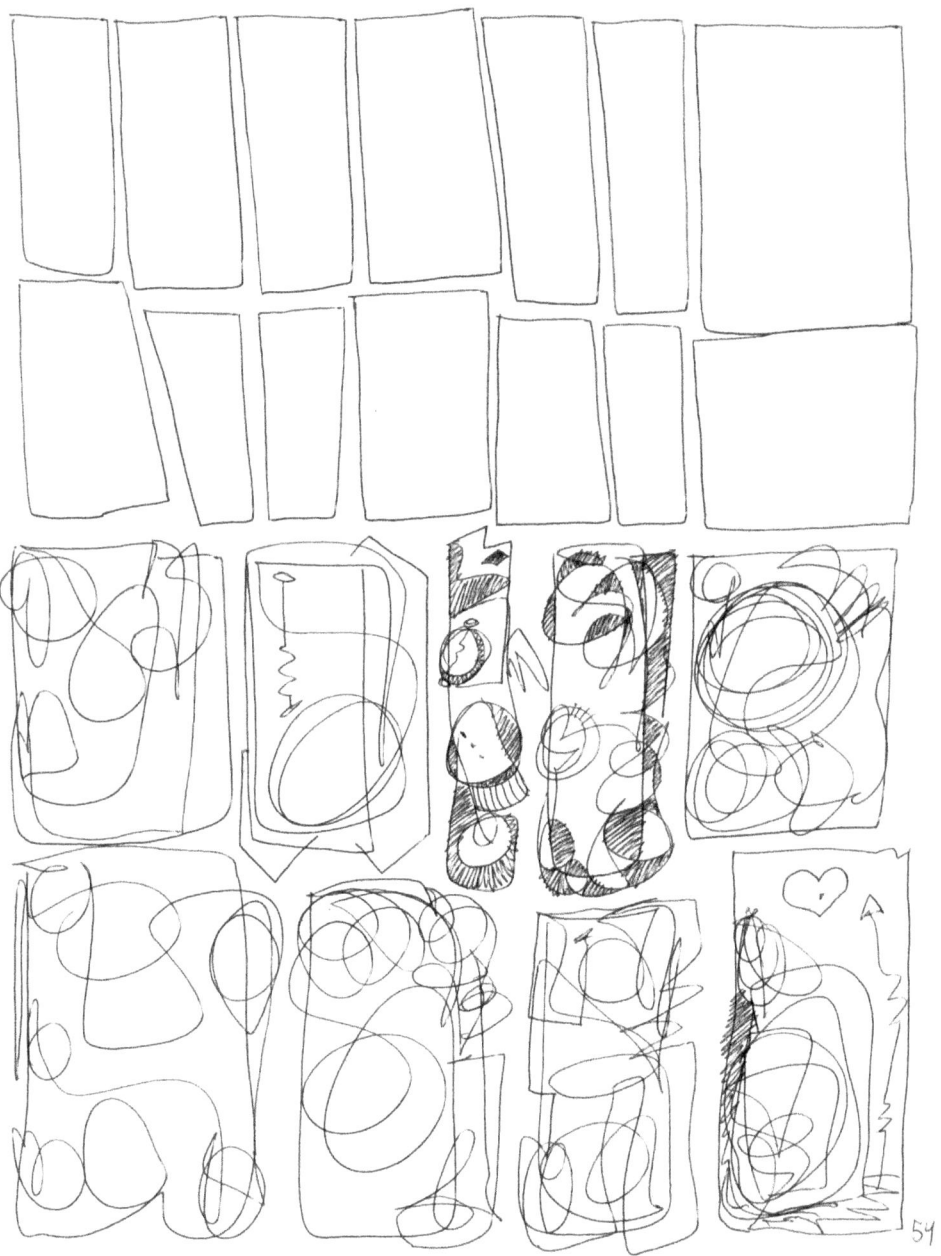

54

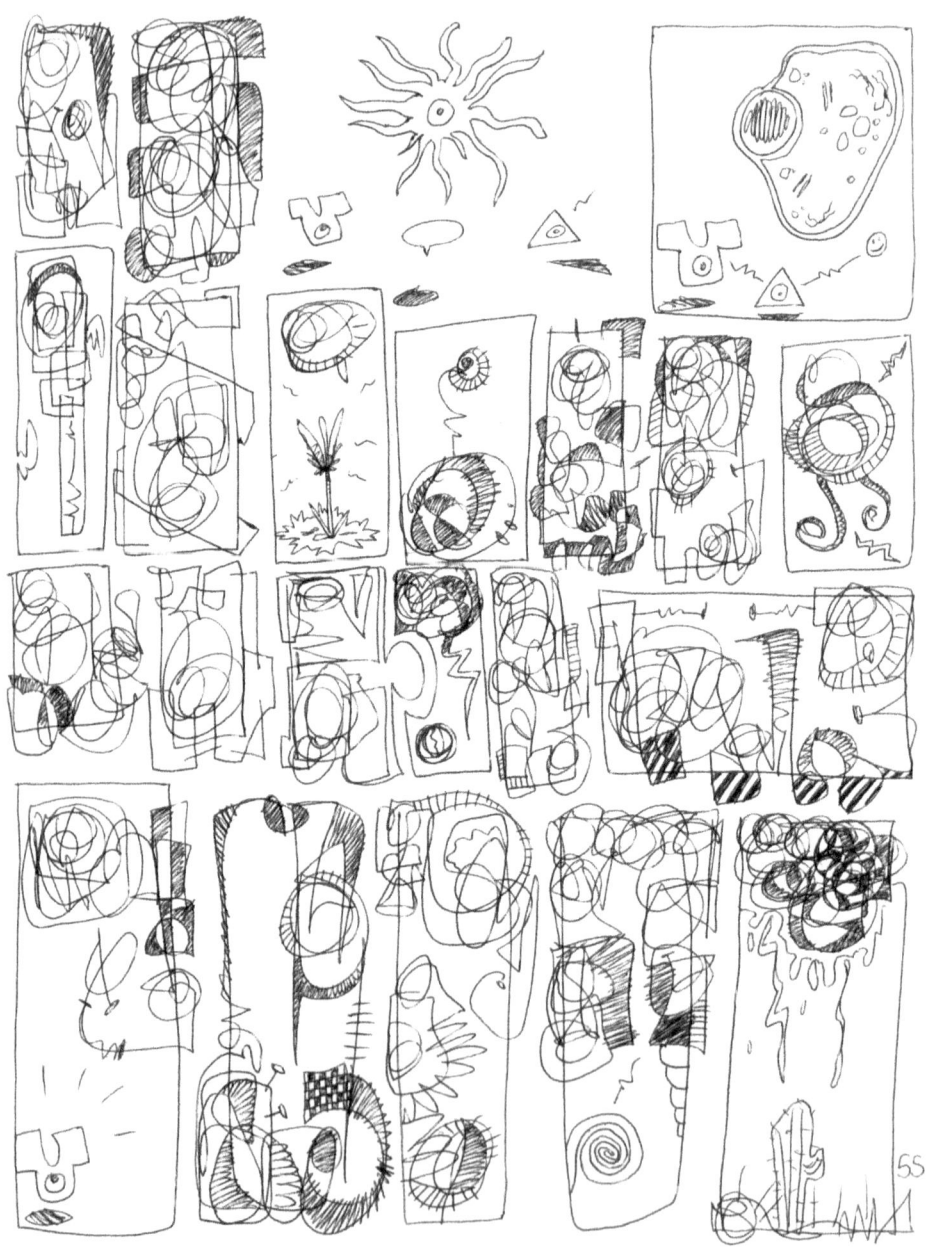

55

60

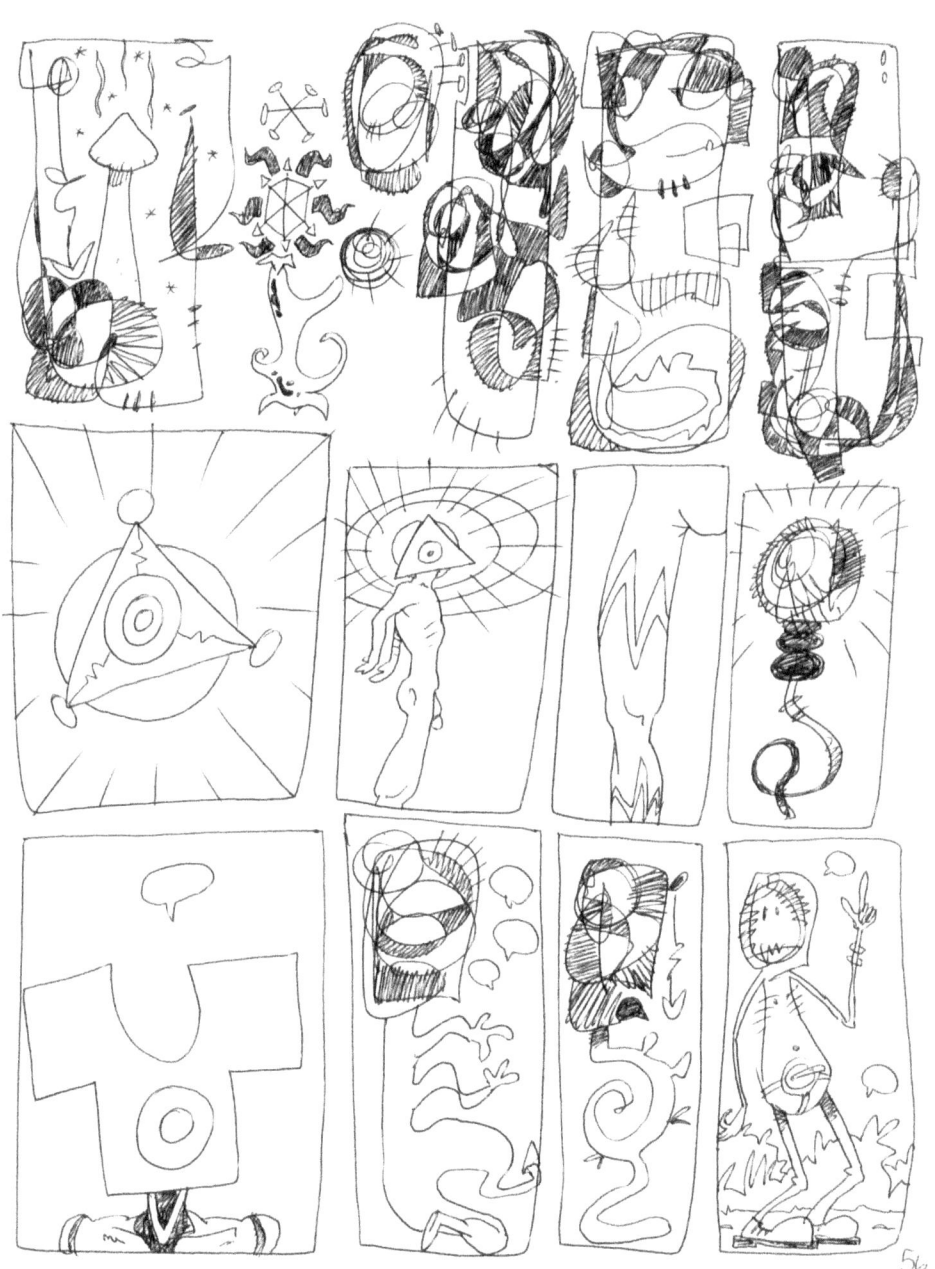

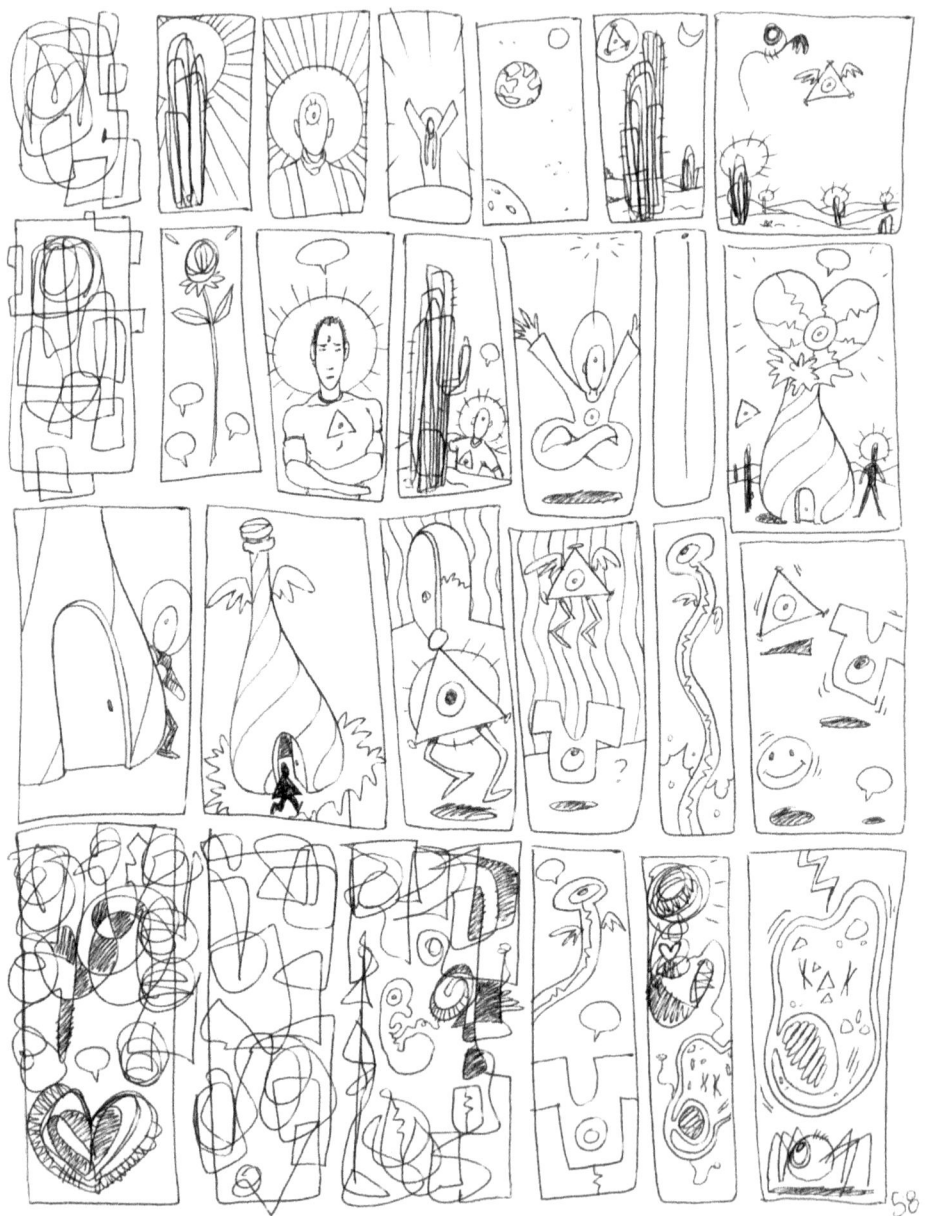

58

62

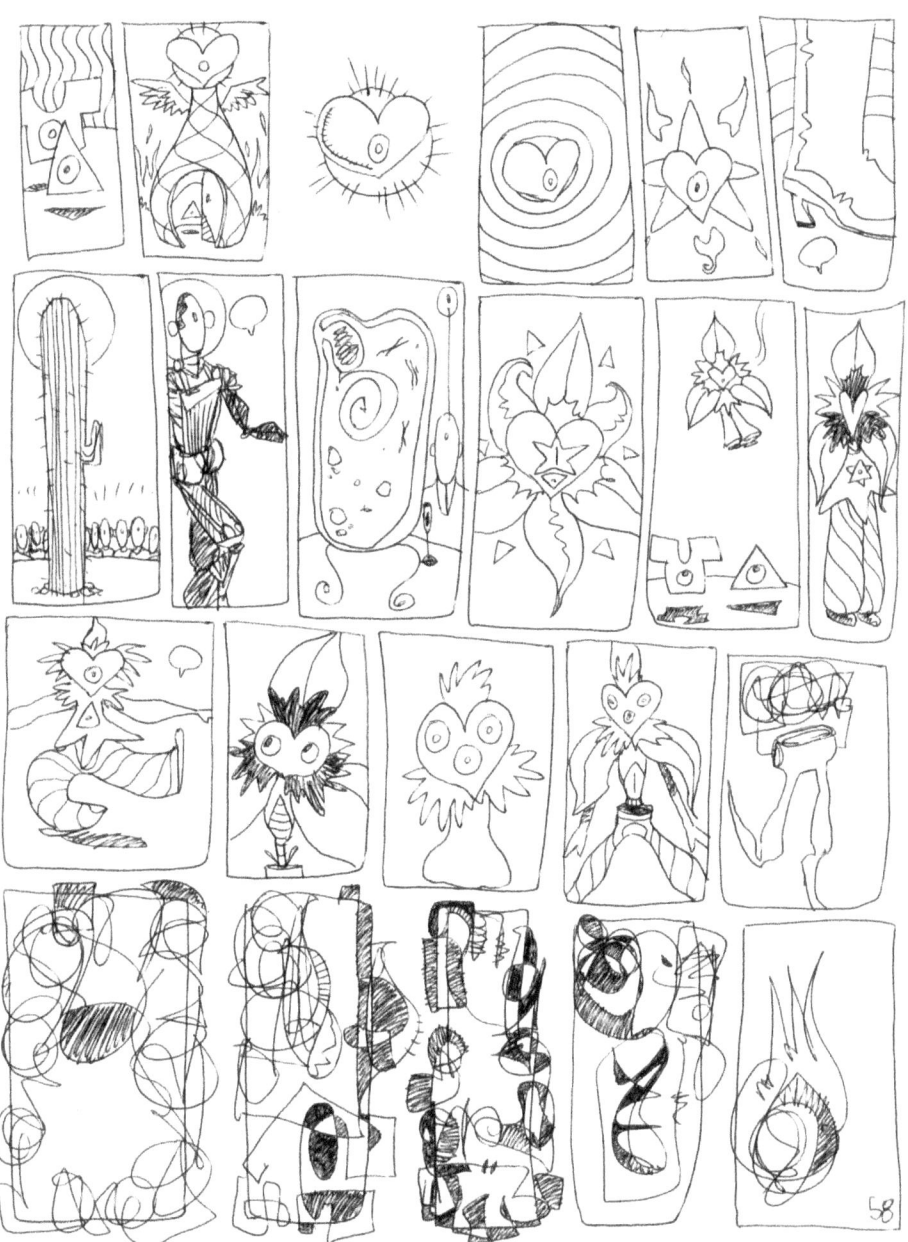

63

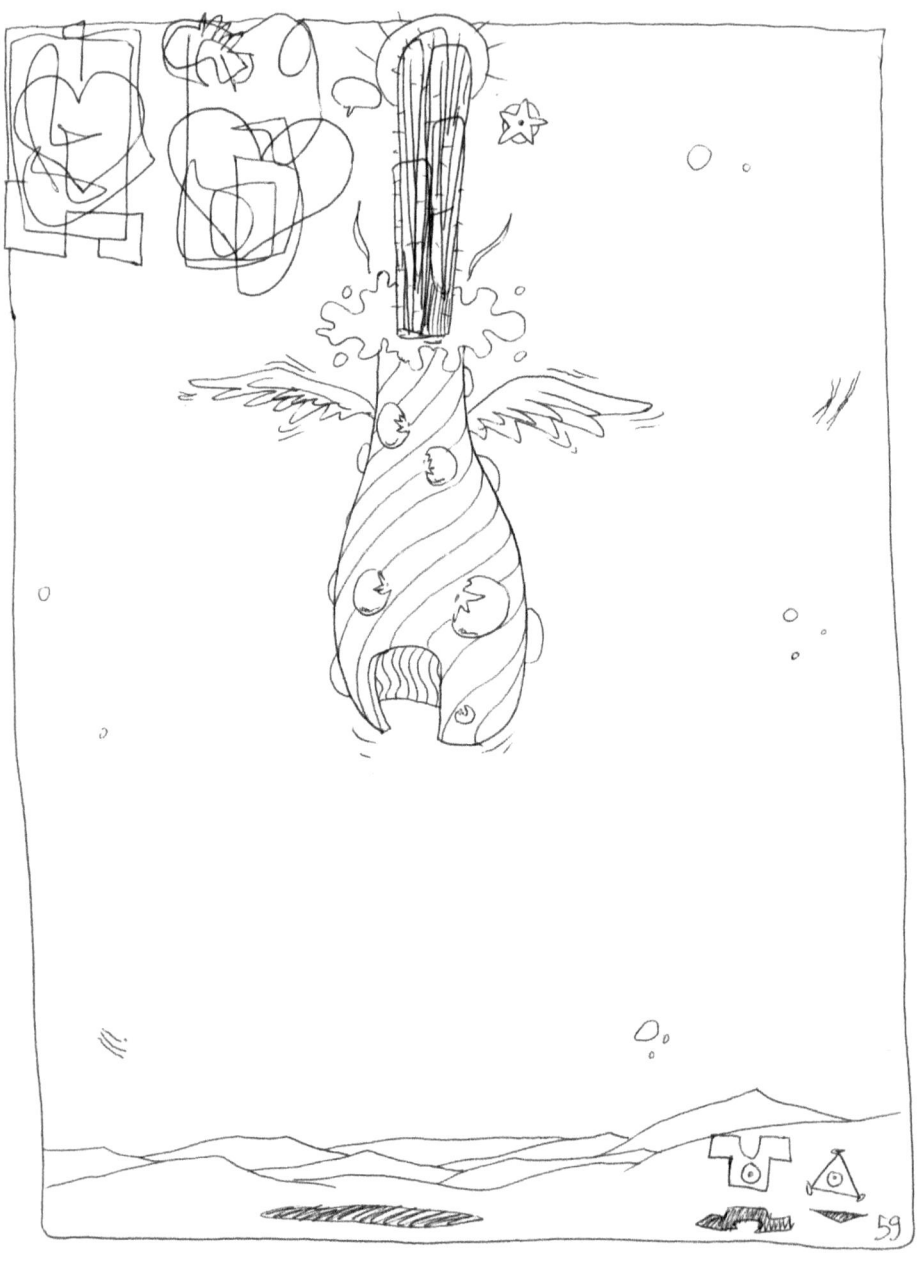

59

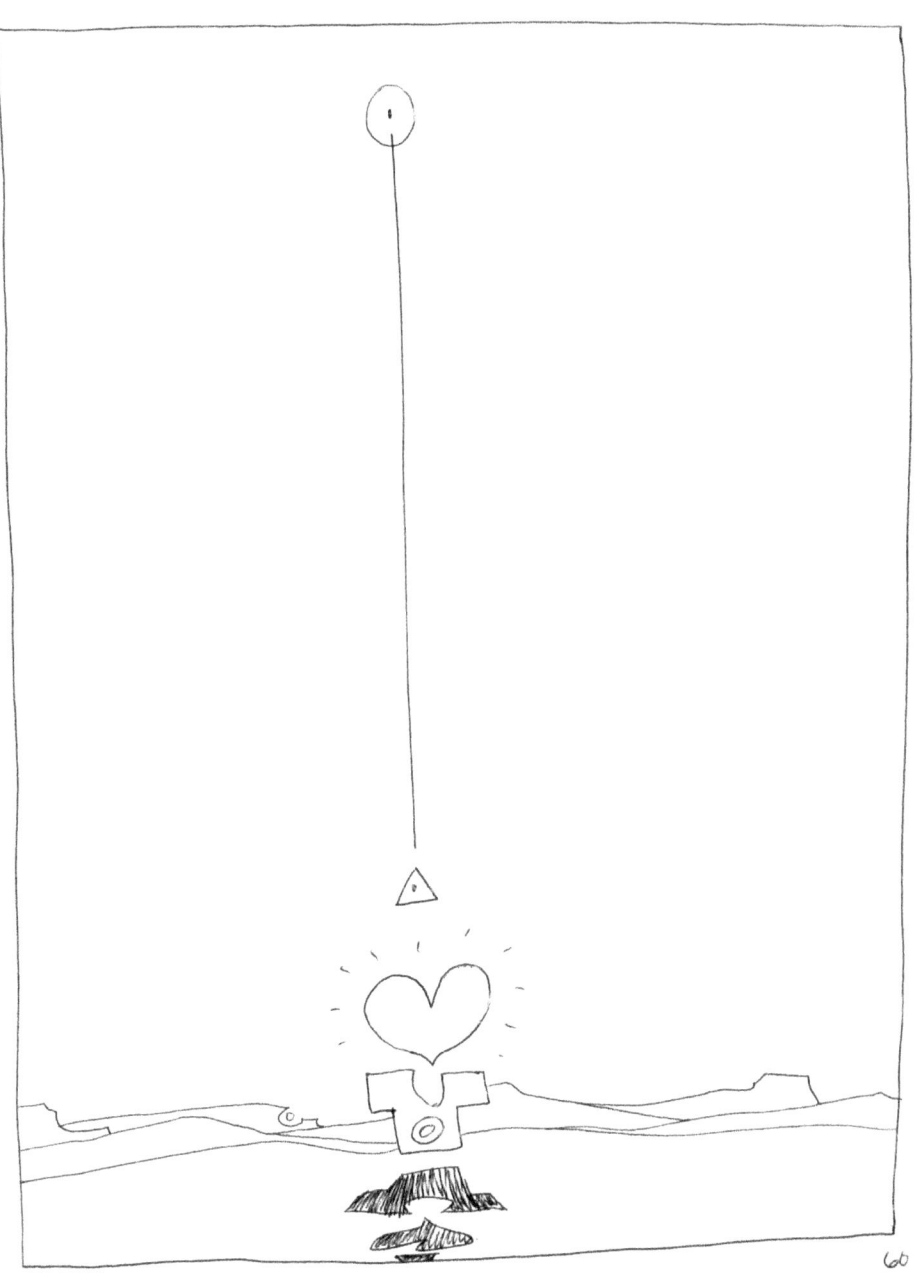

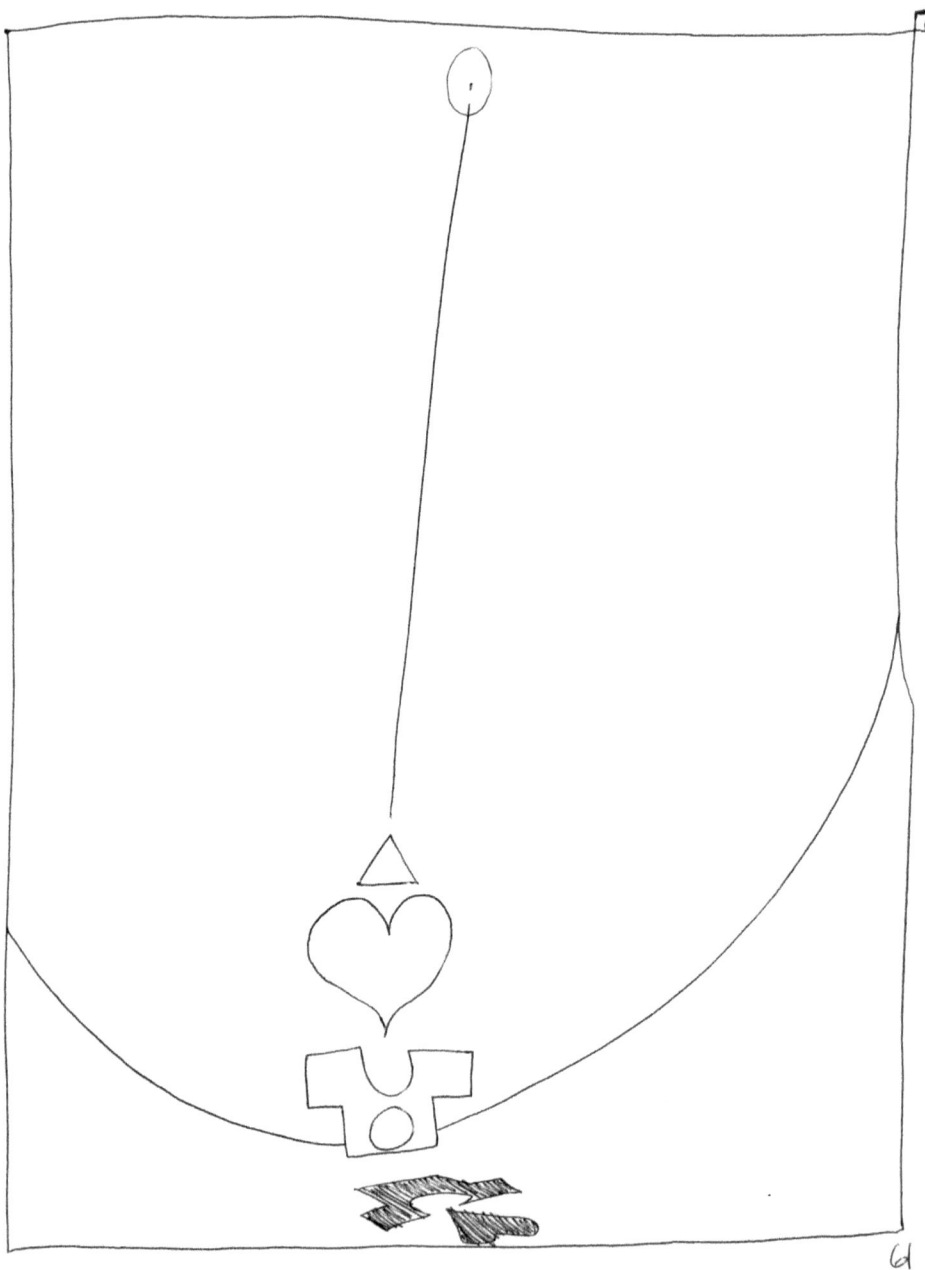

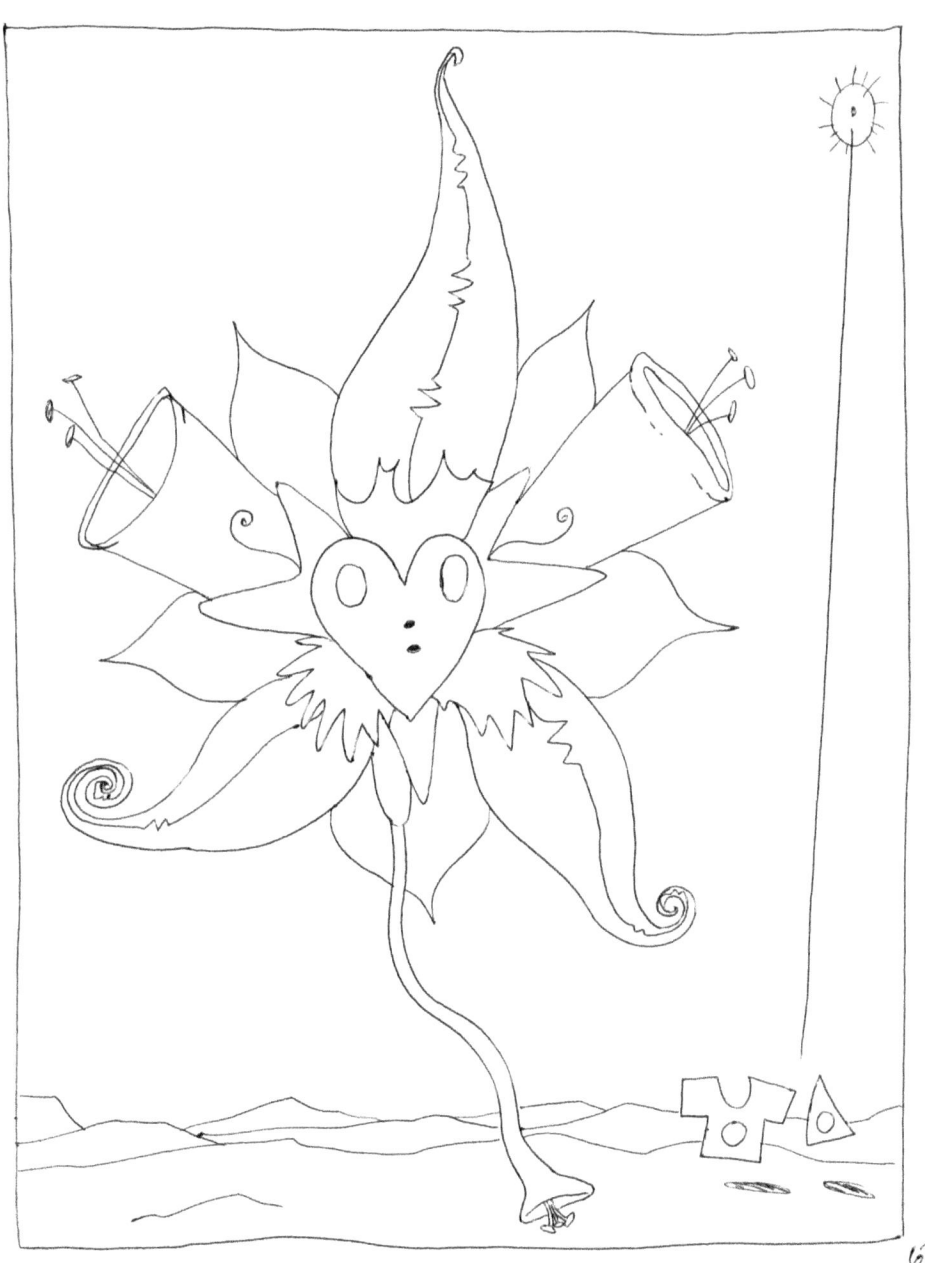

62

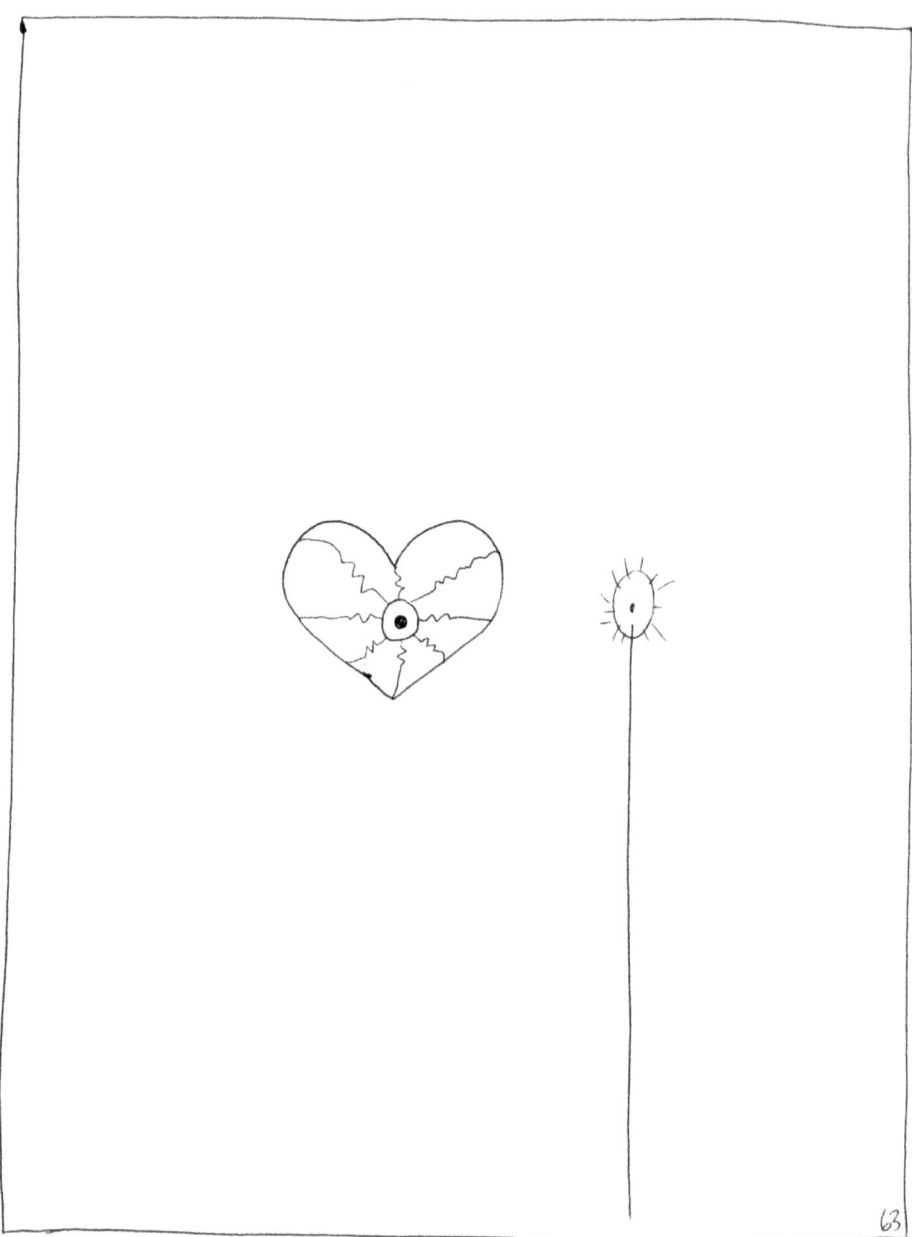

63

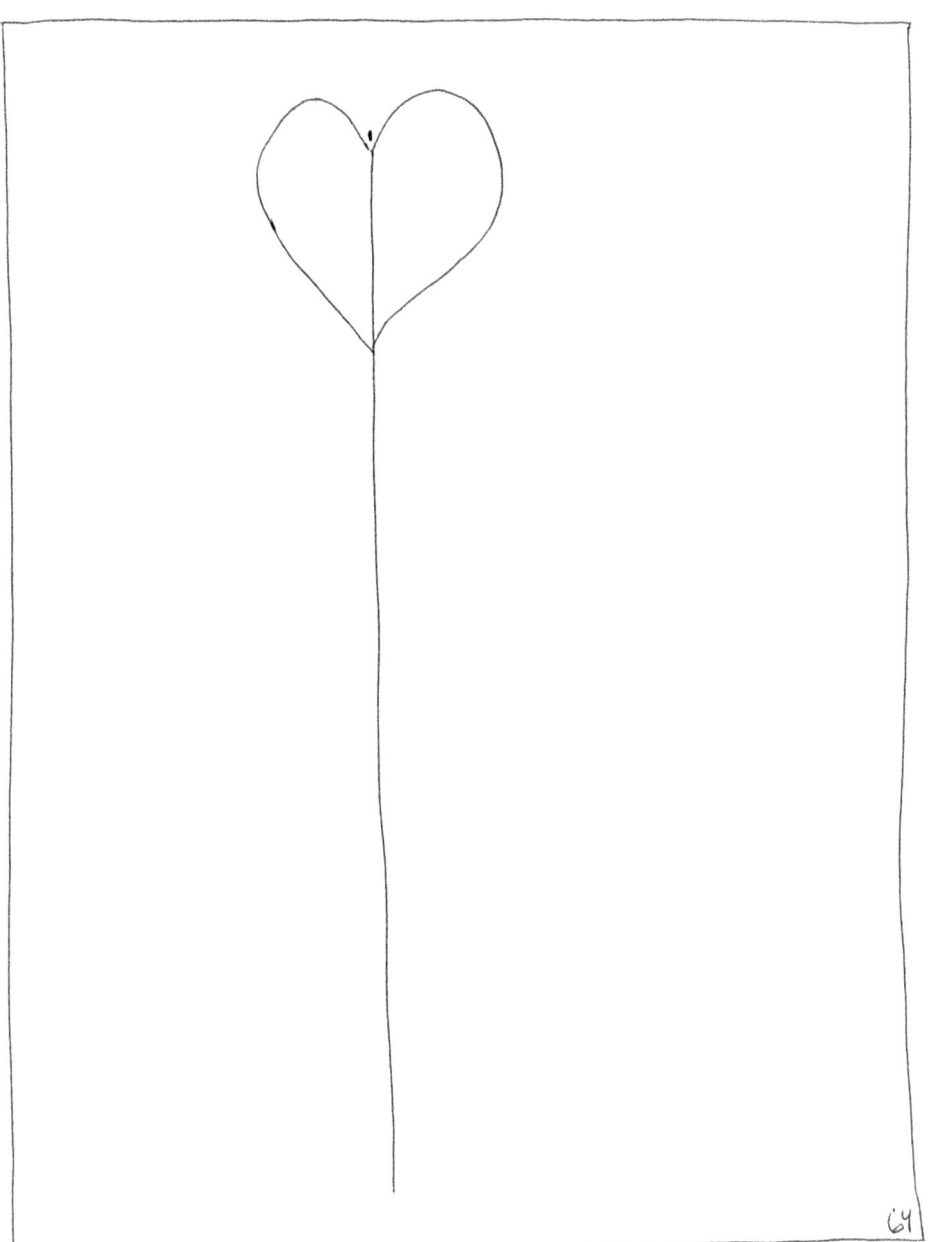

64

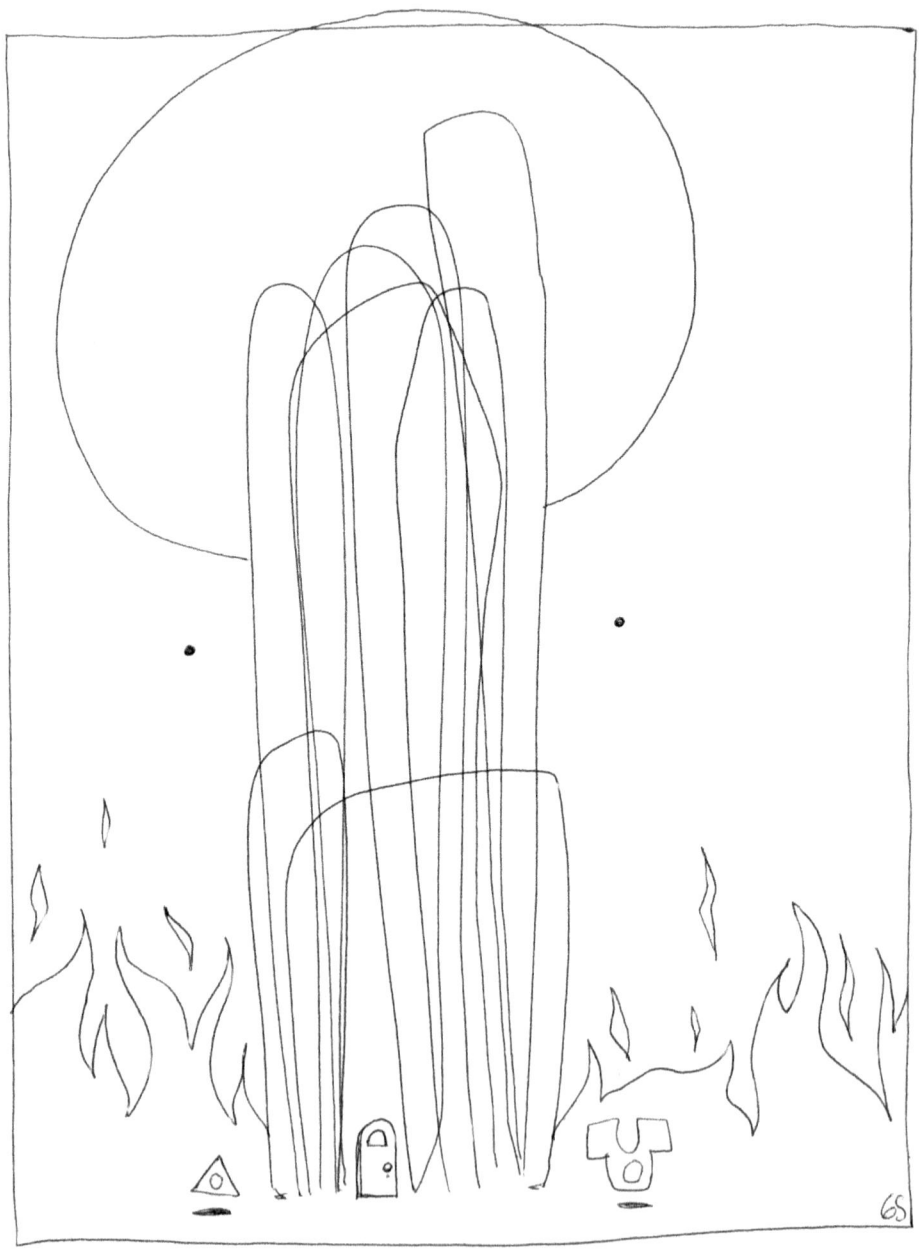

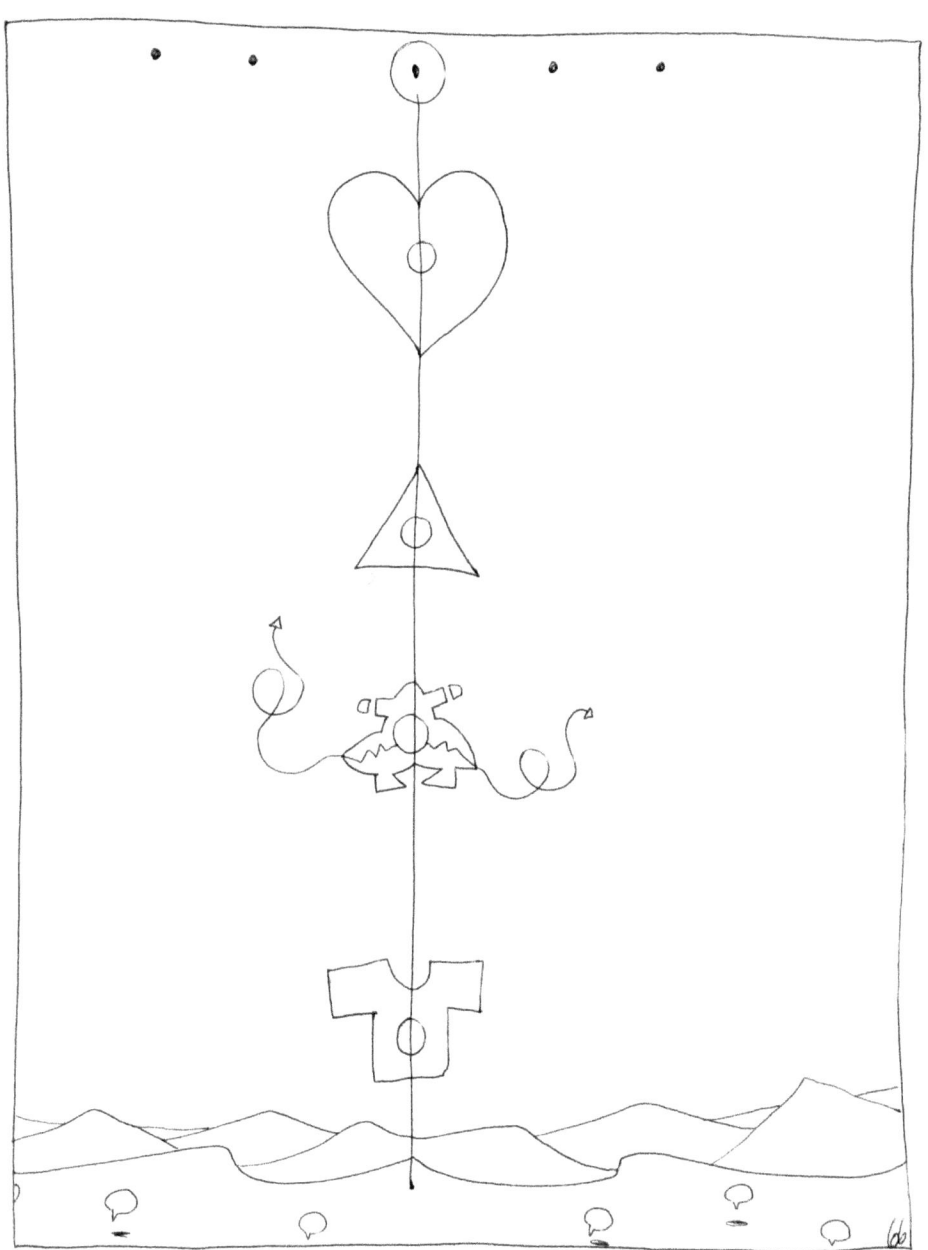

71

67

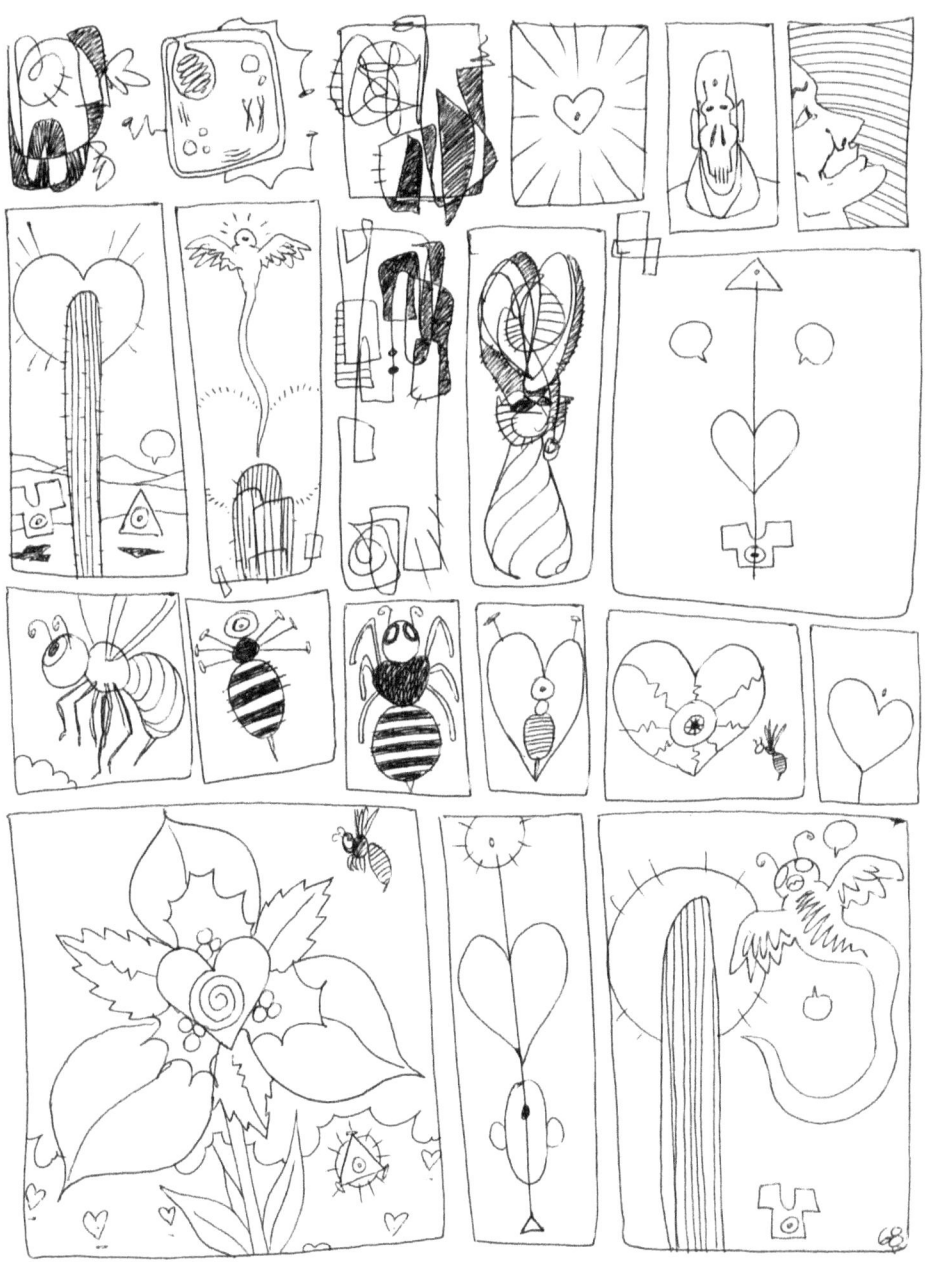

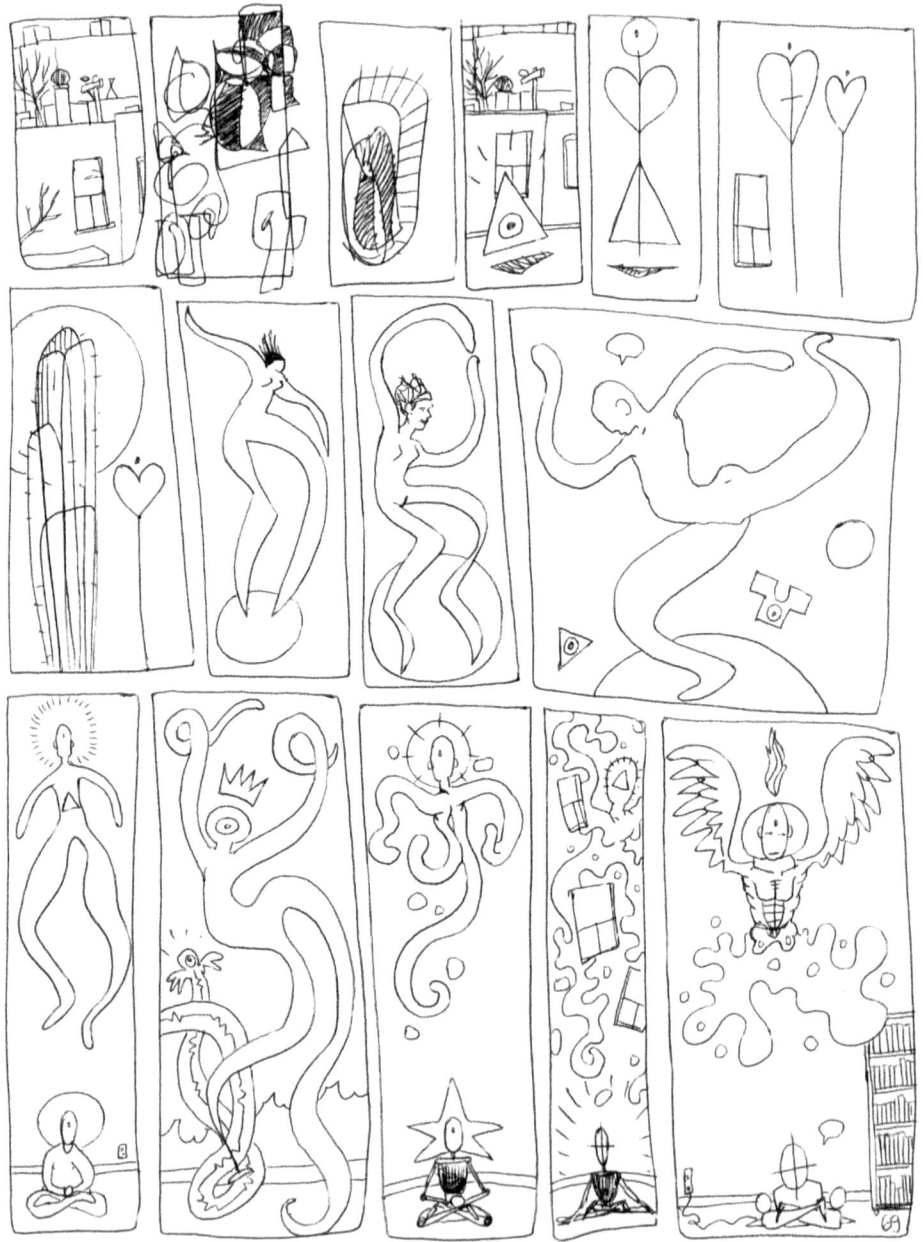

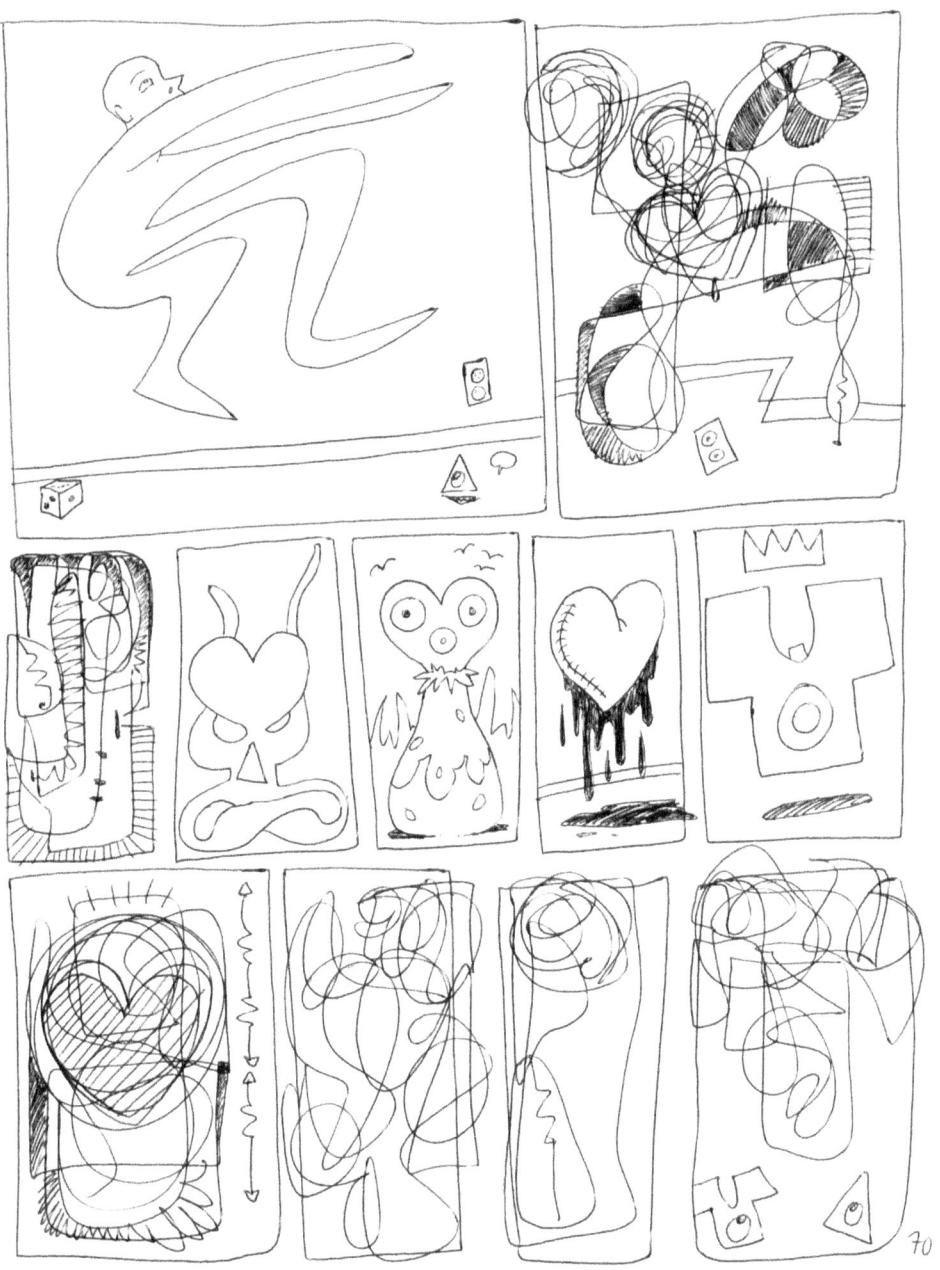

75

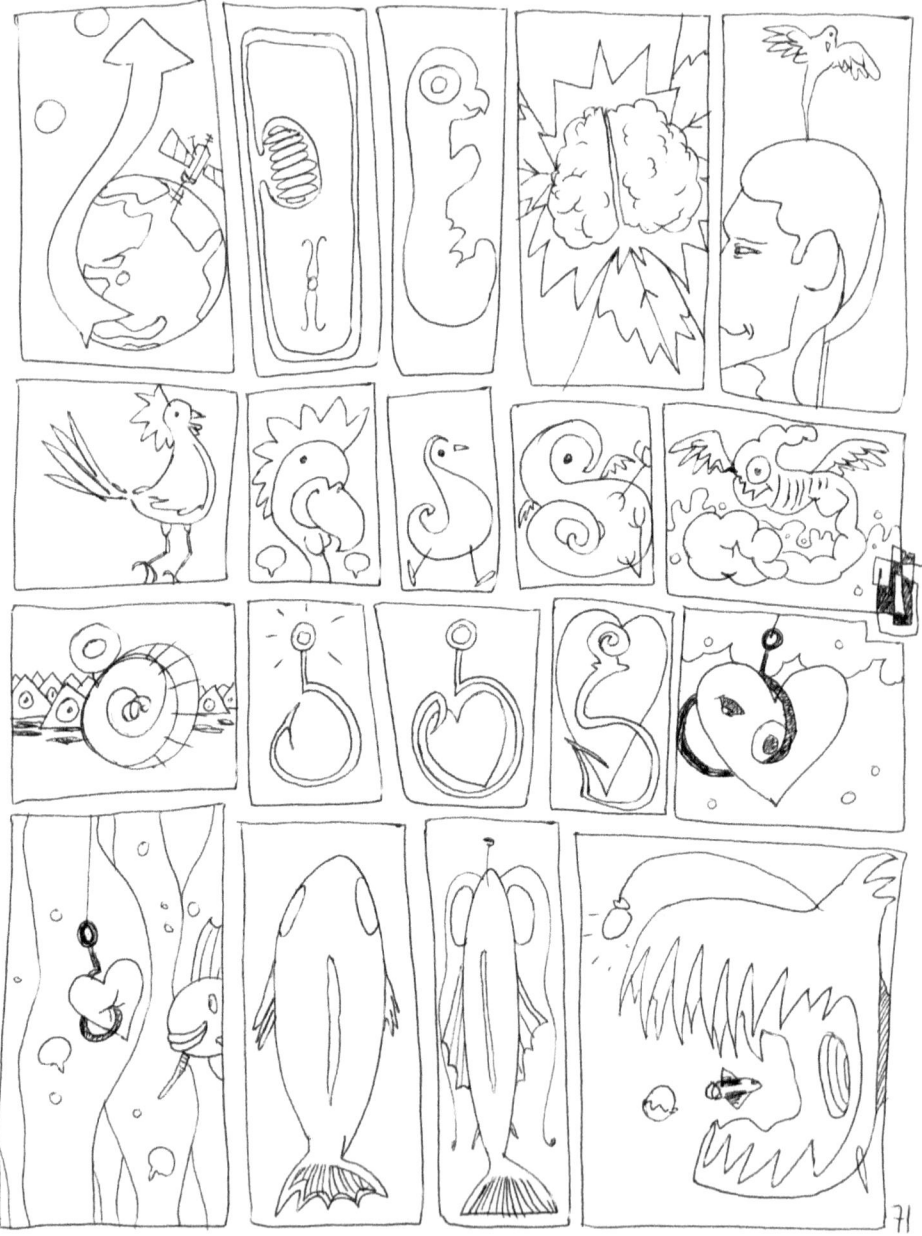

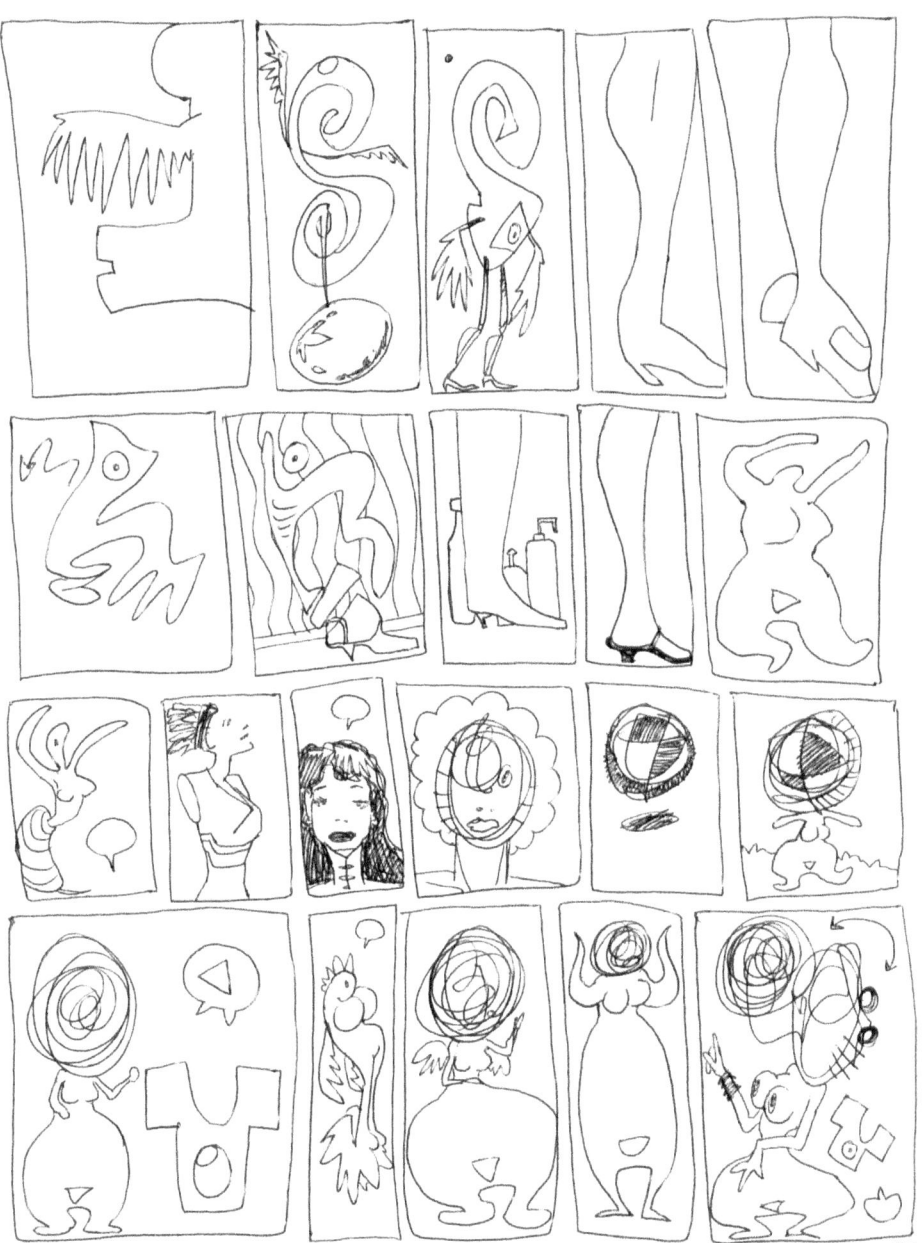

77

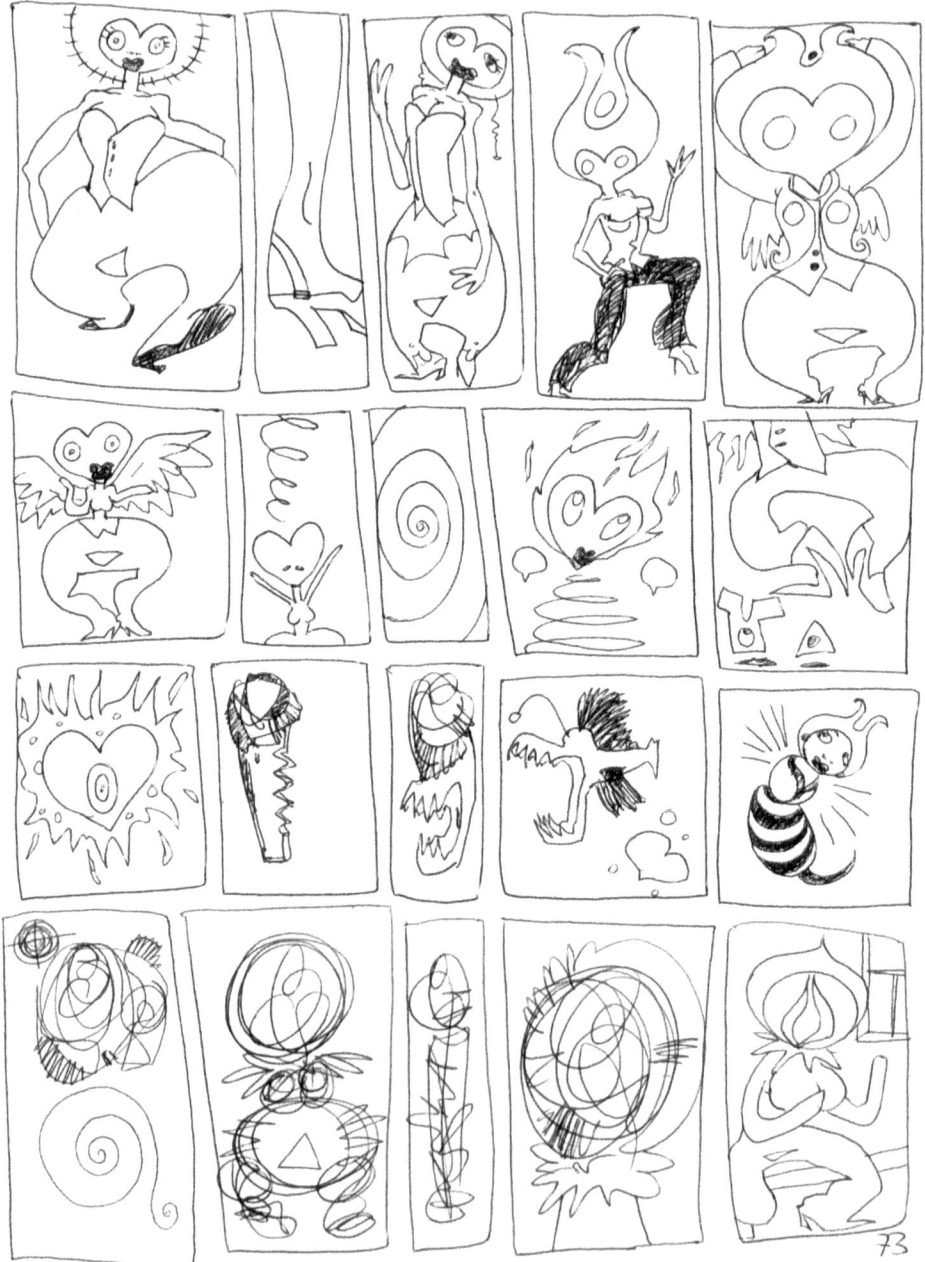

73

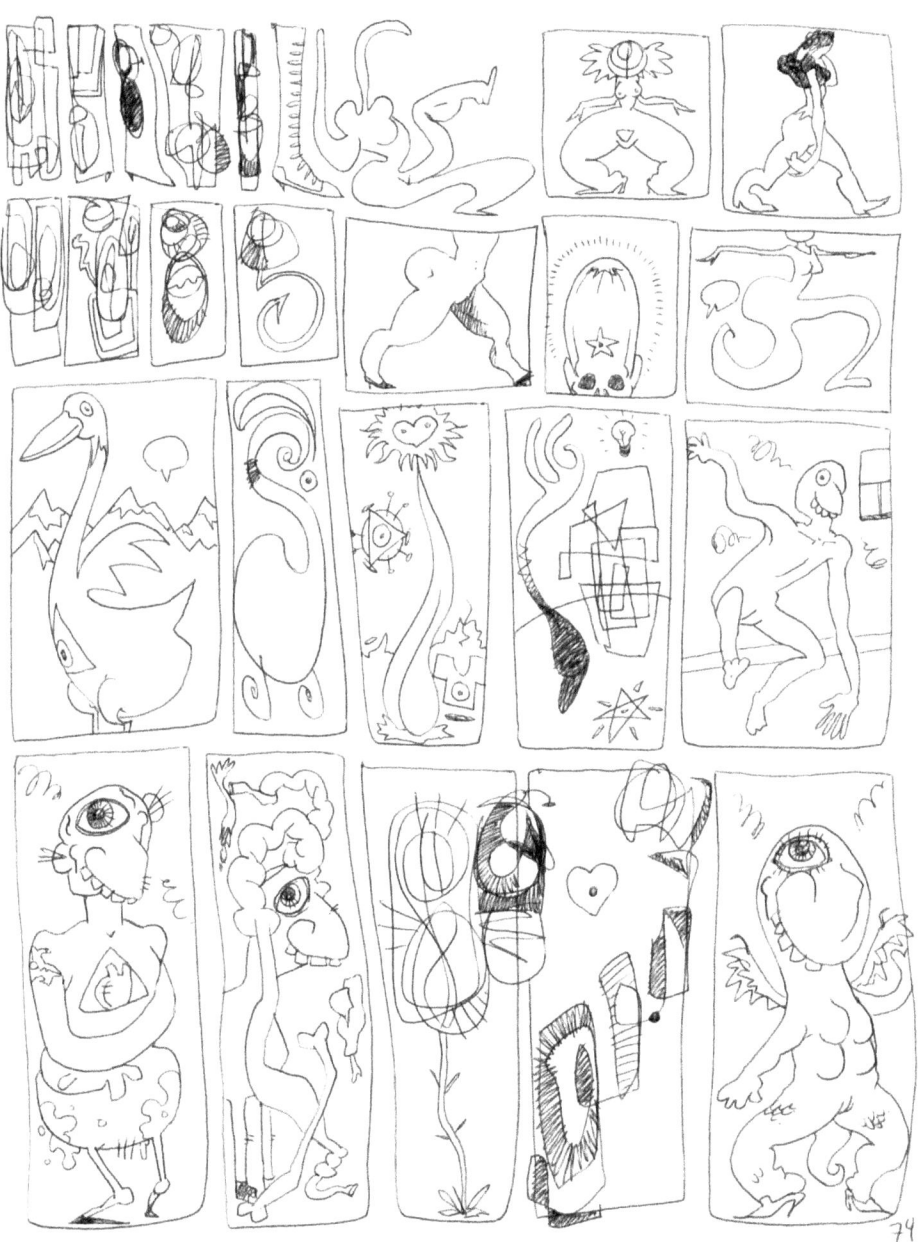

74

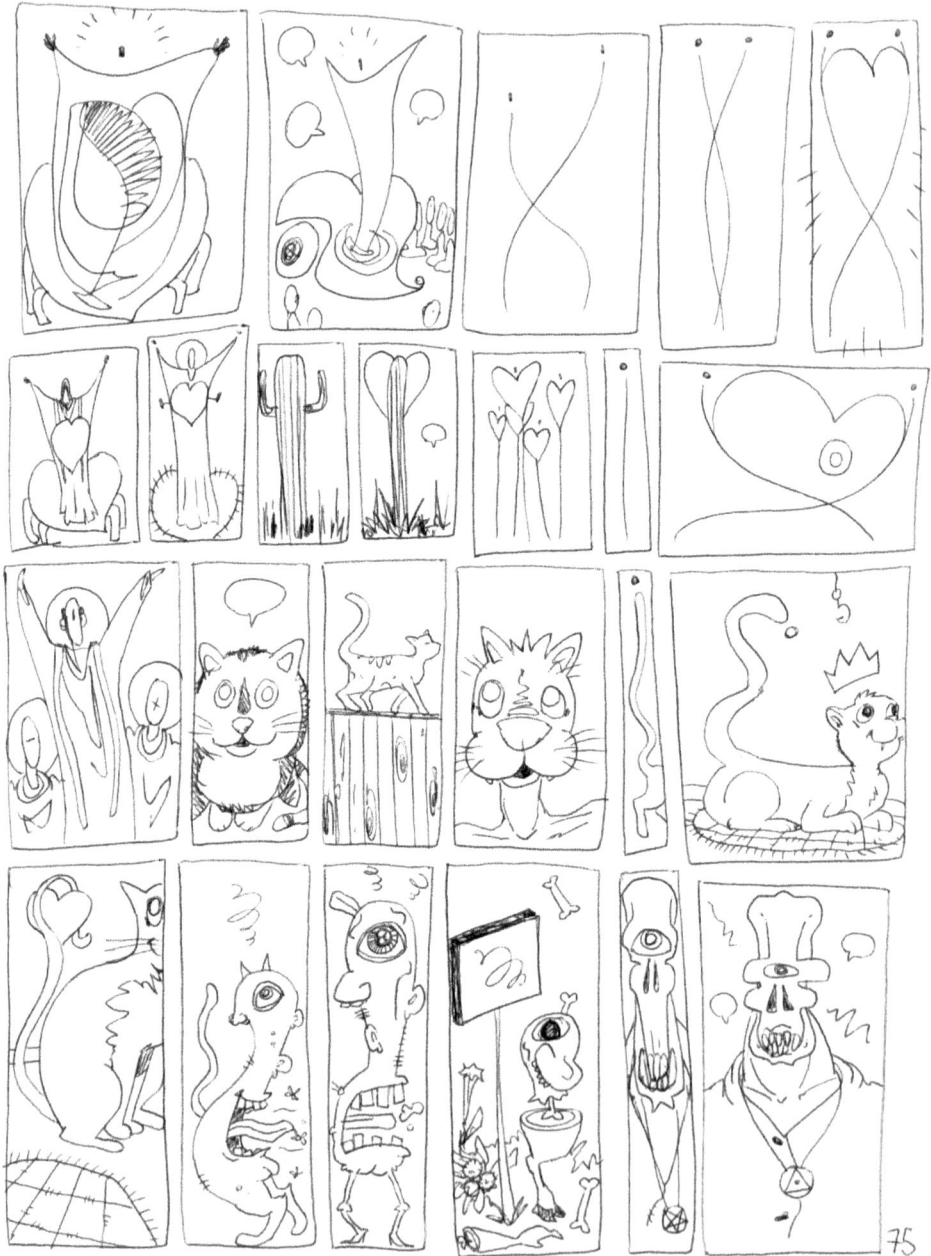

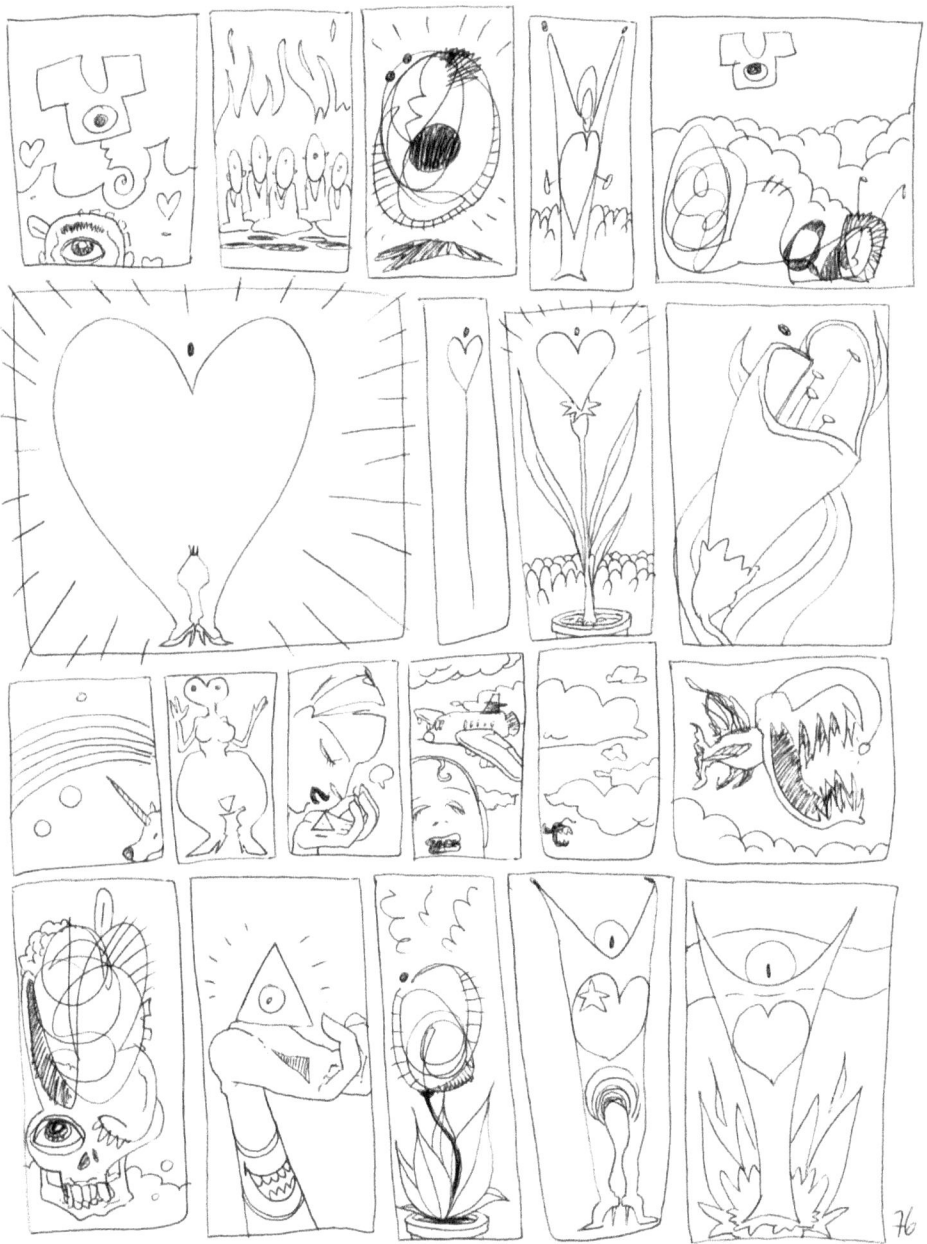

81

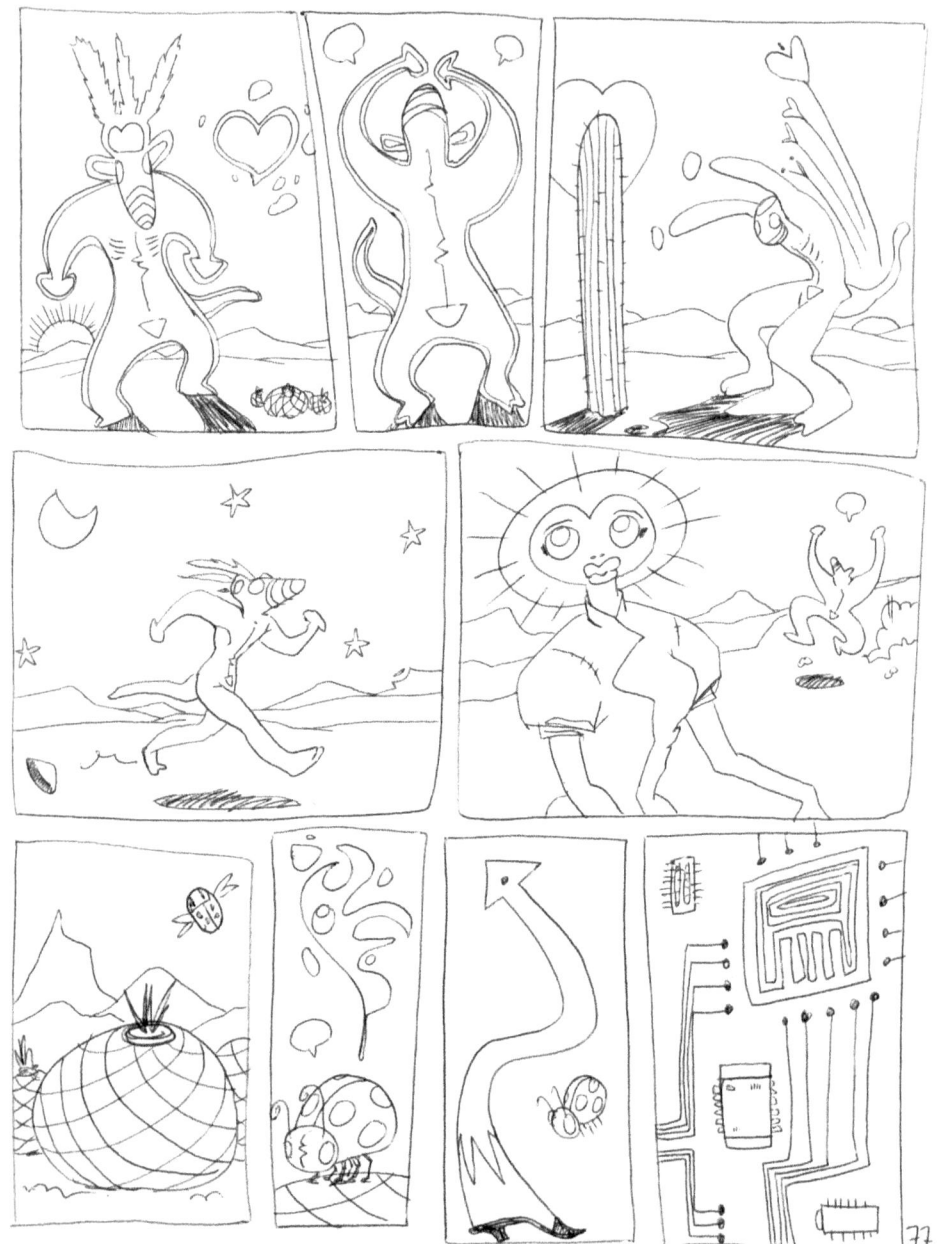

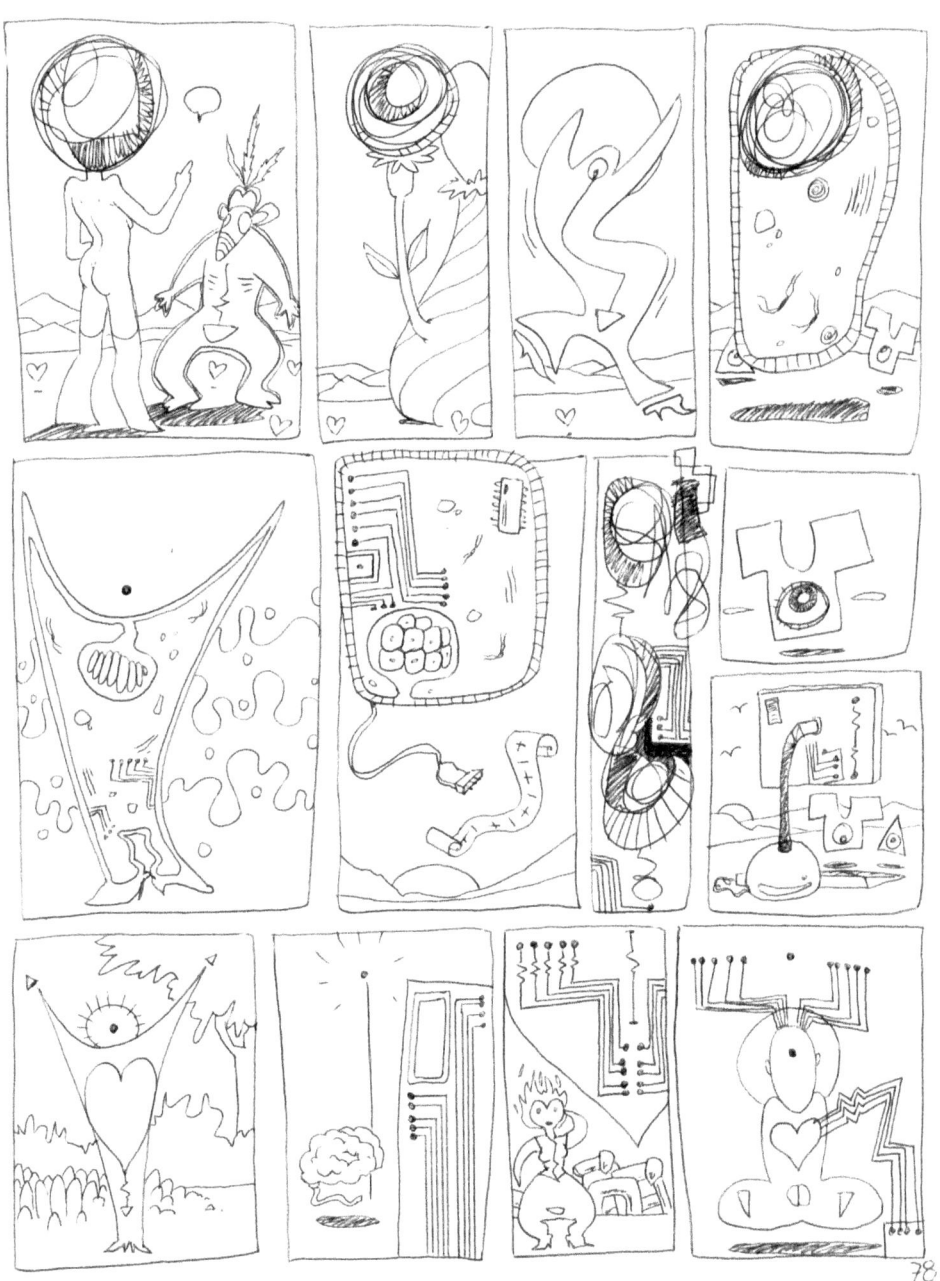

78

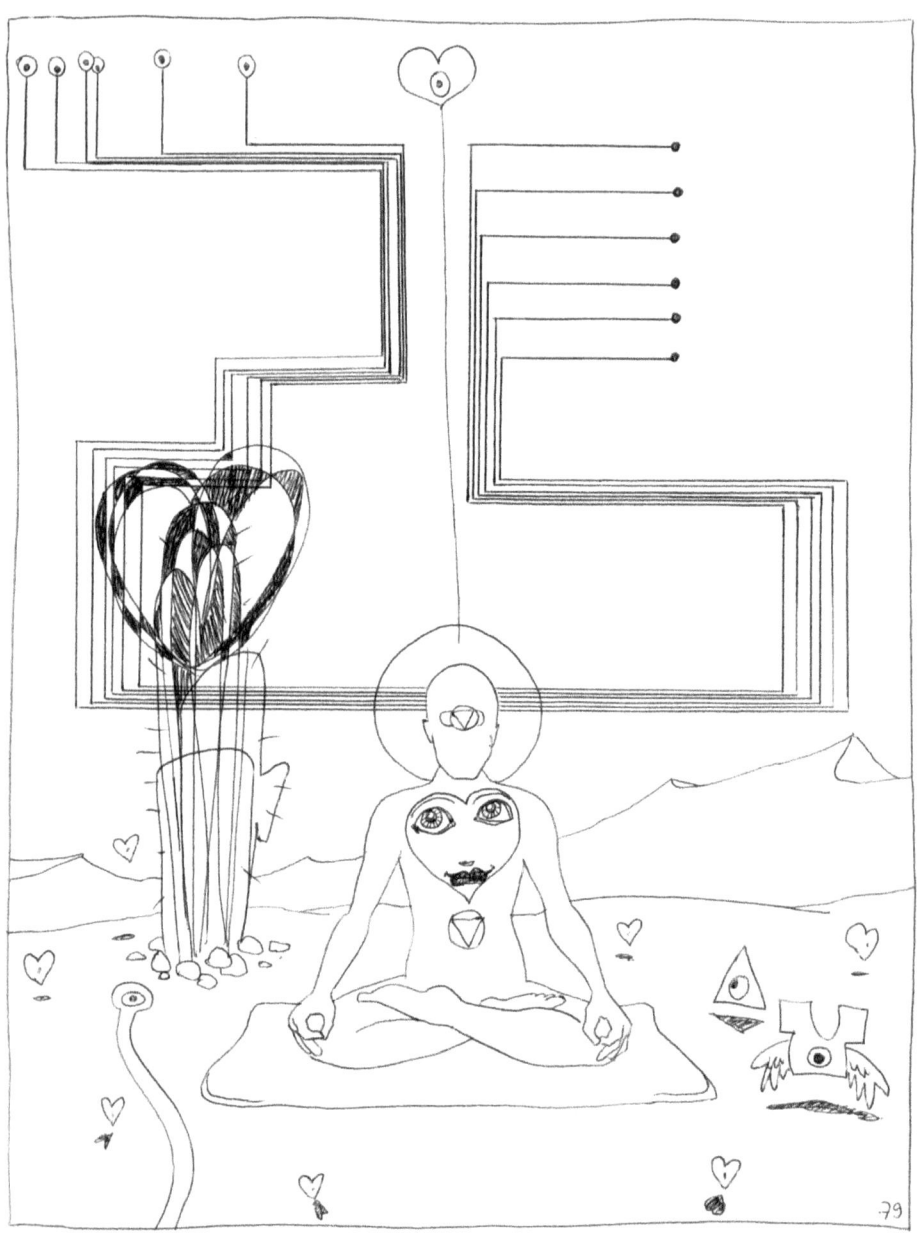

84

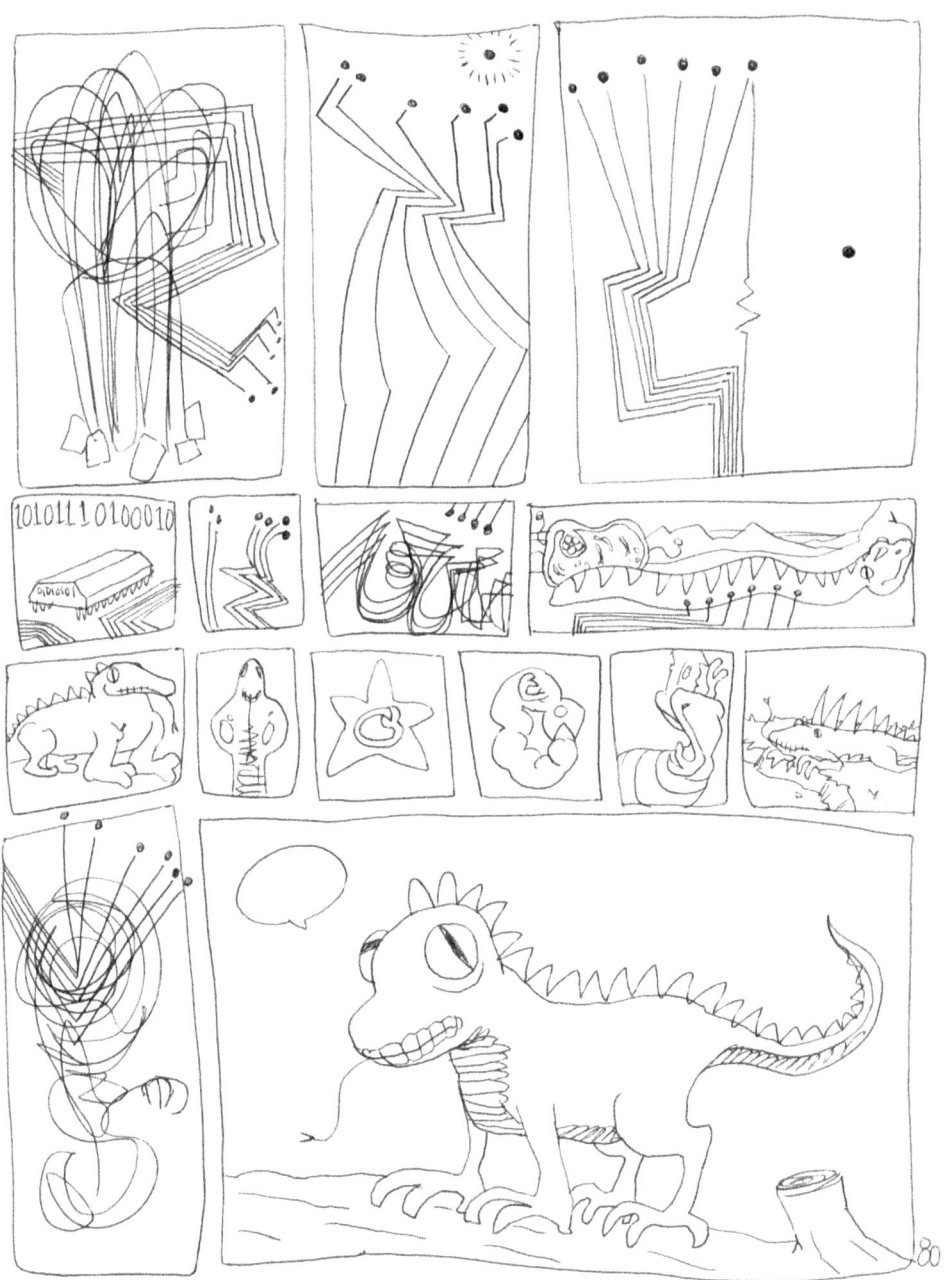

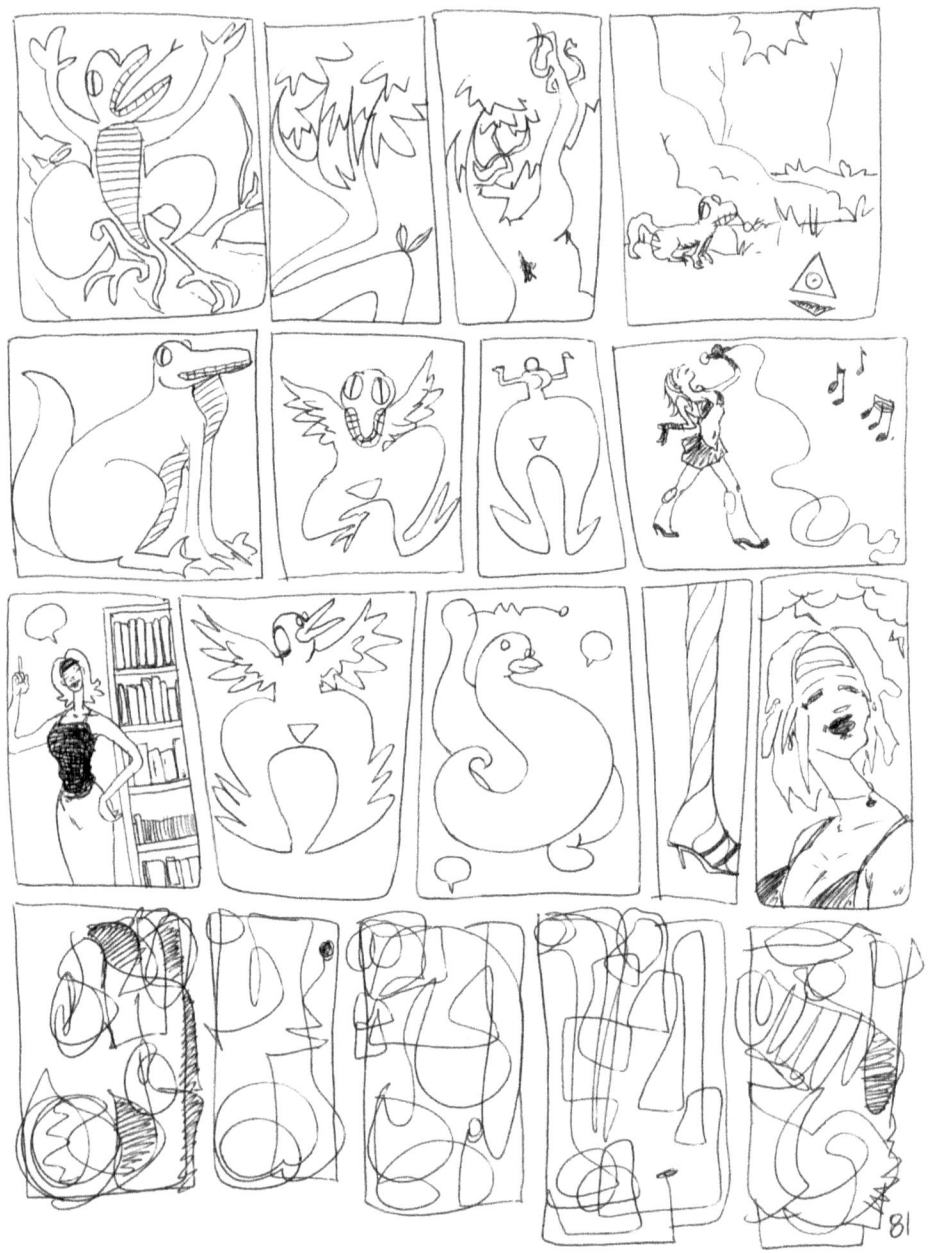

86

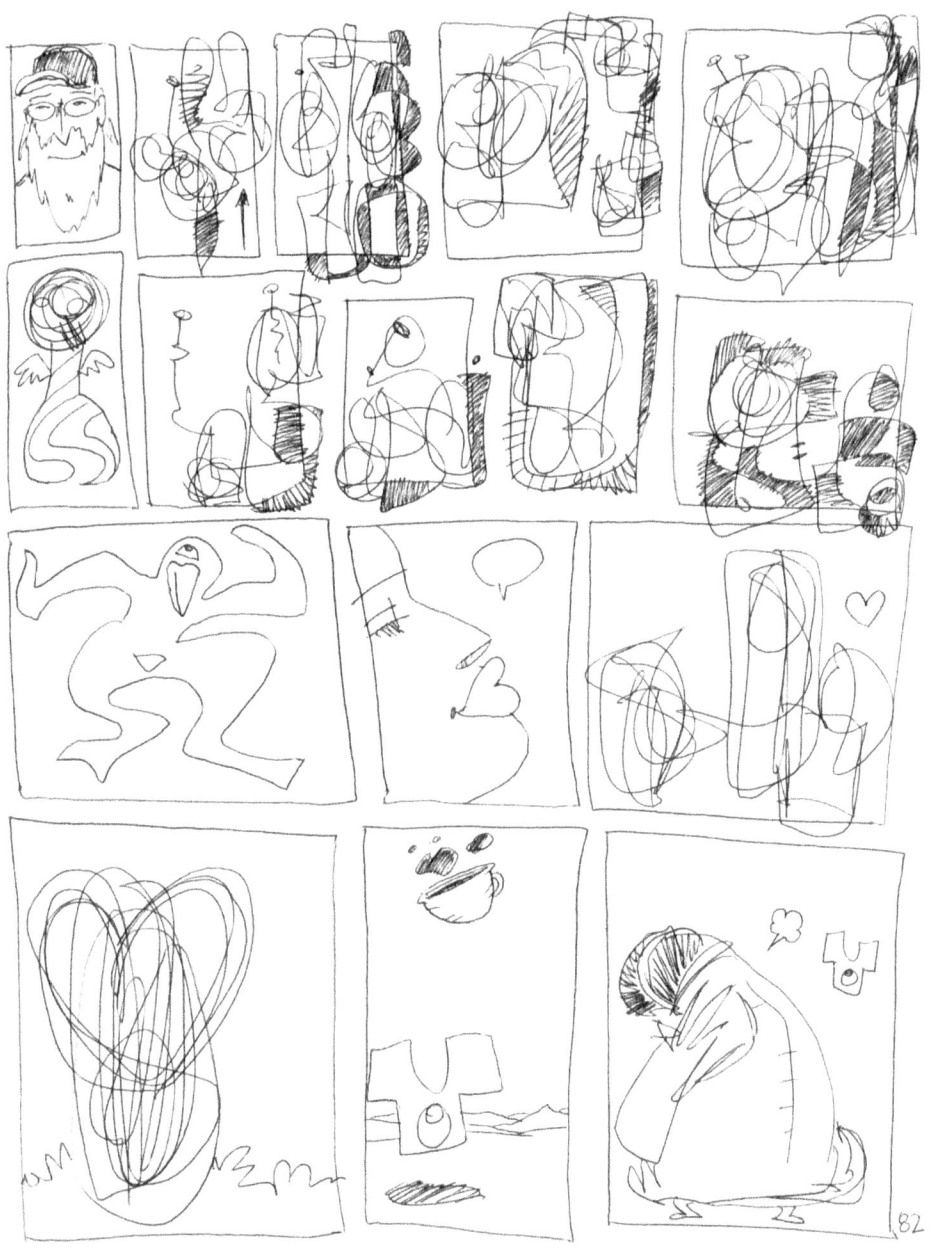

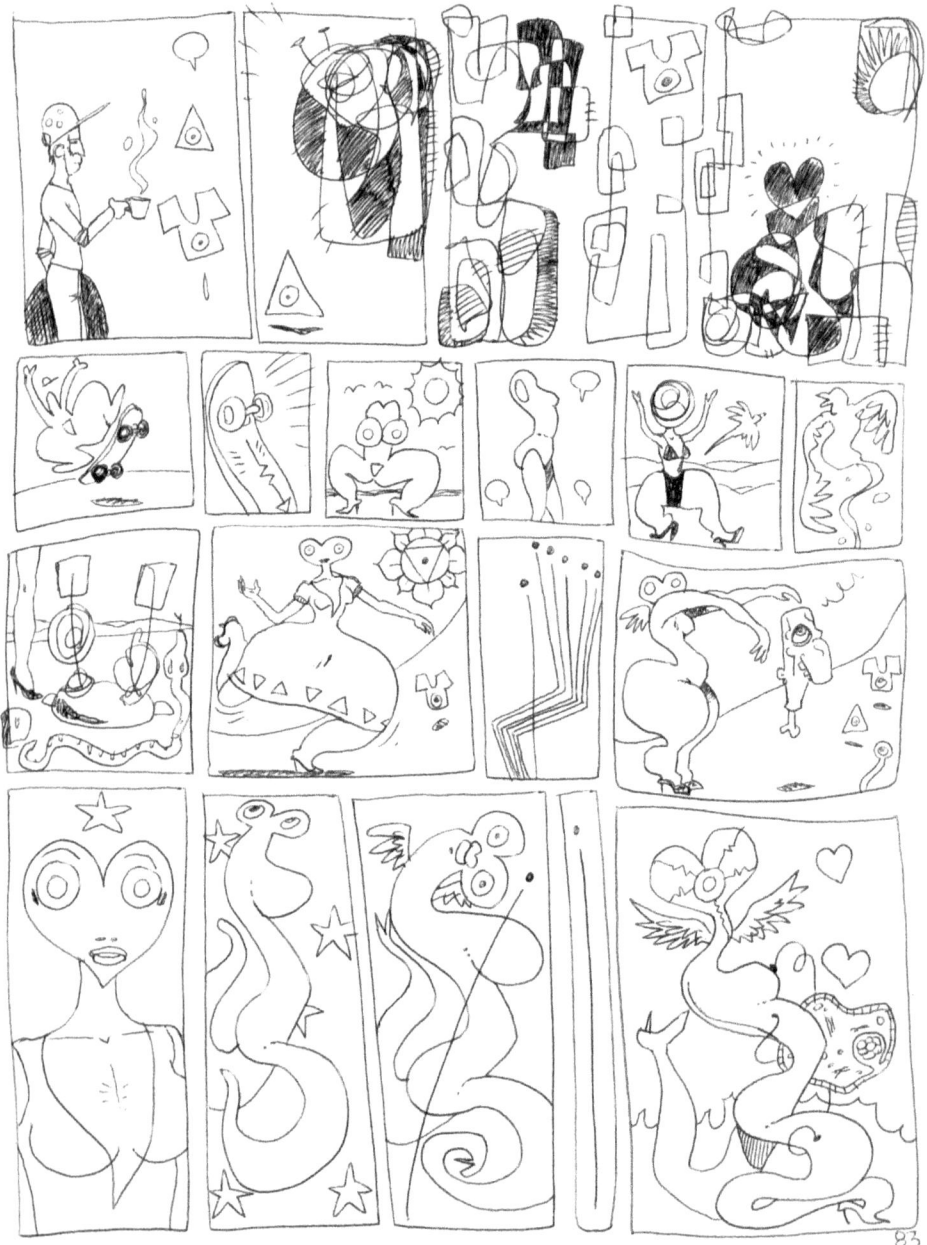

83

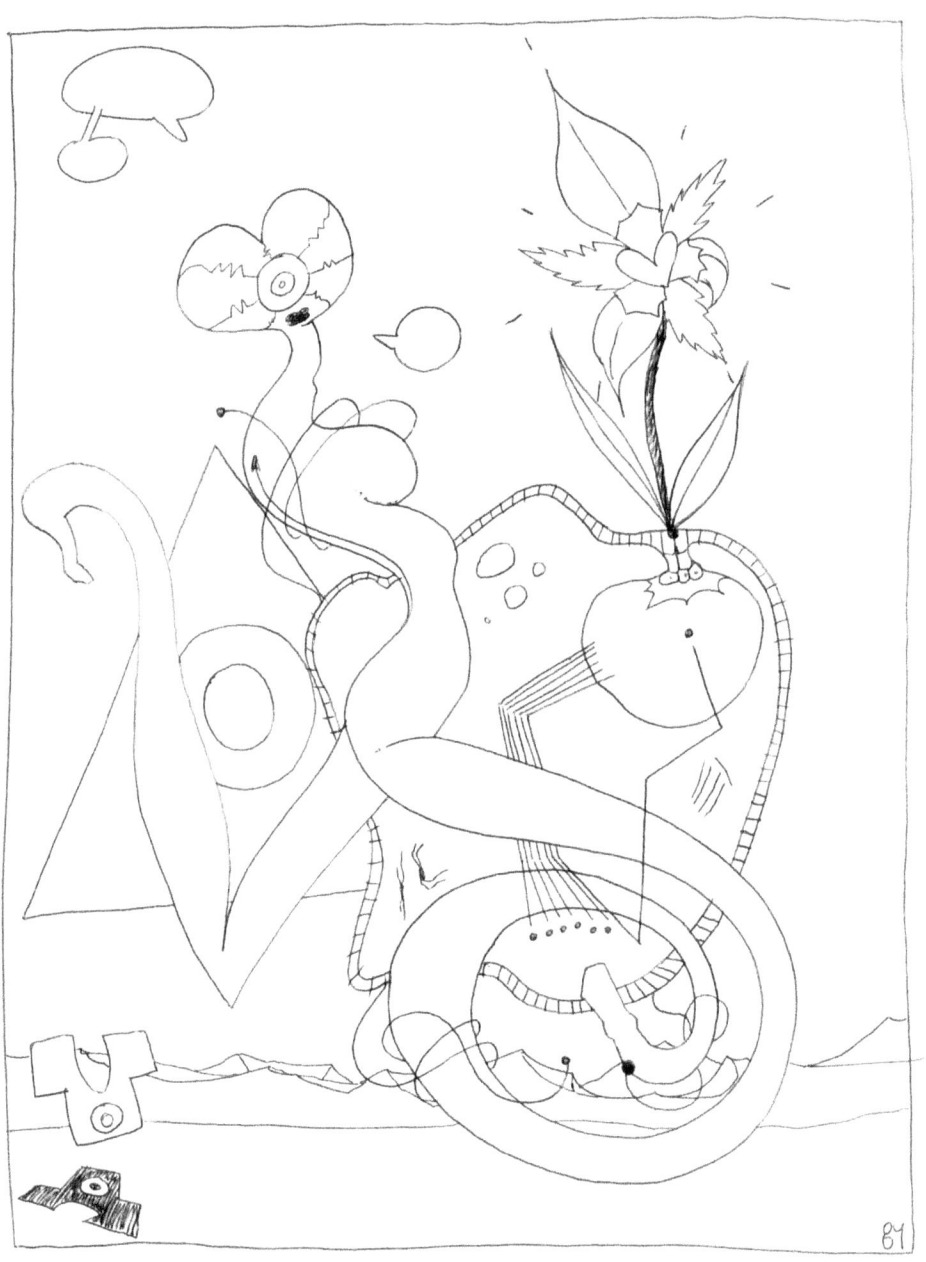

89

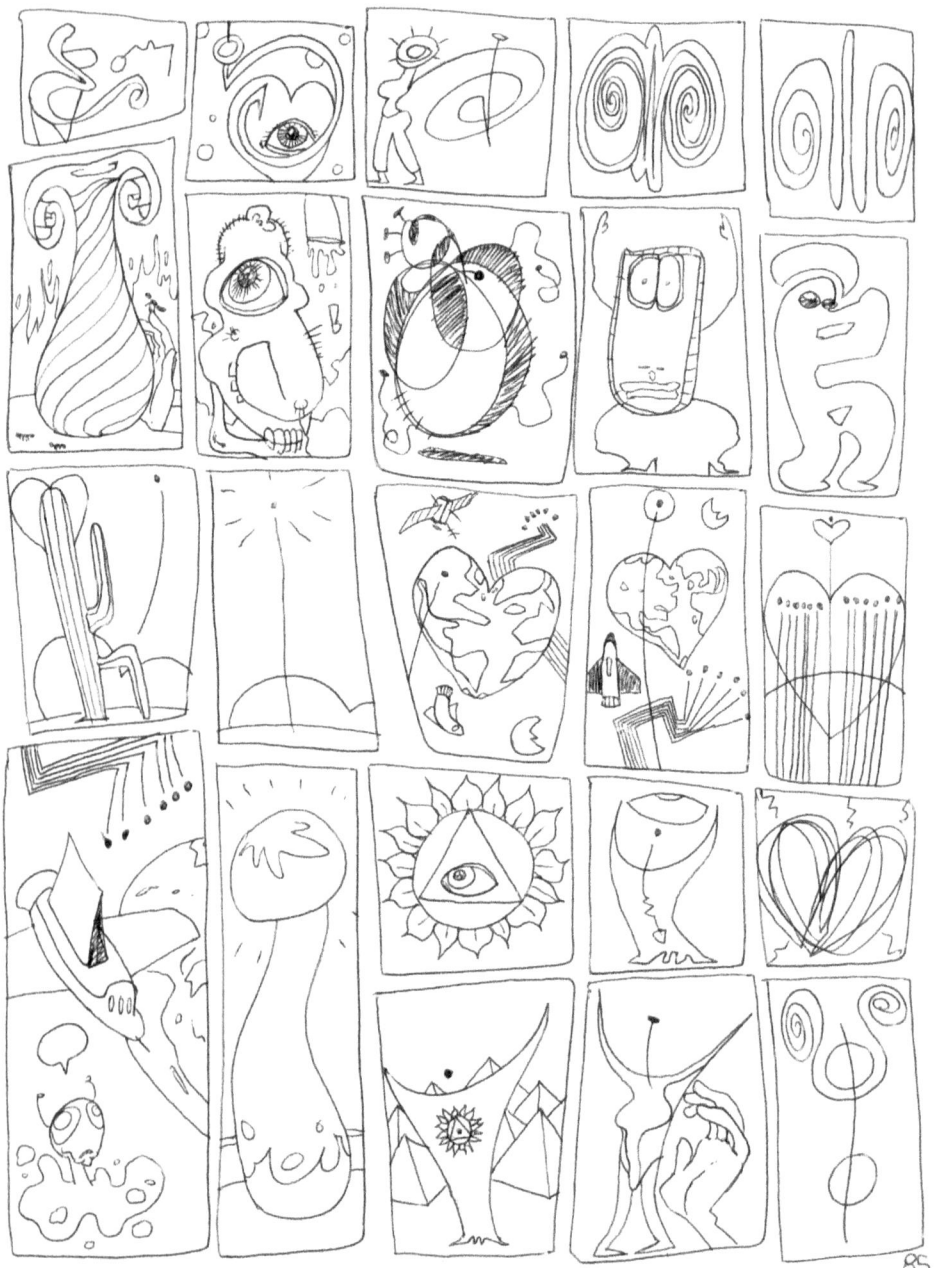

85

90

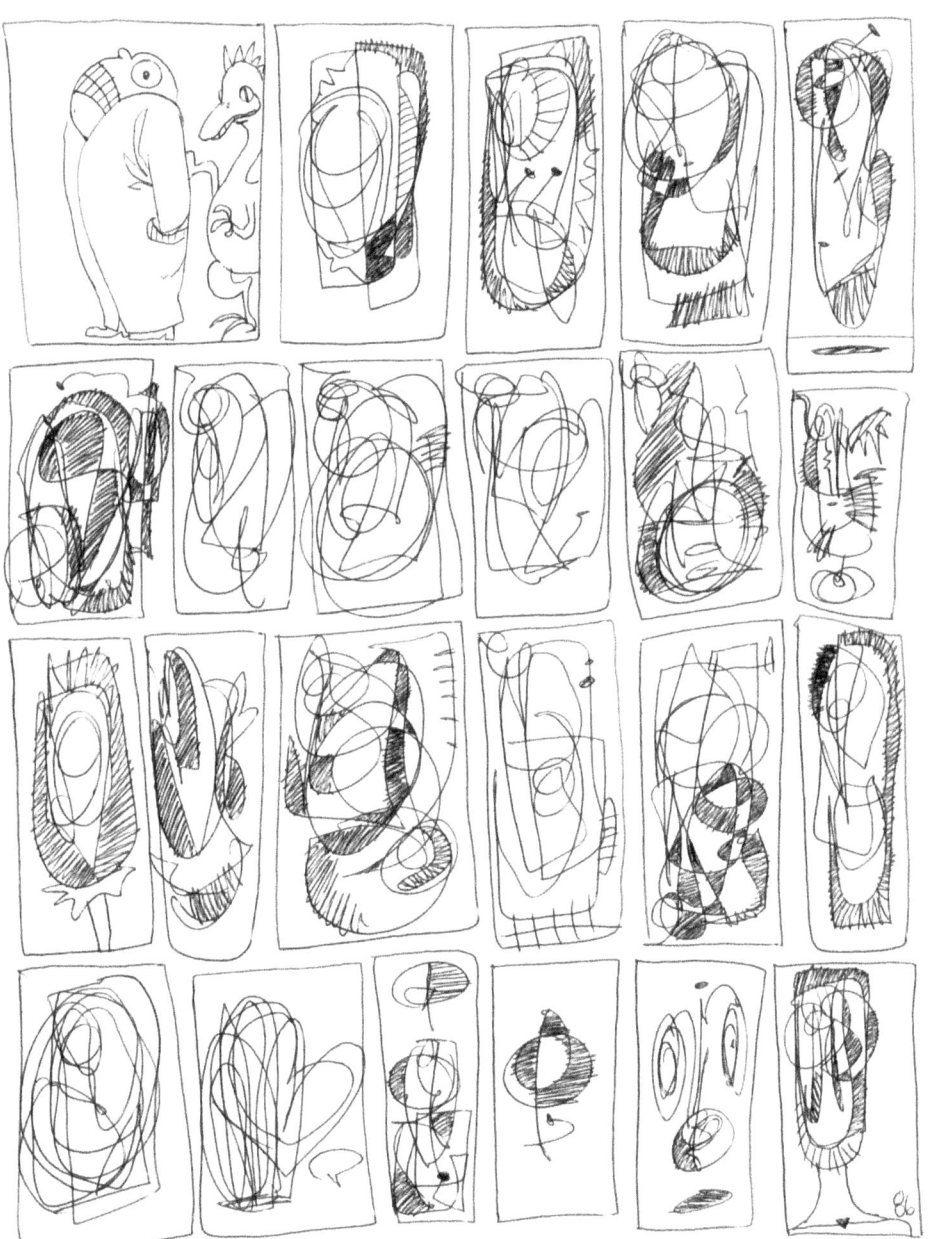

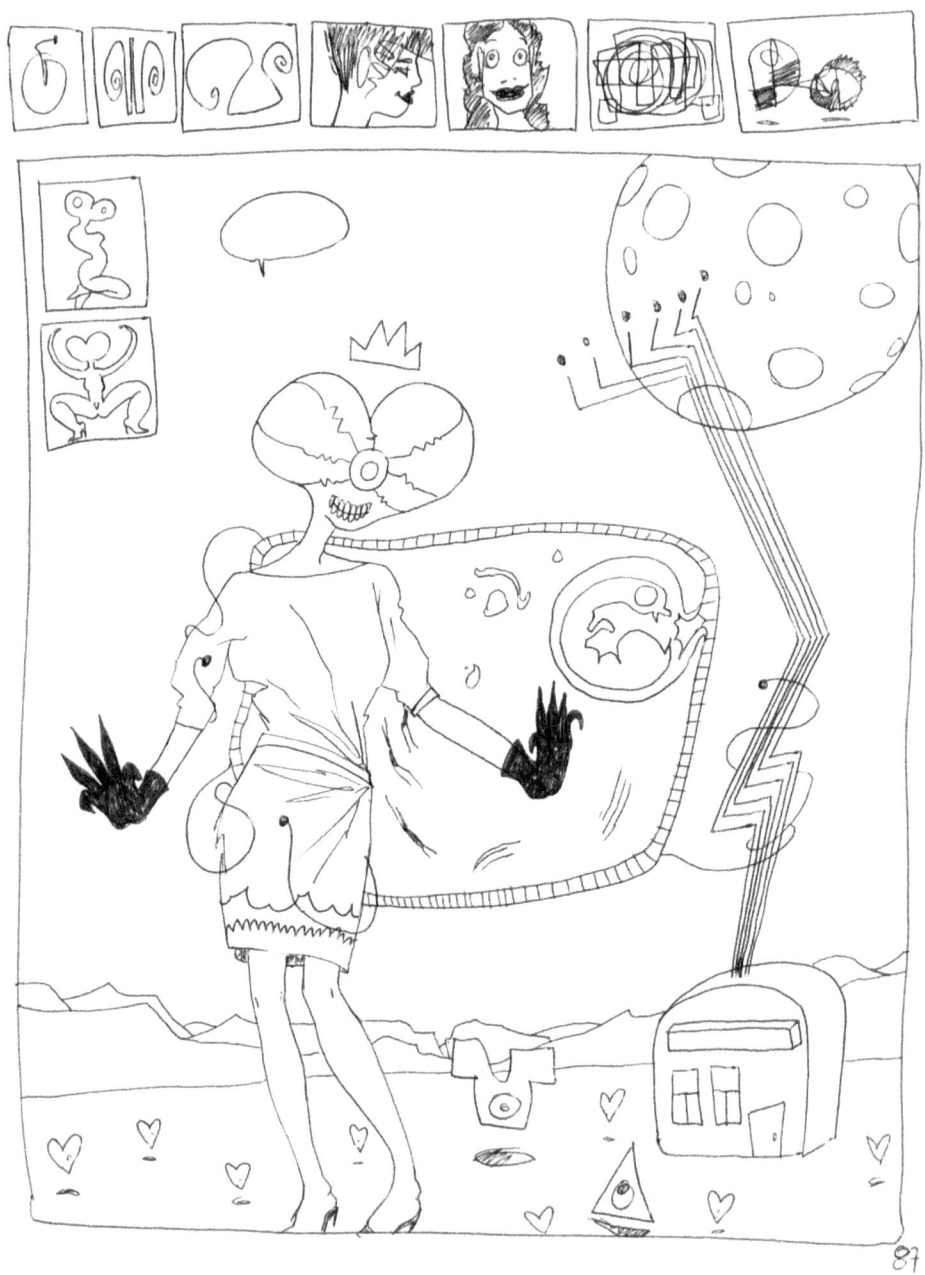

92

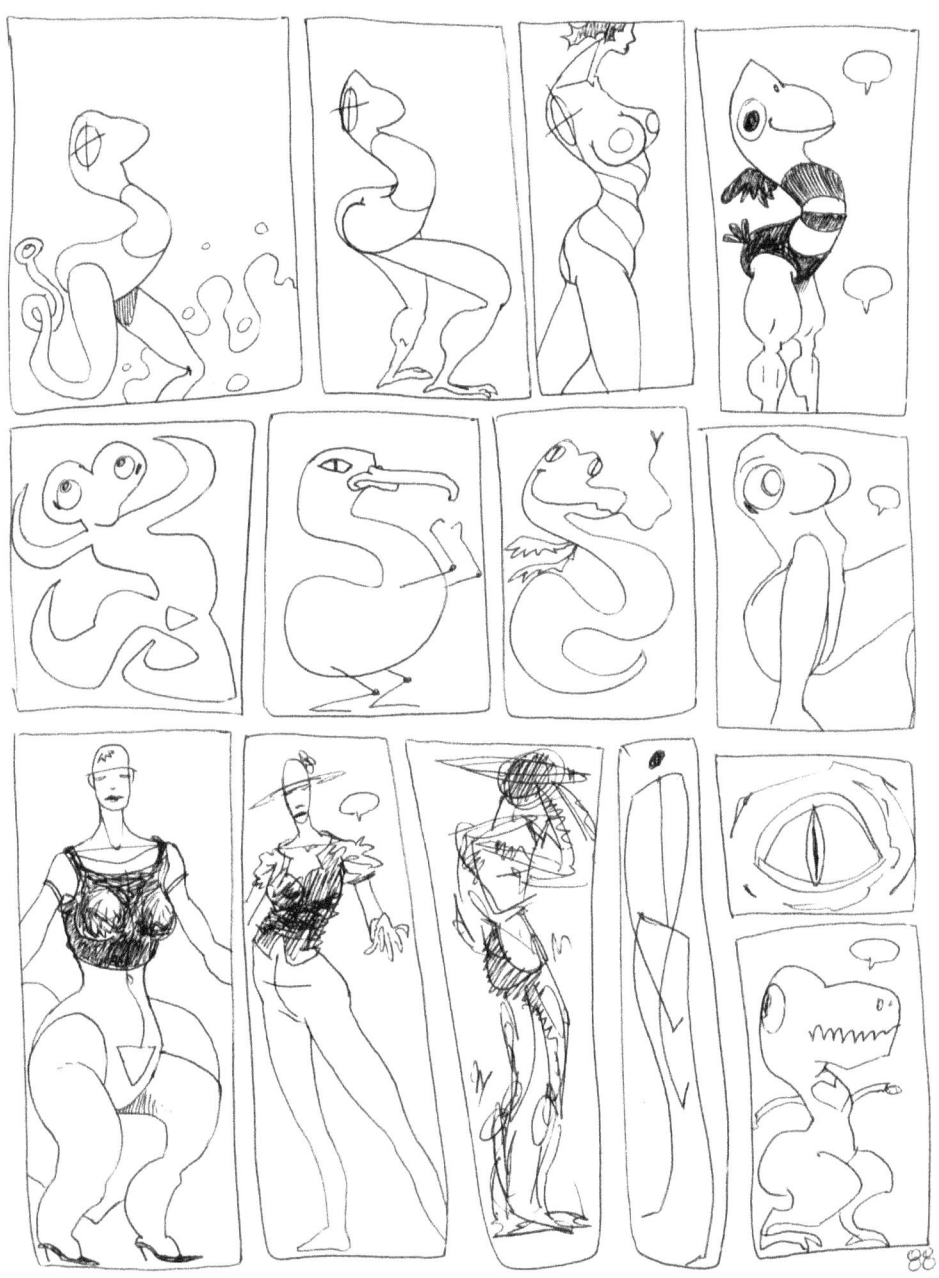

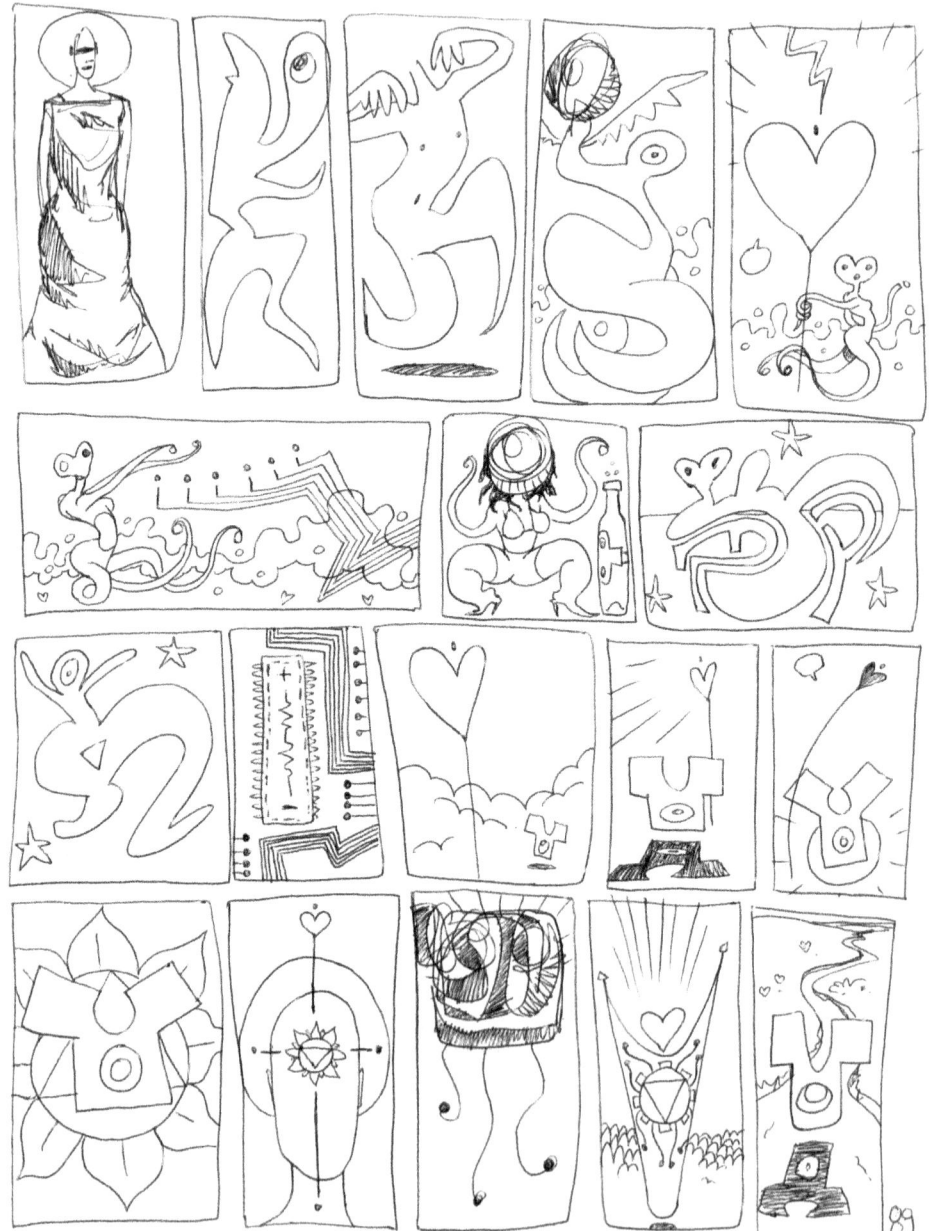

94

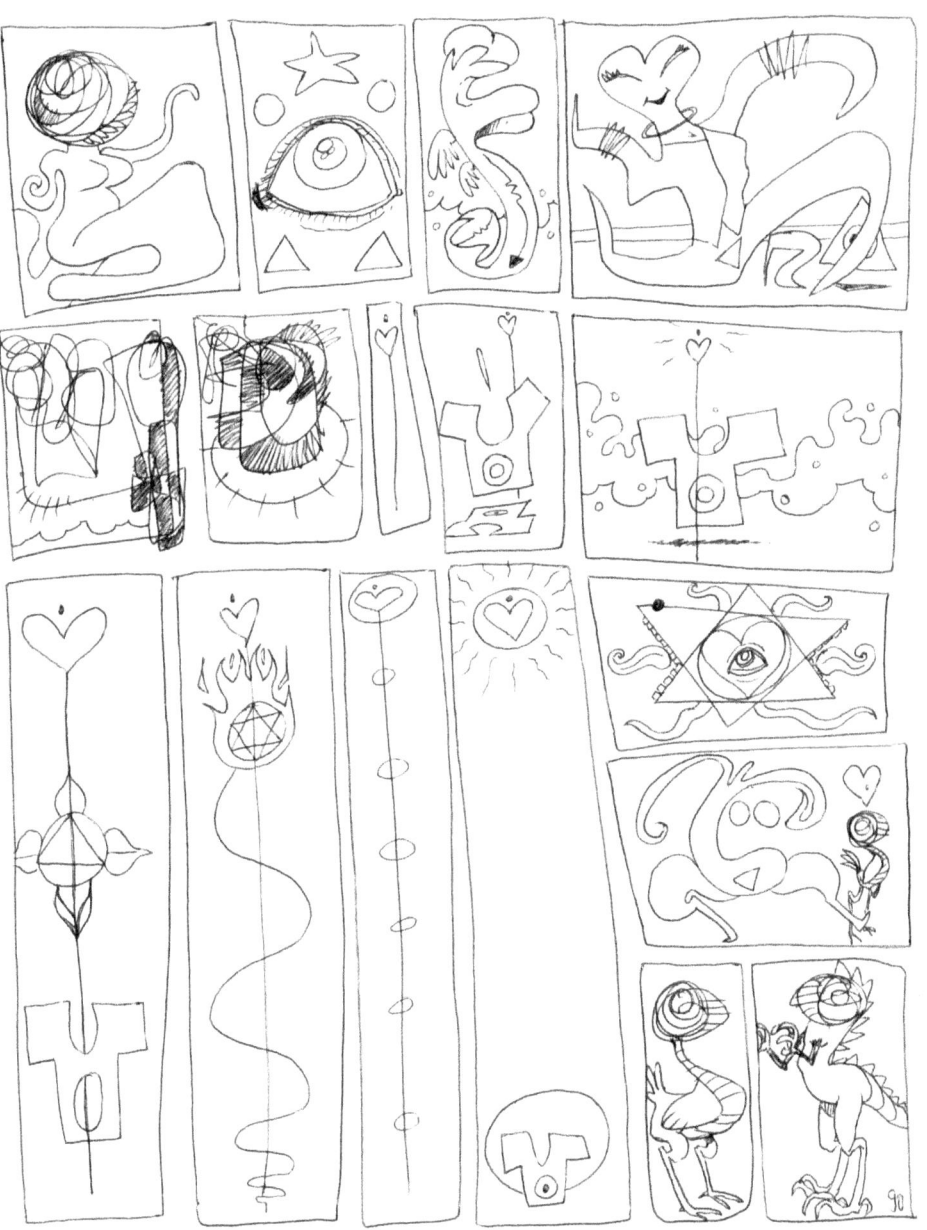

95

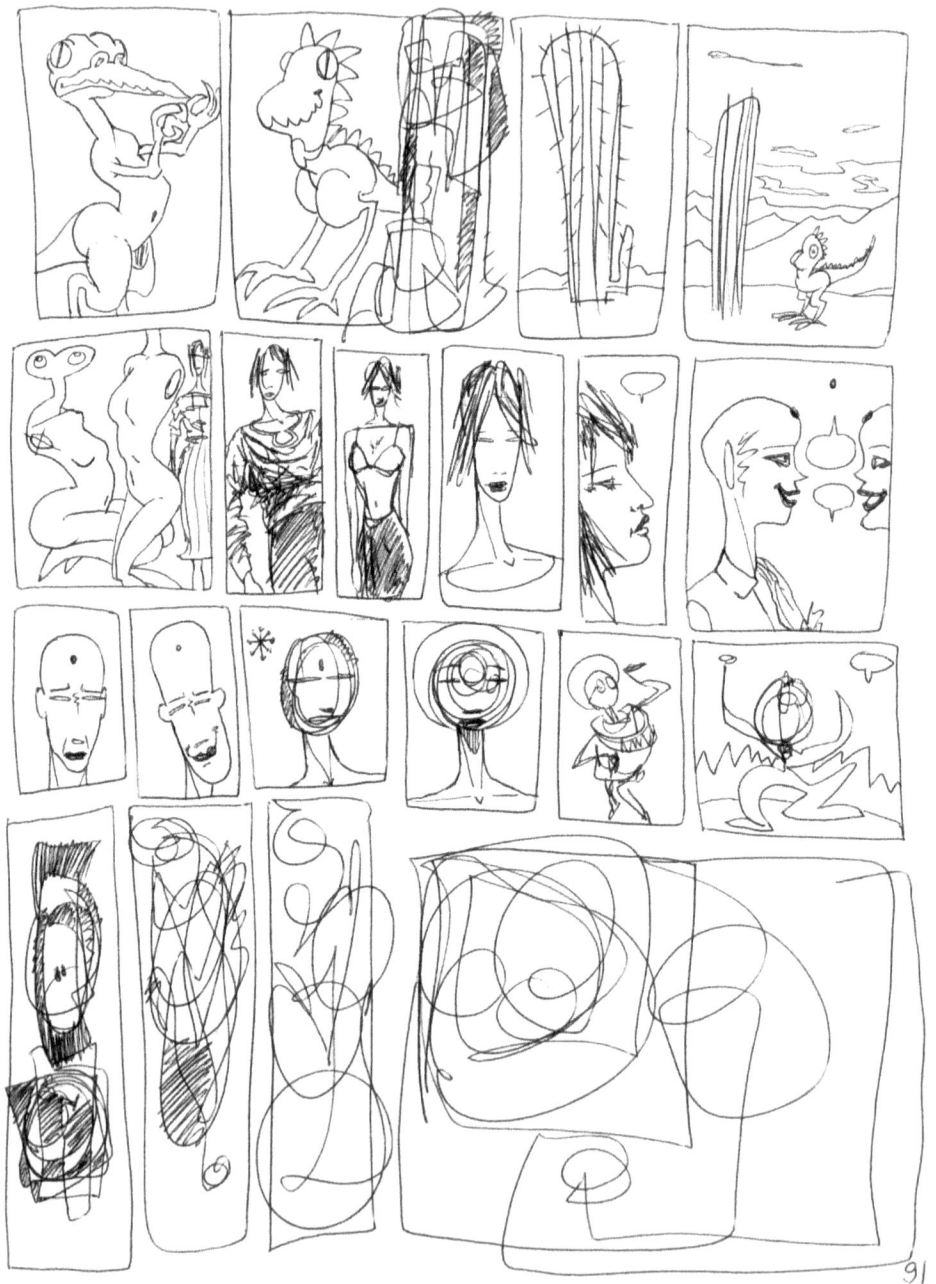

91

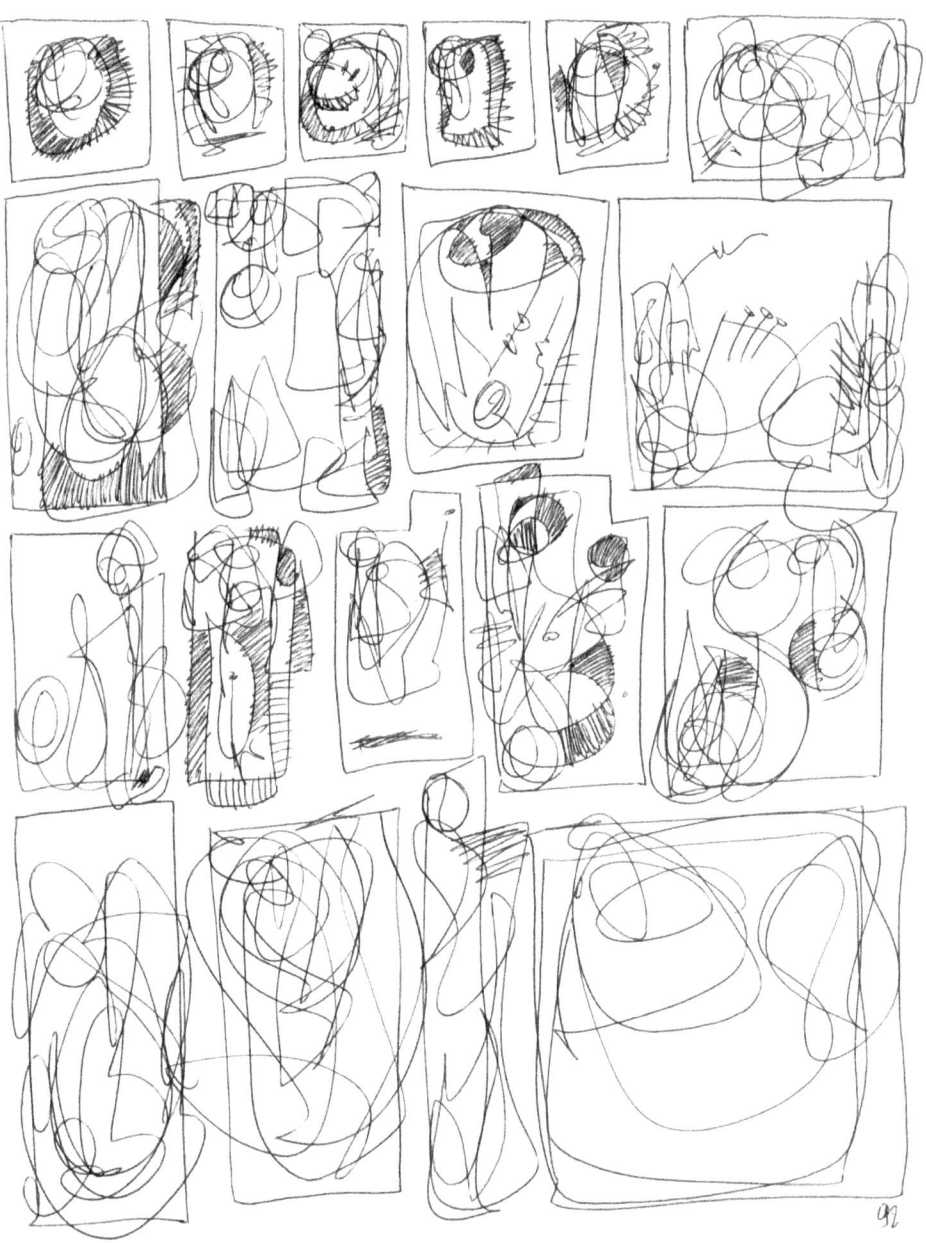

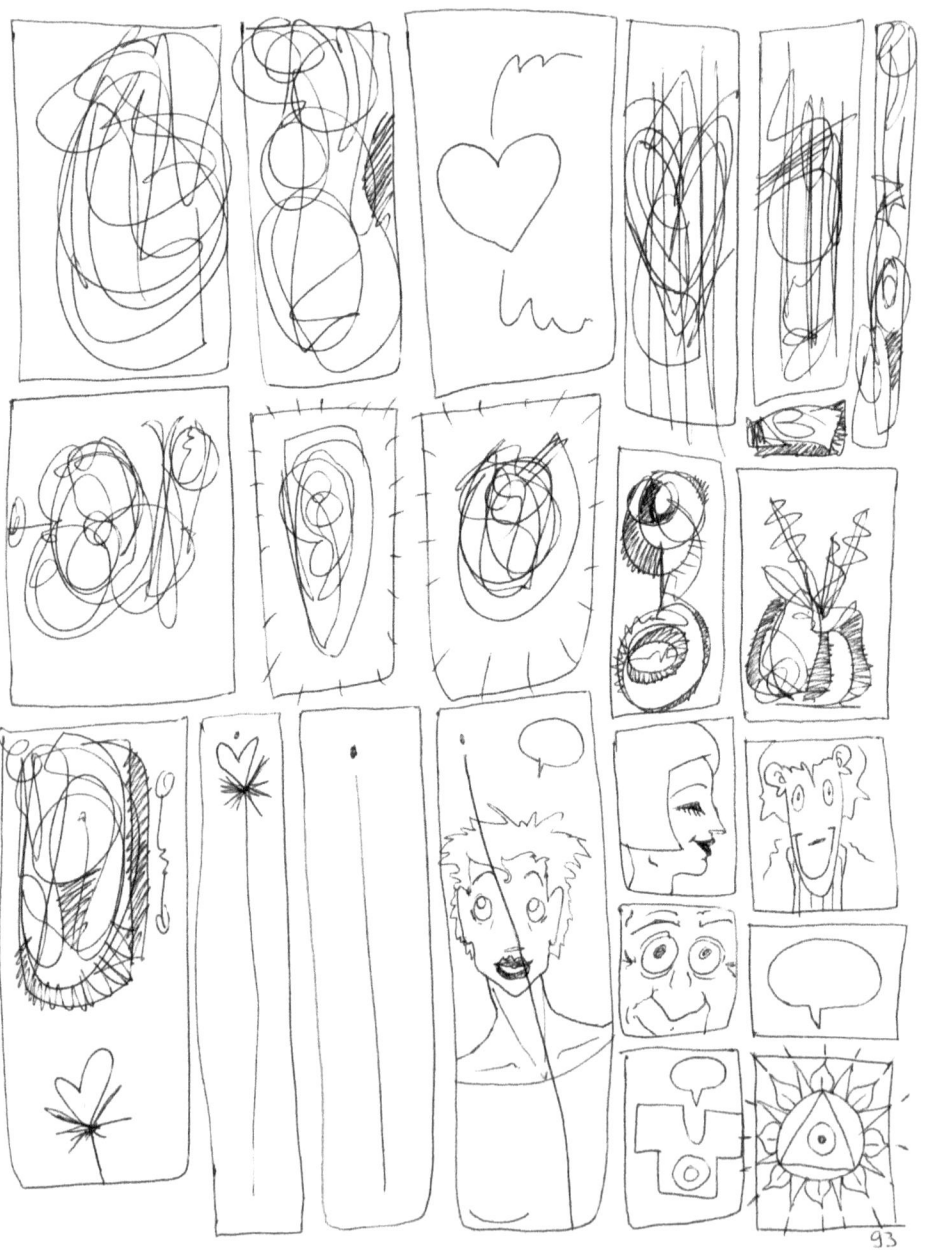

93

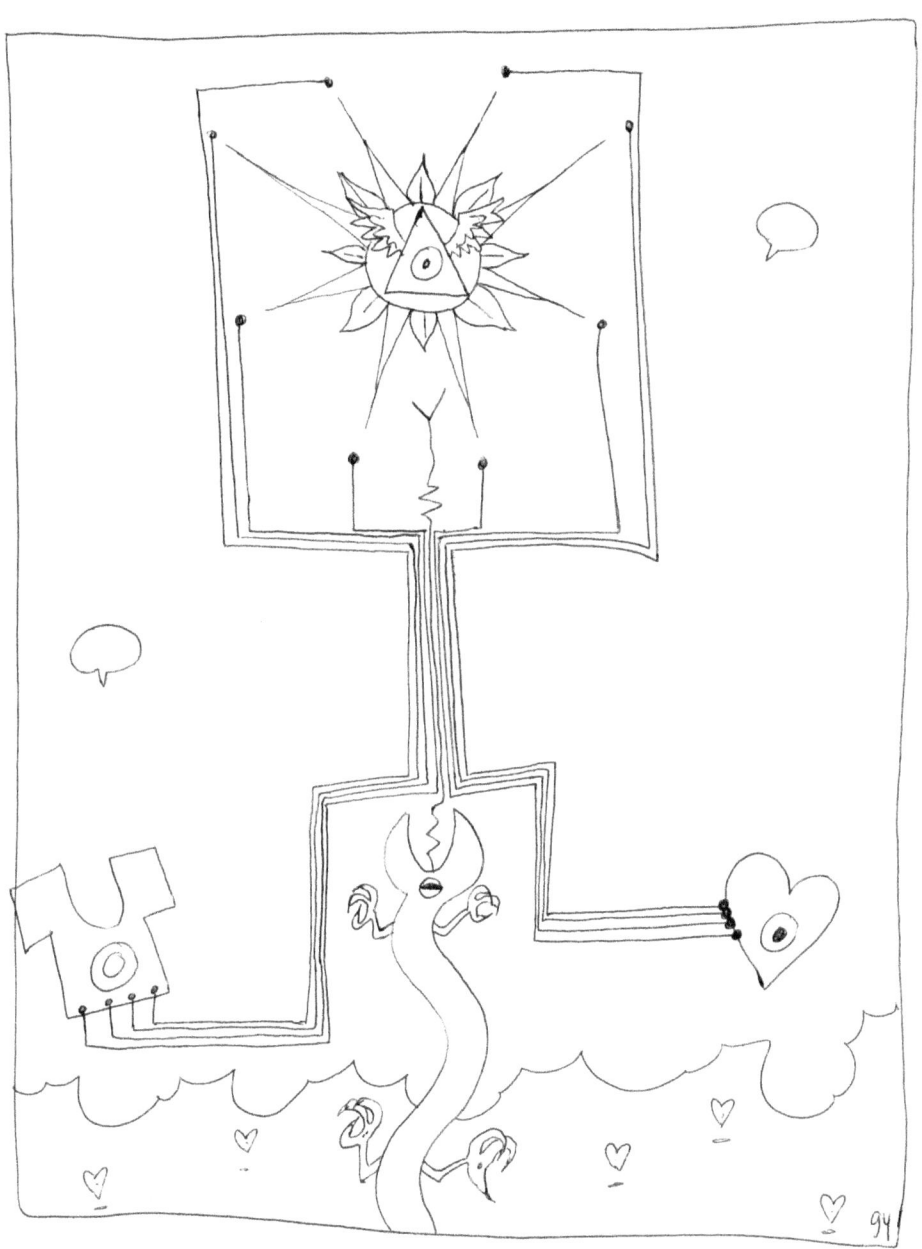

99

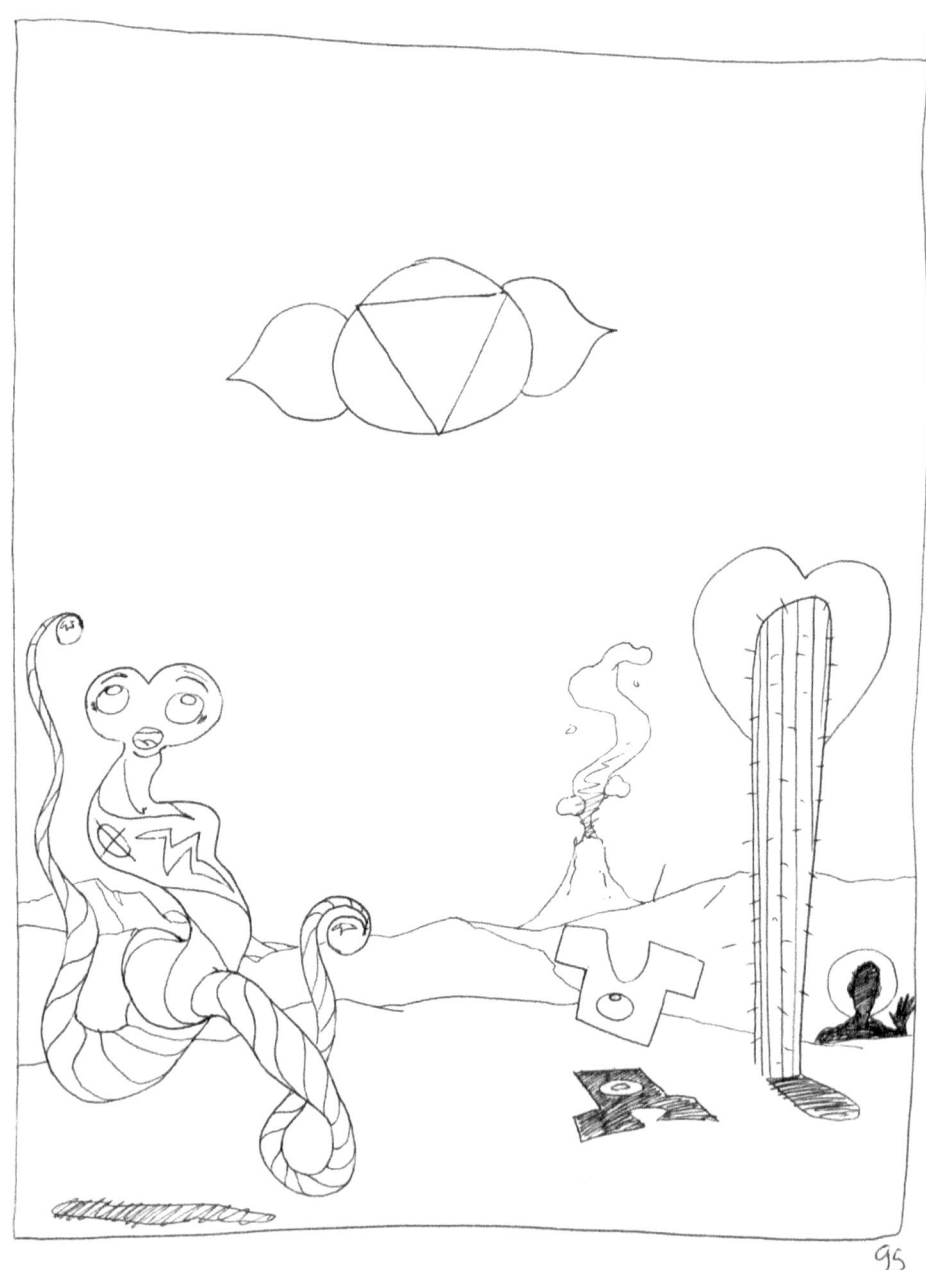

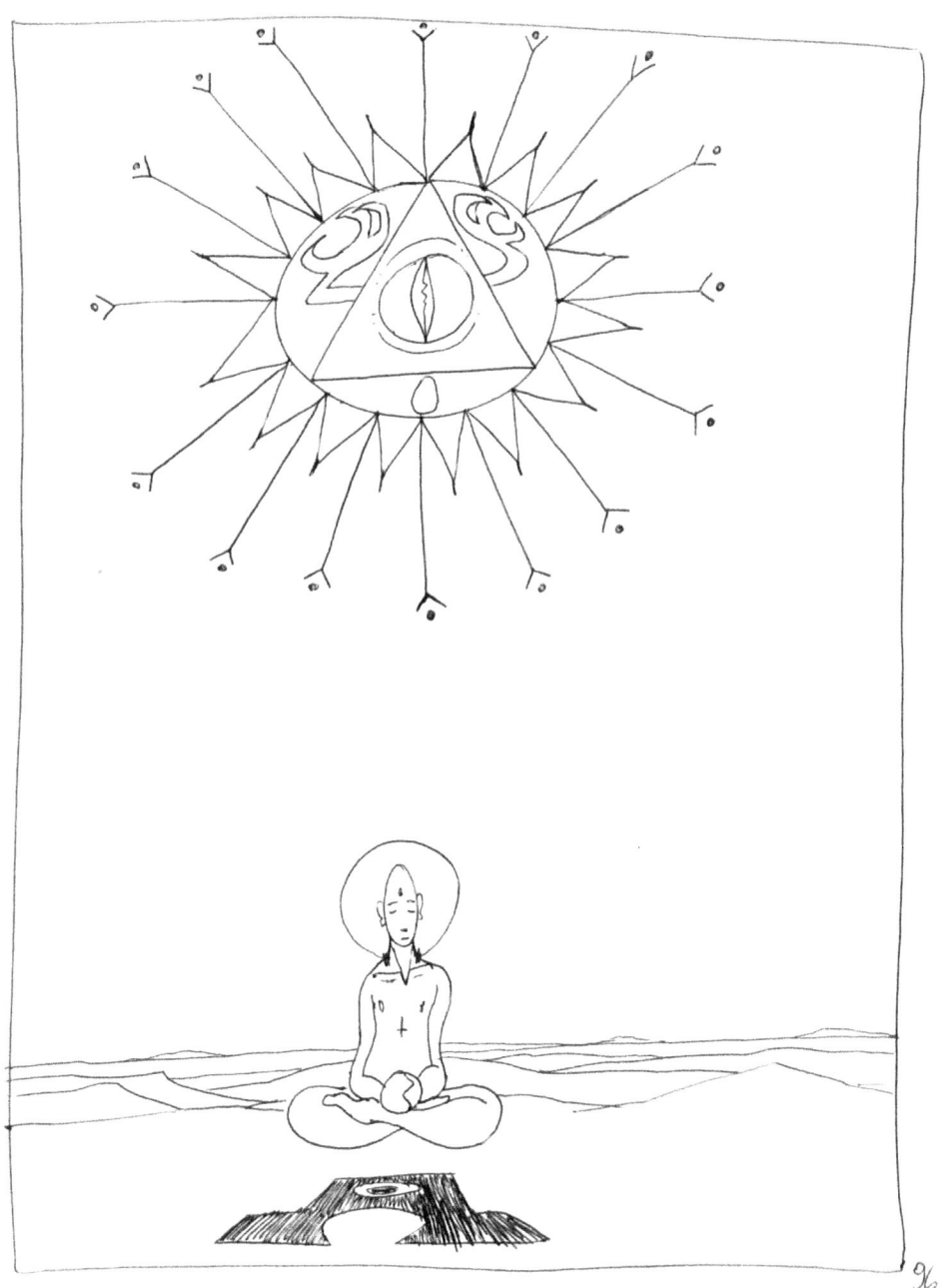

101

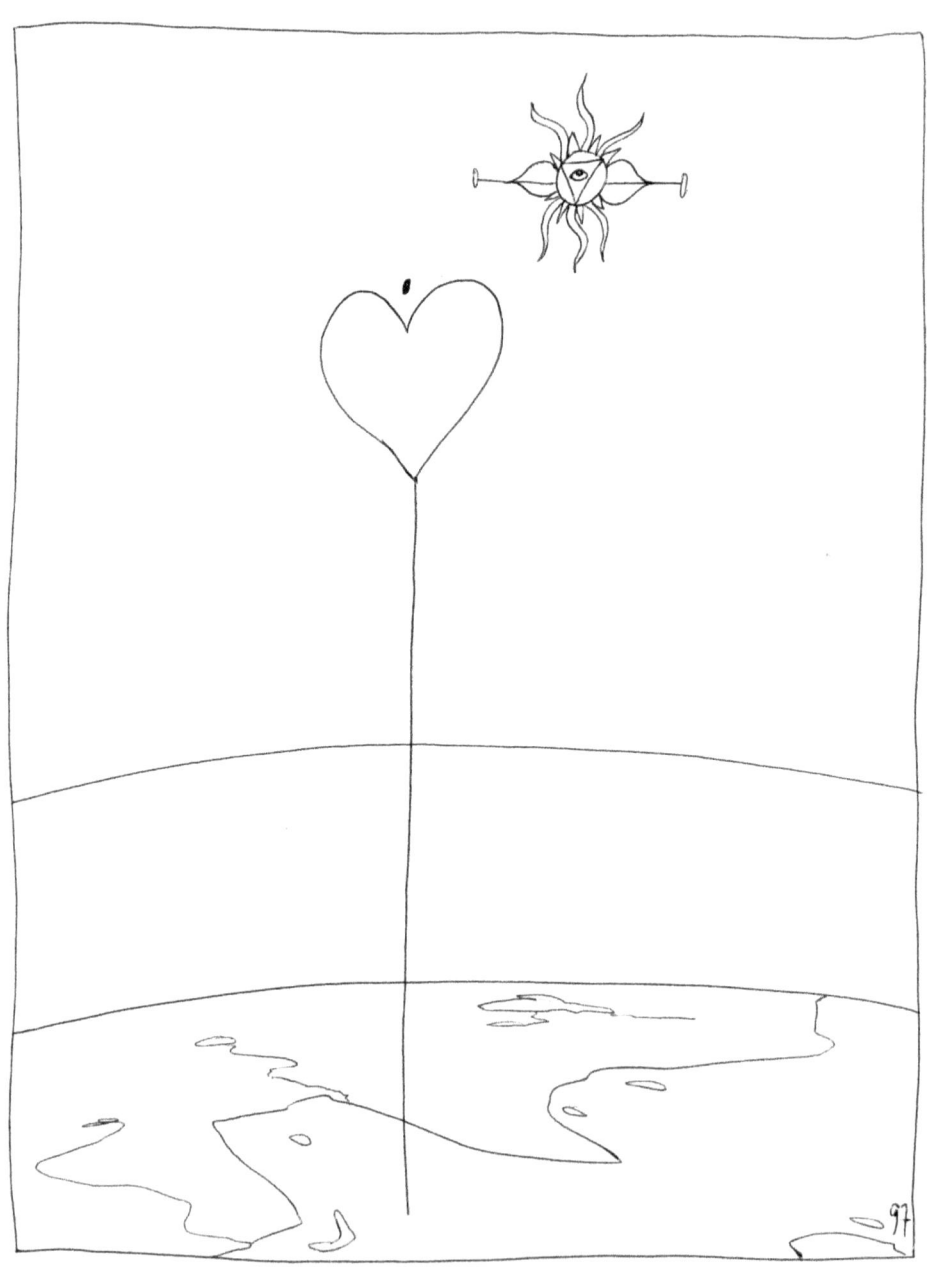

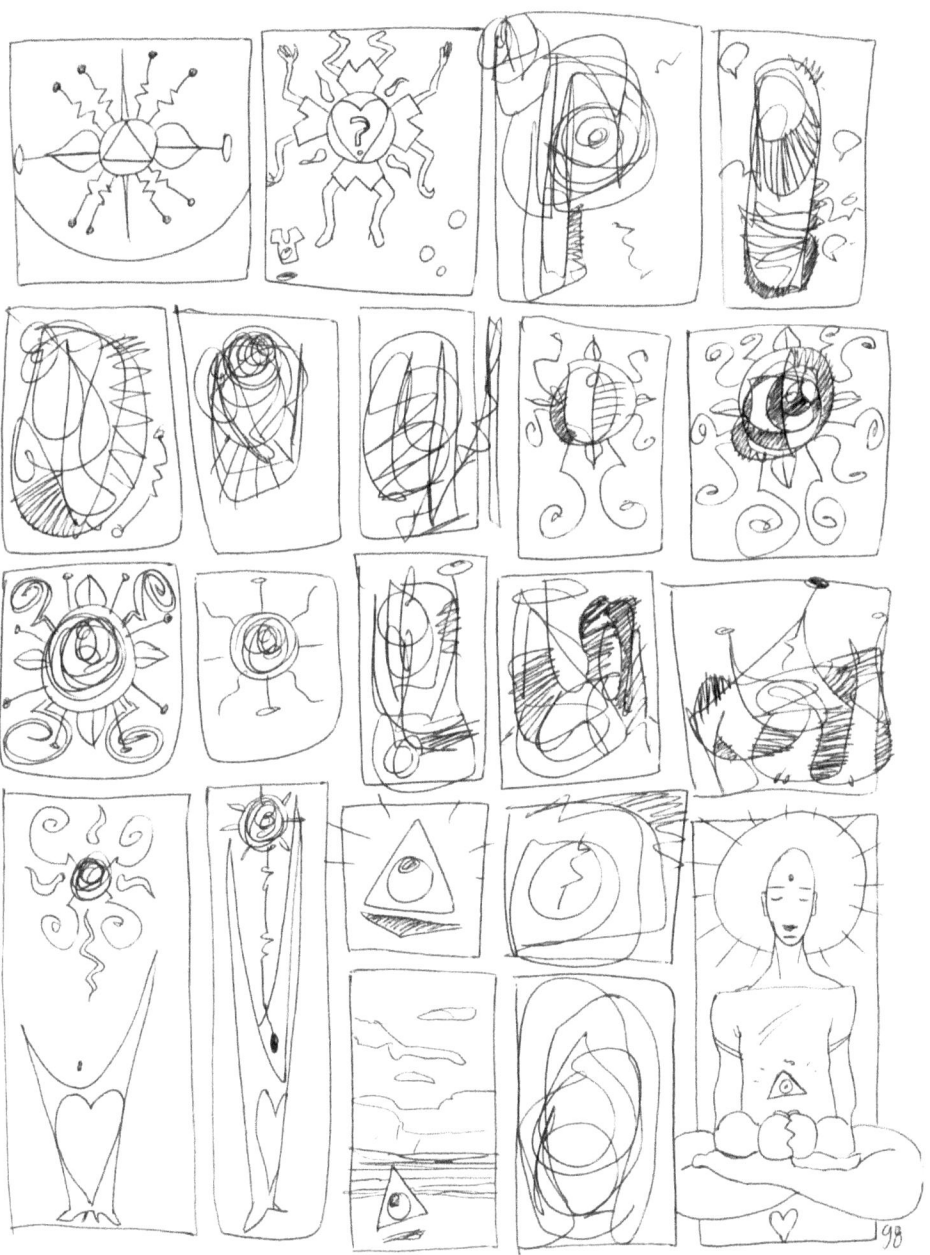

103

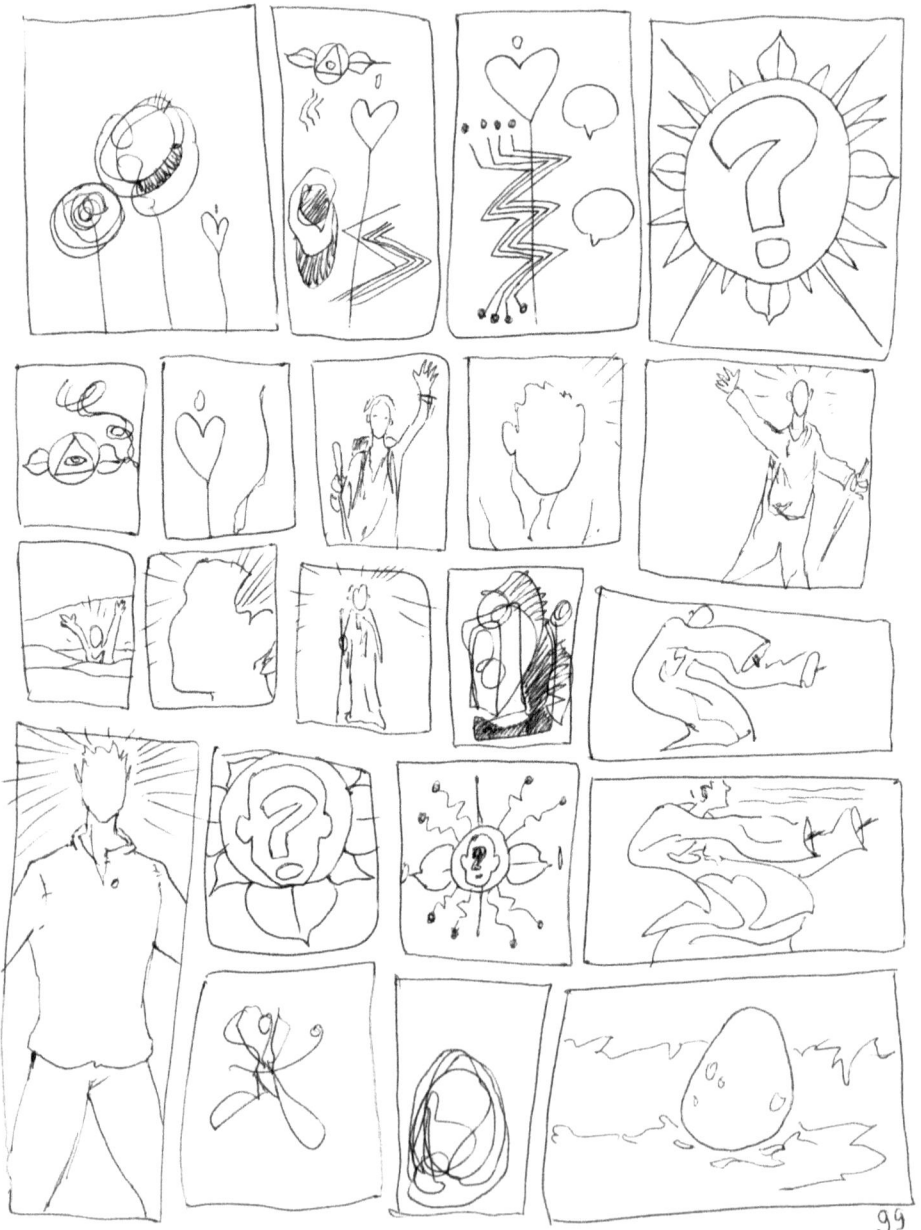

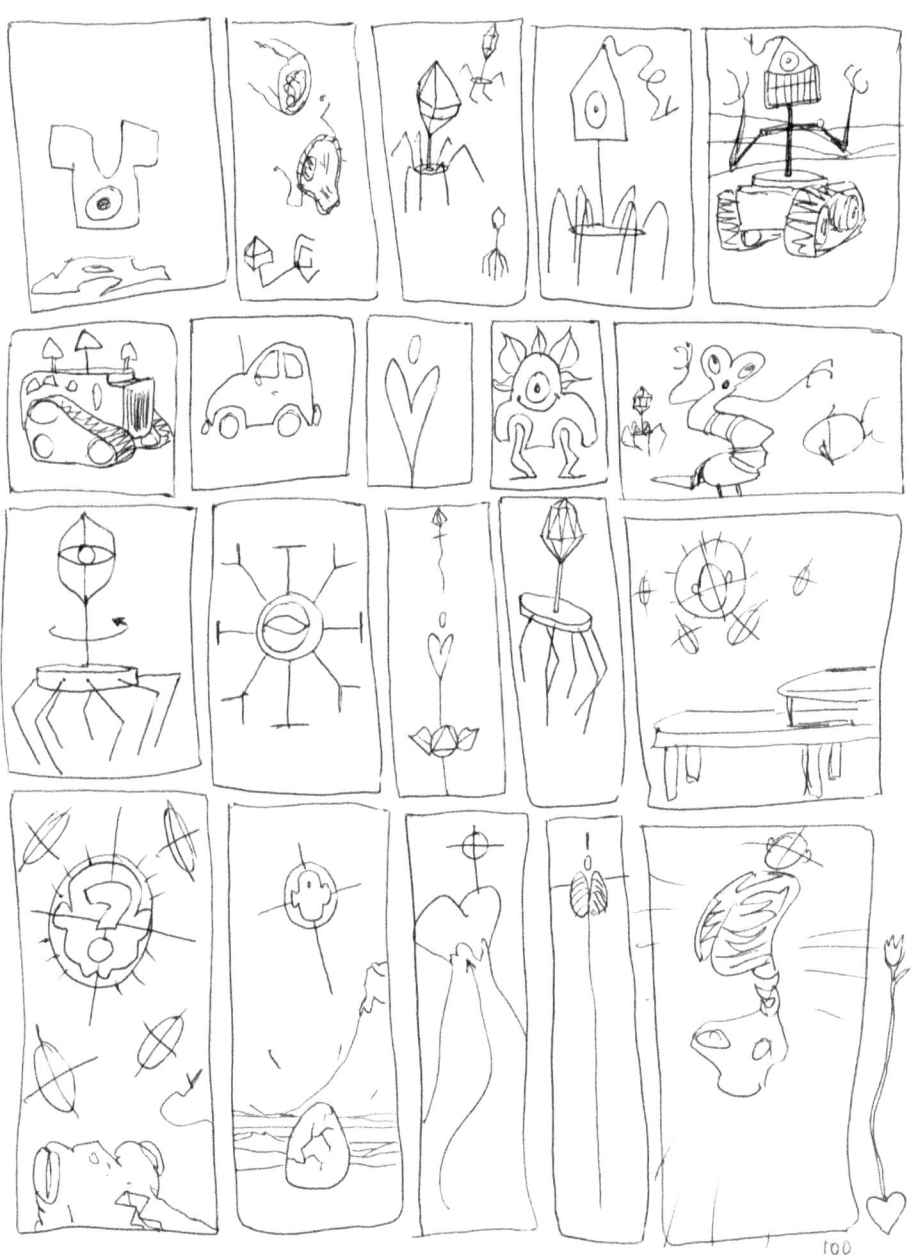

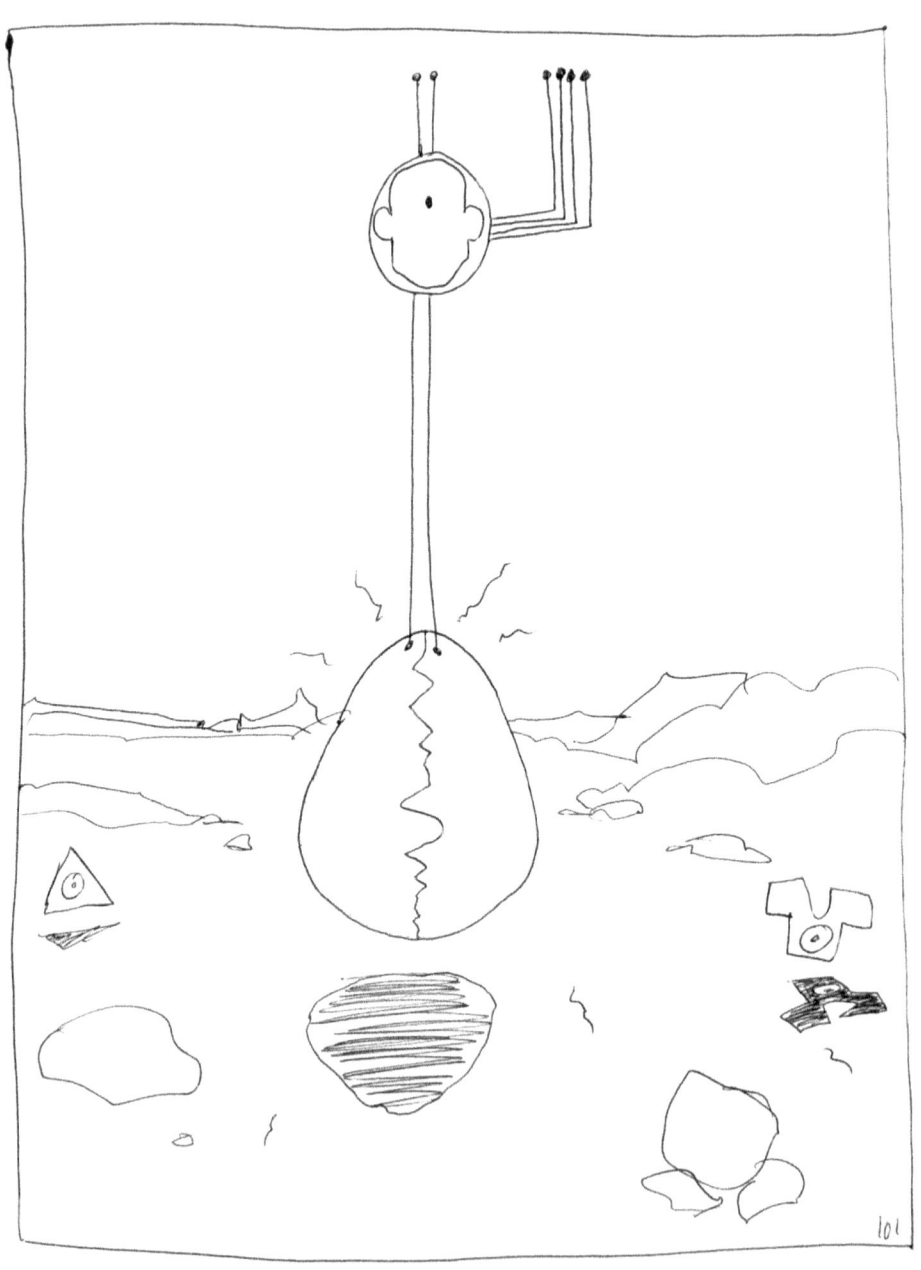

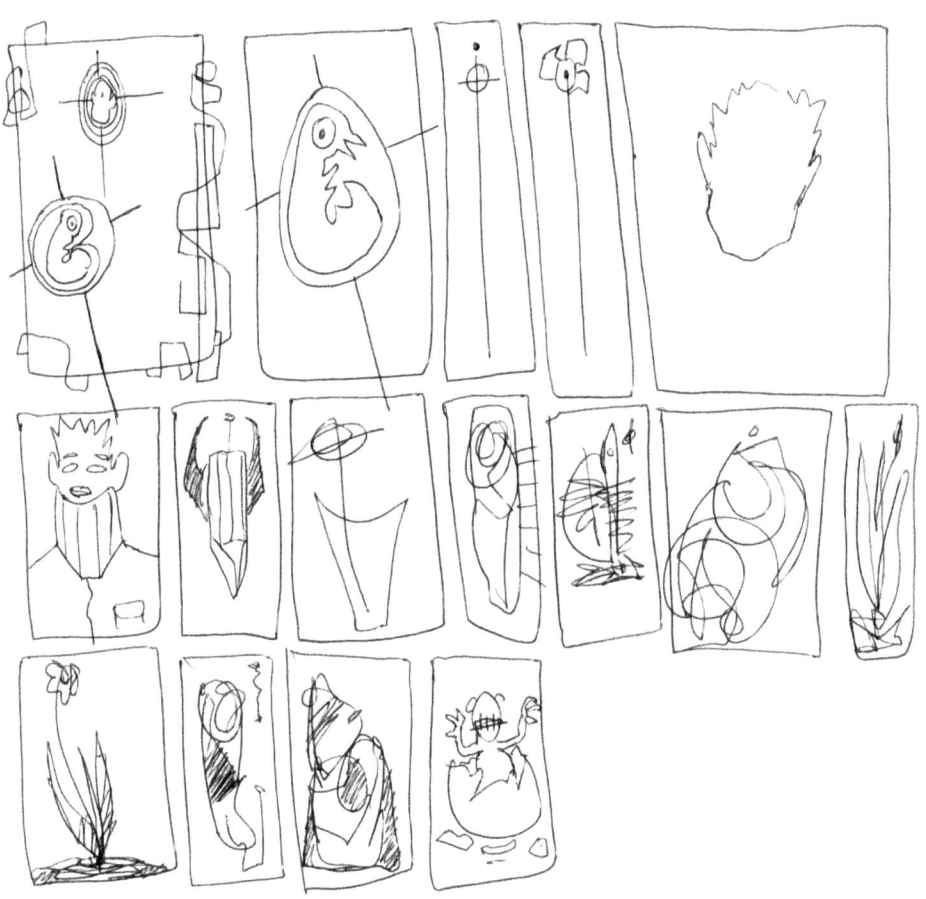

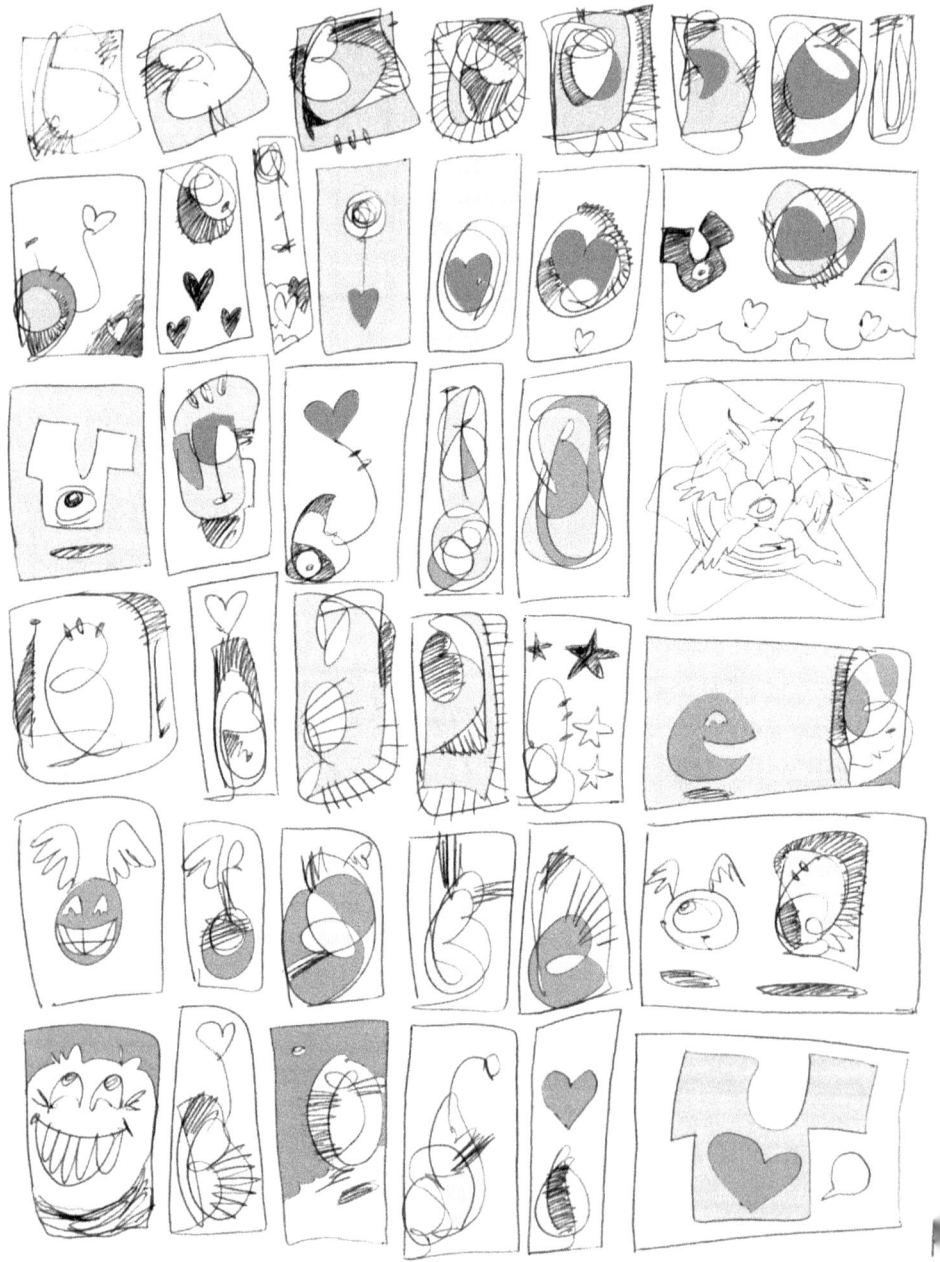

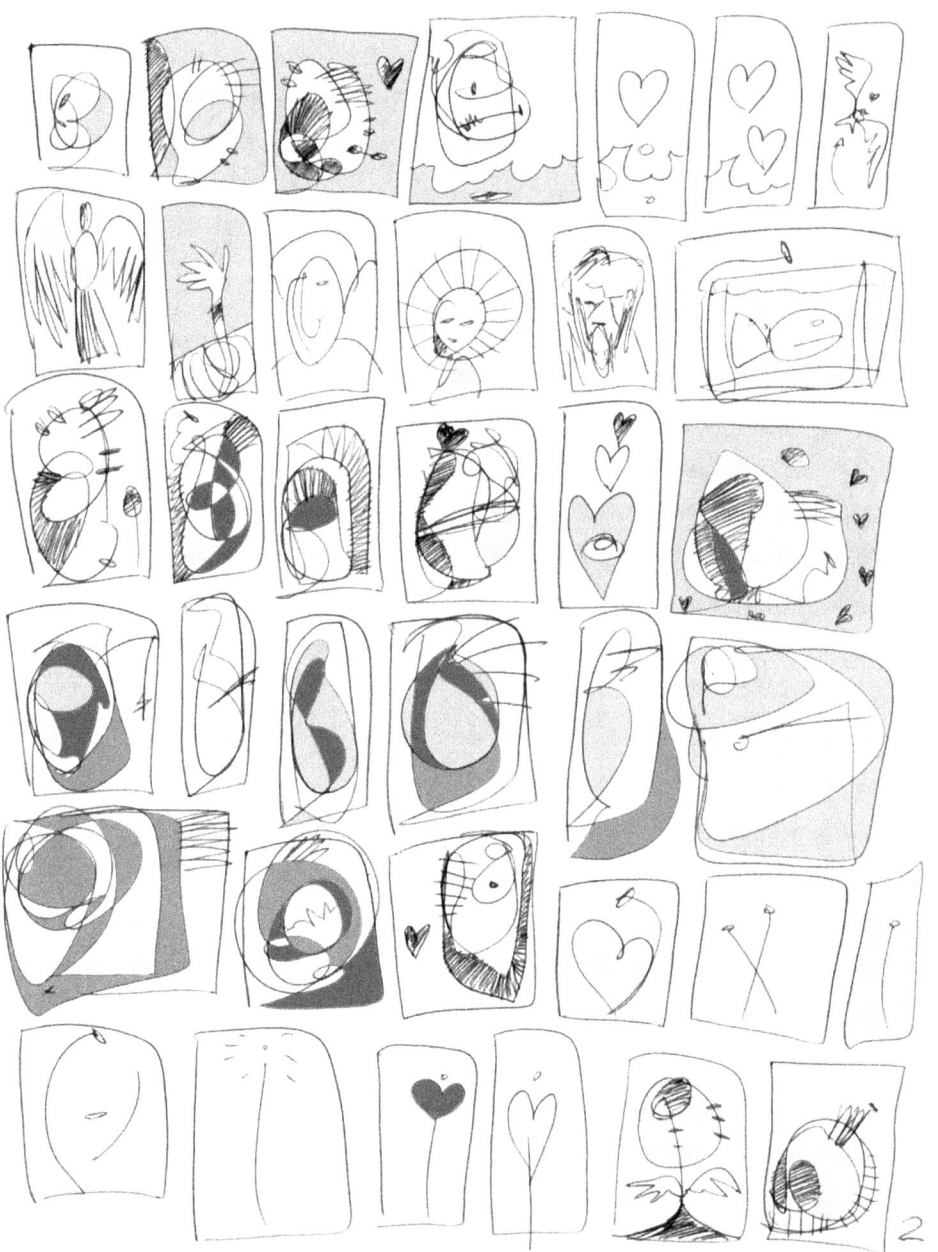

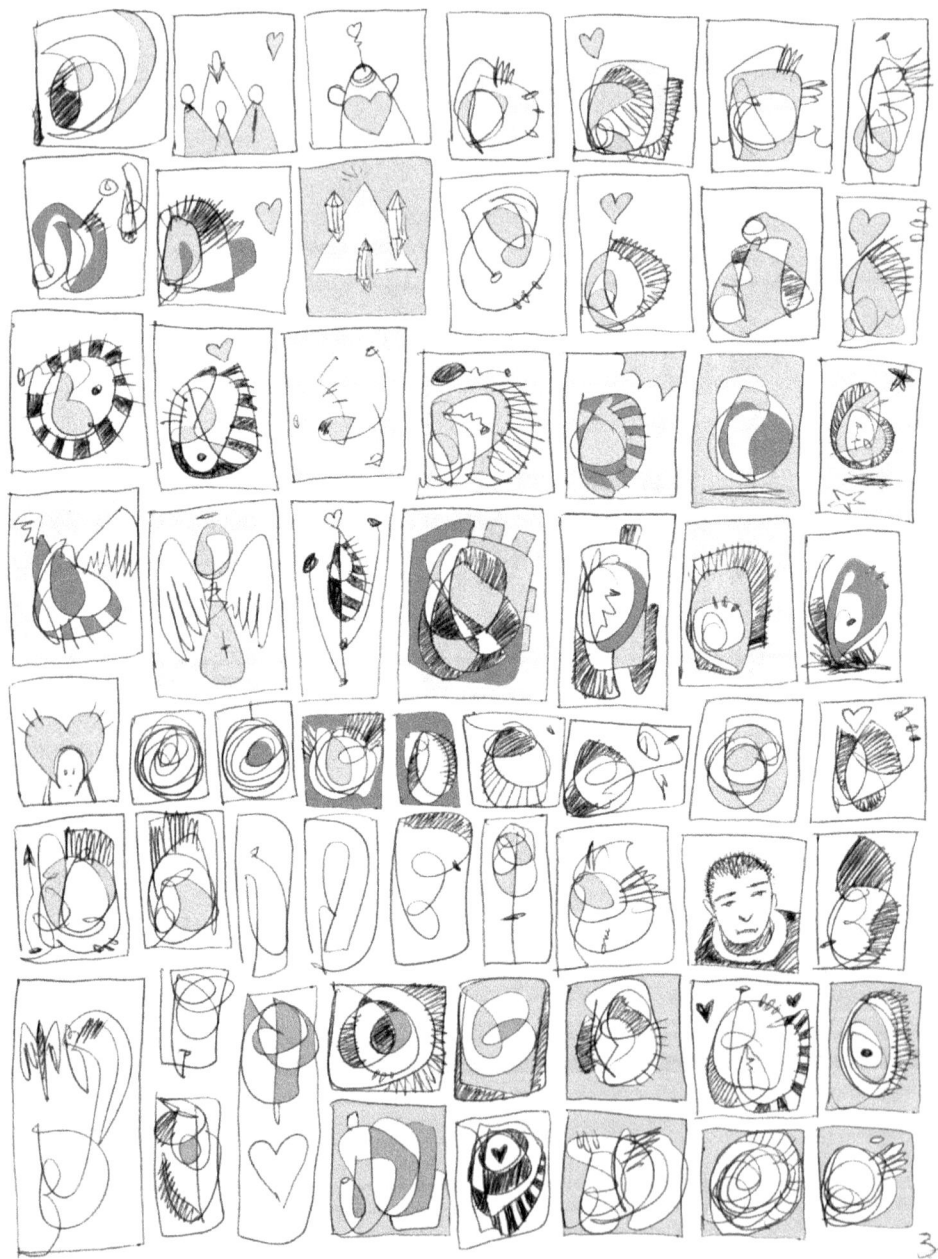

110

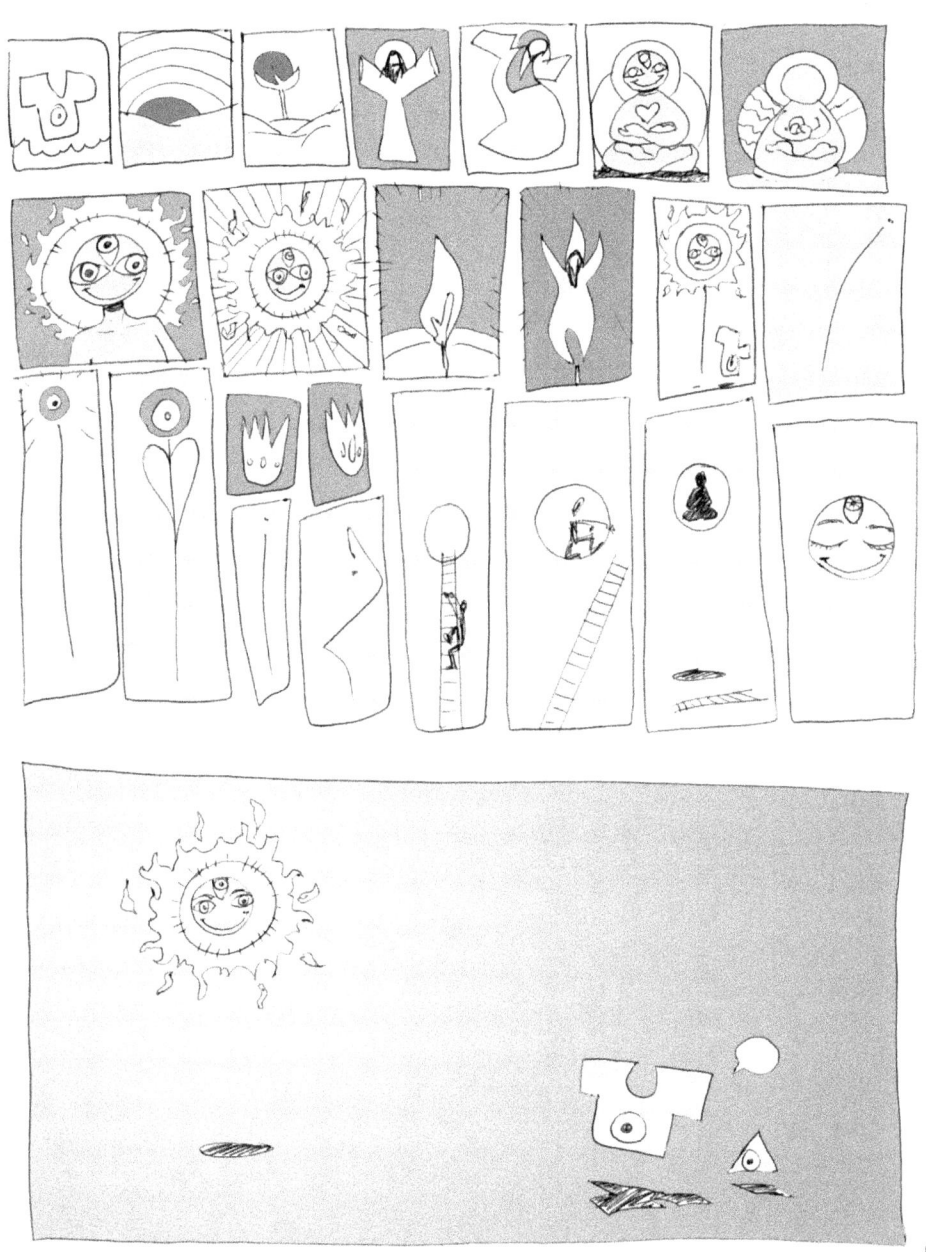

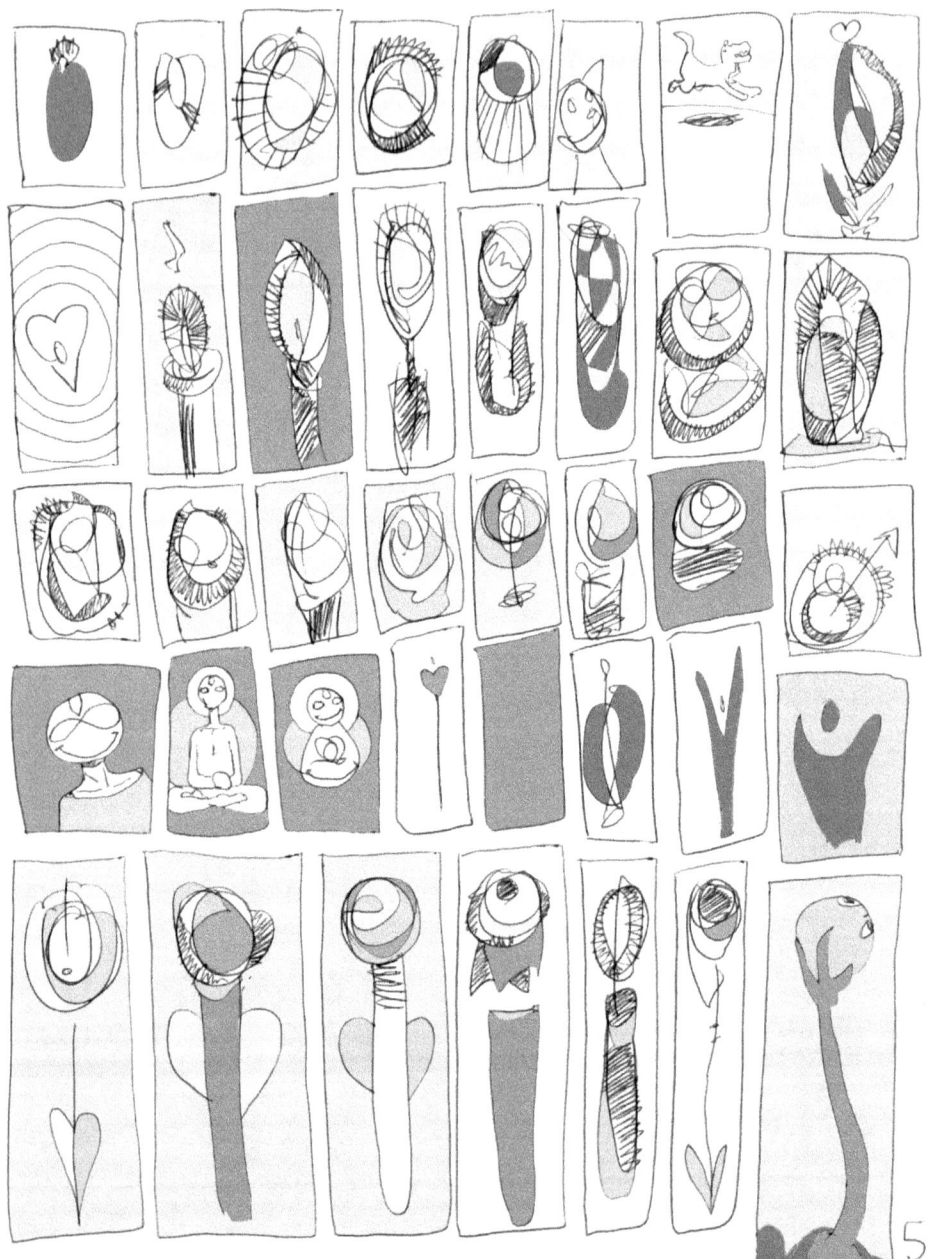

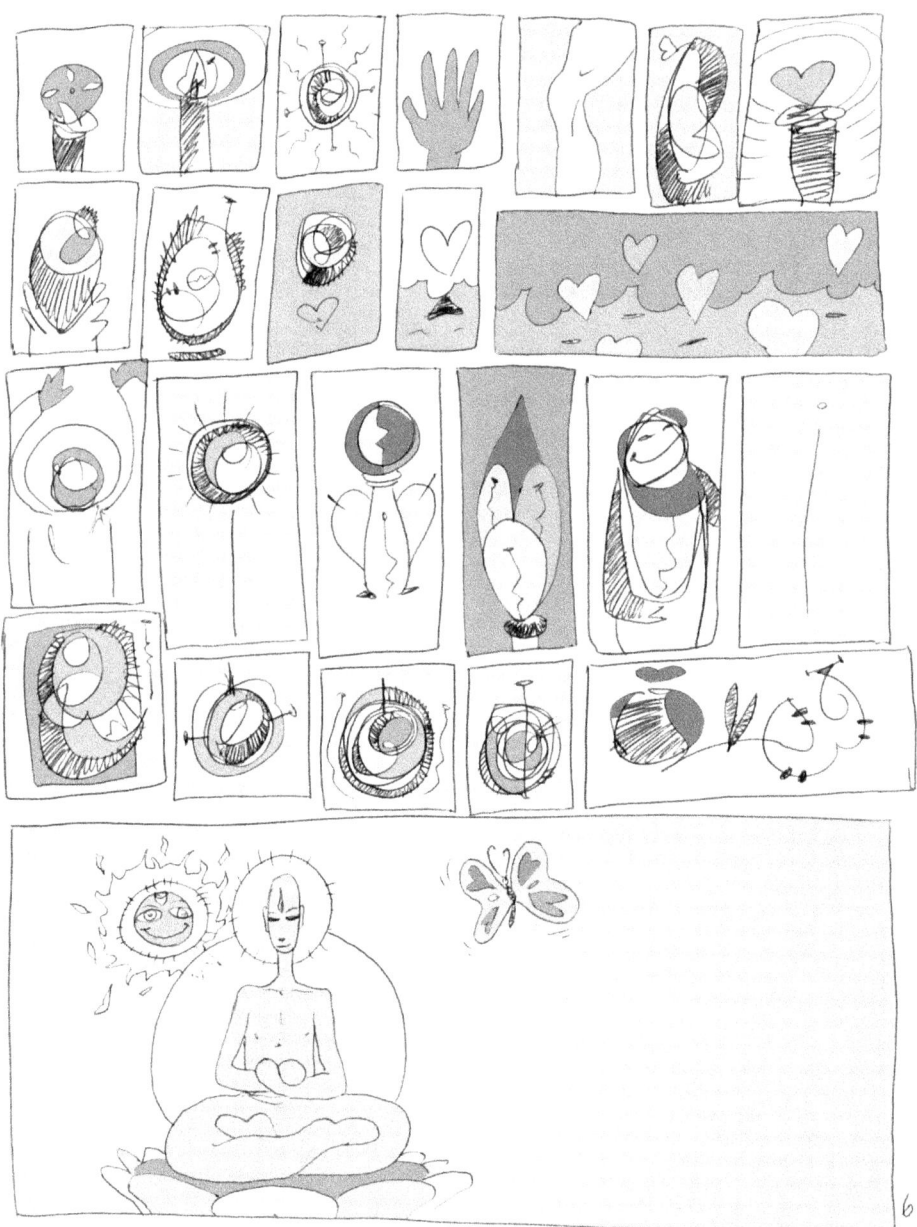

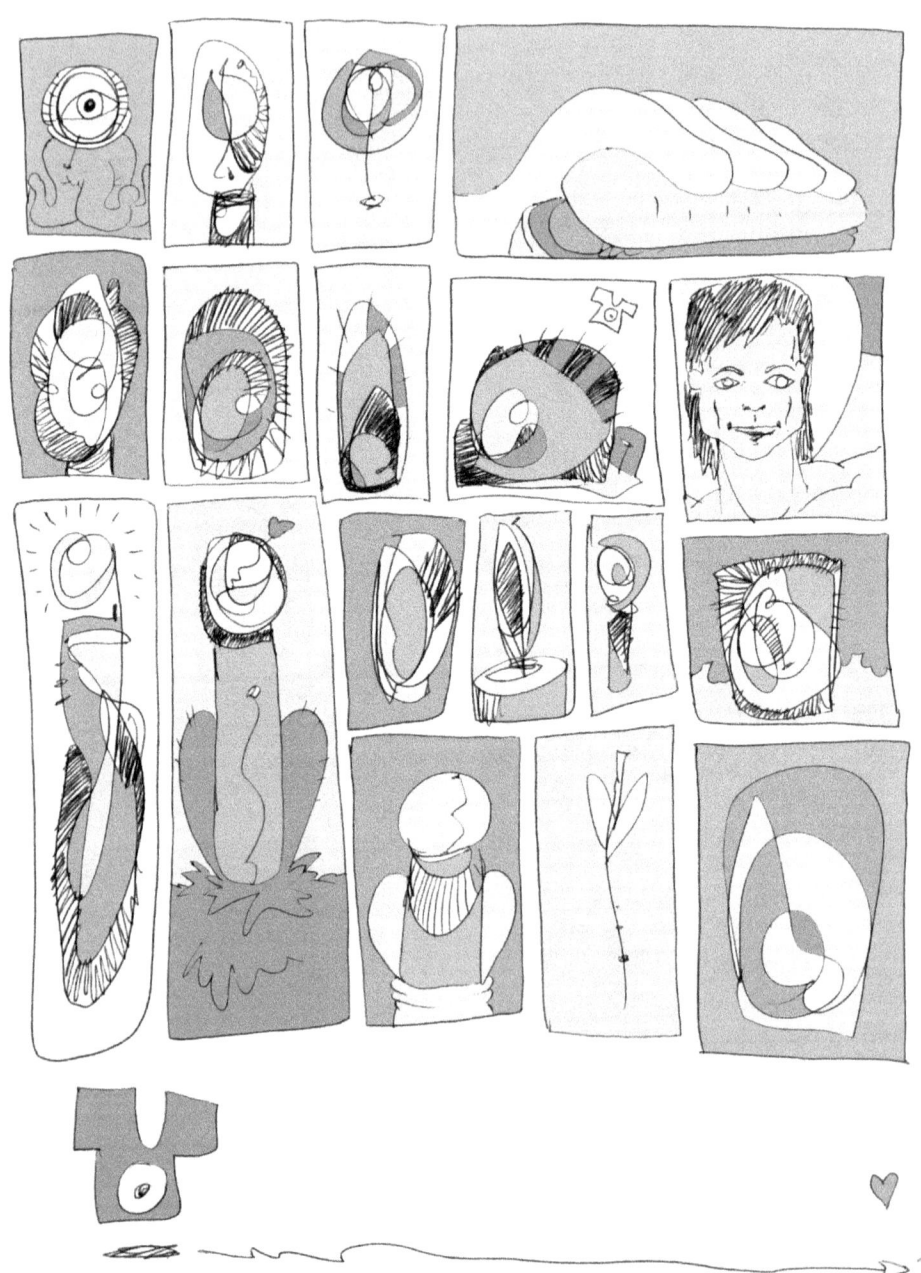

114

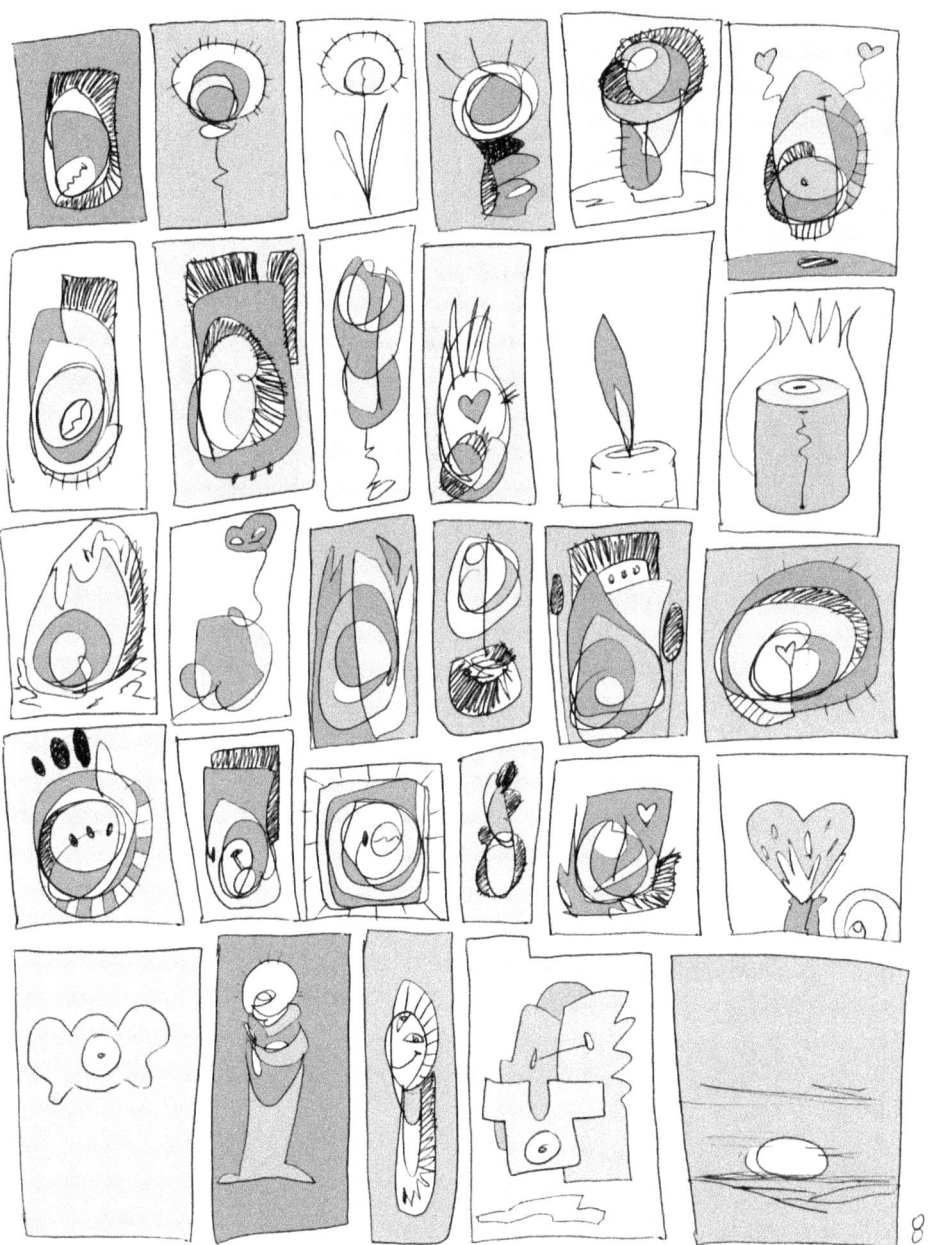

8

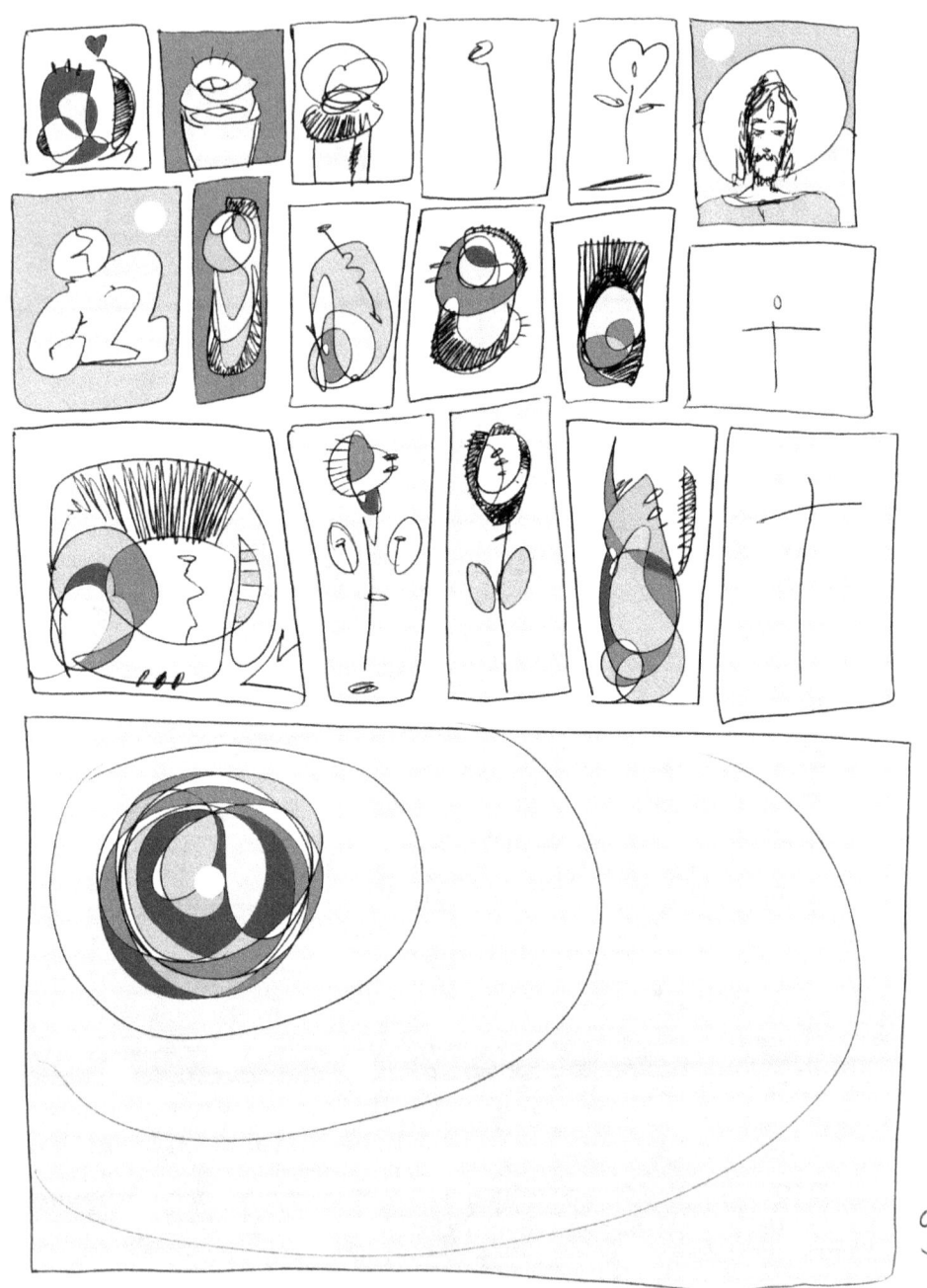

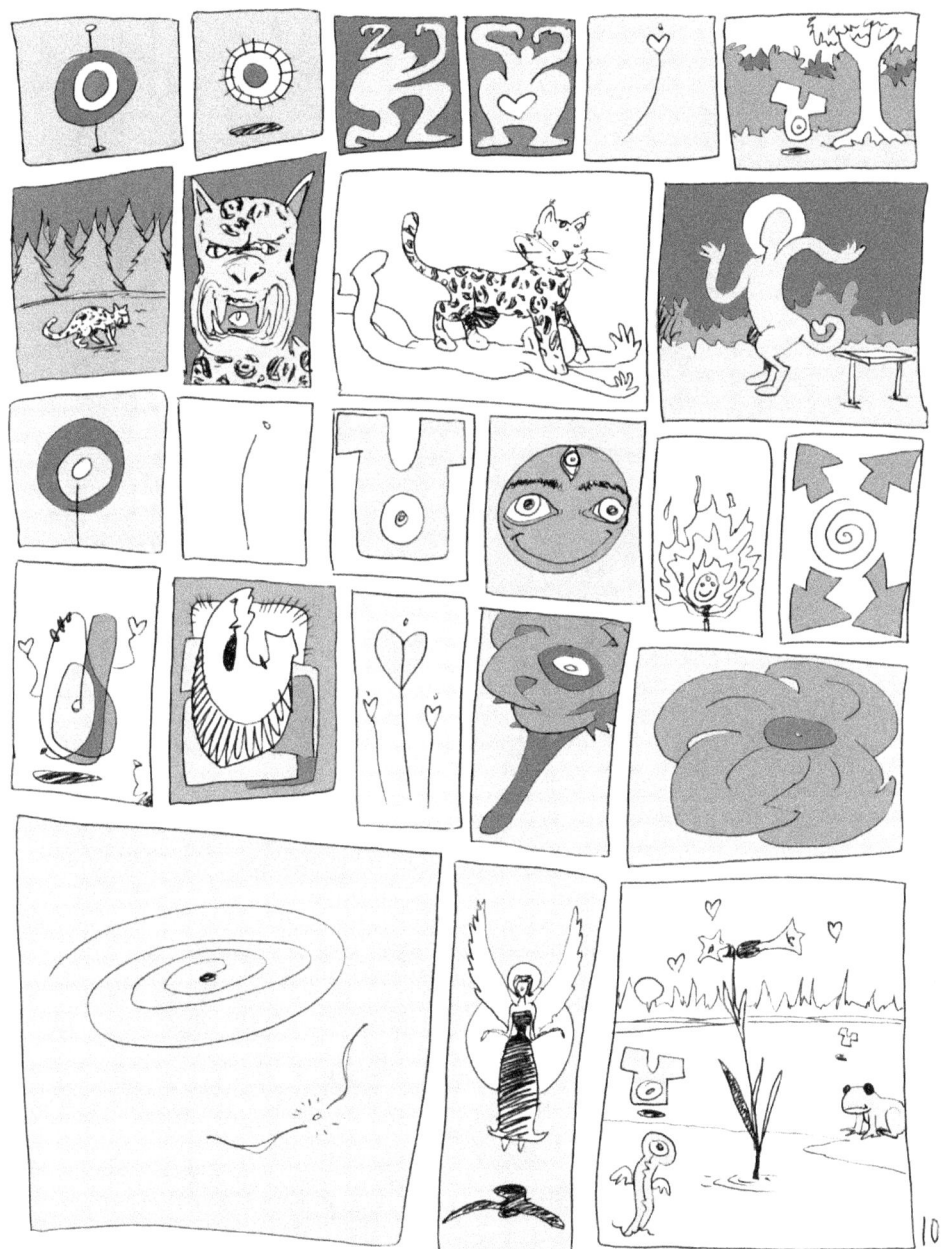

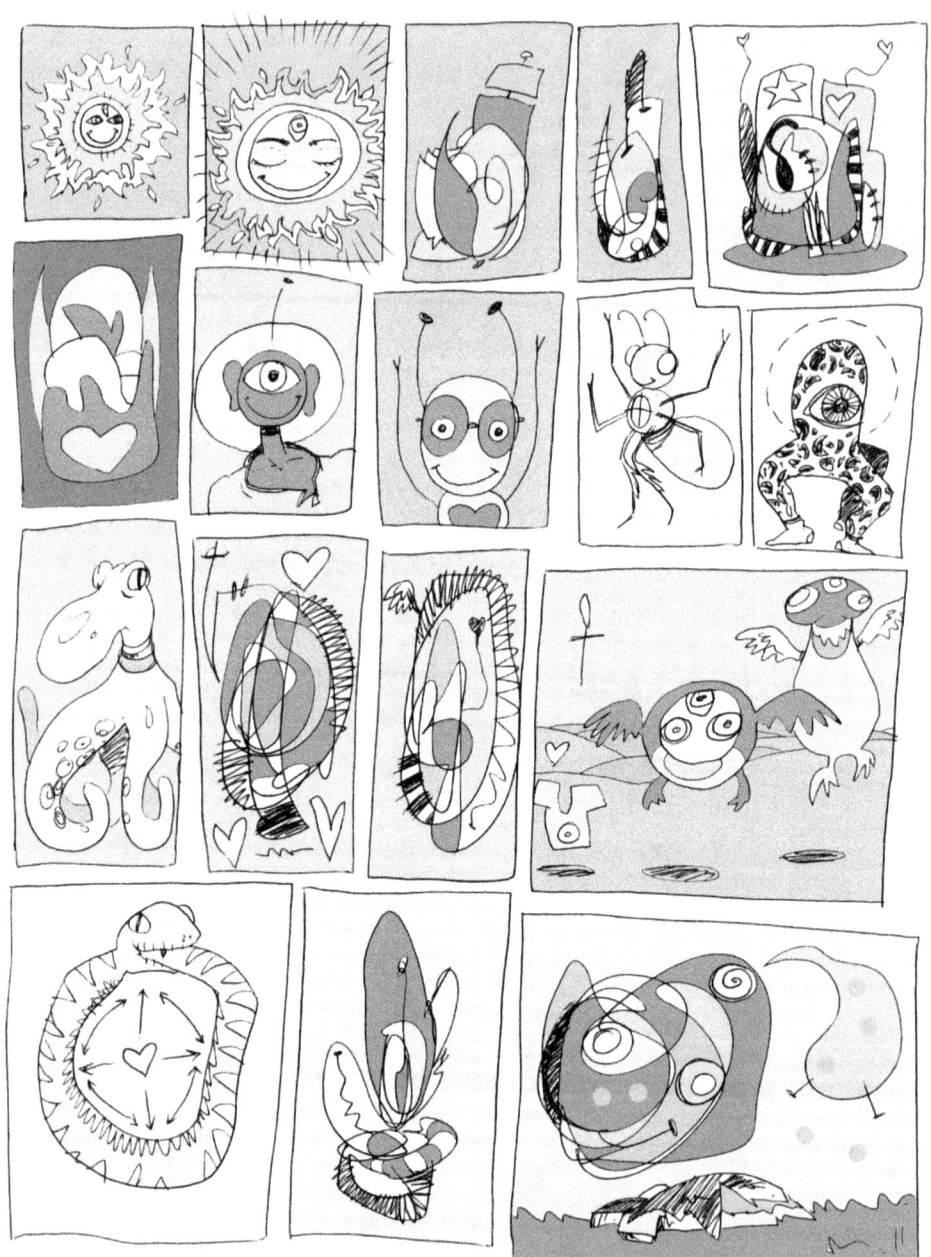

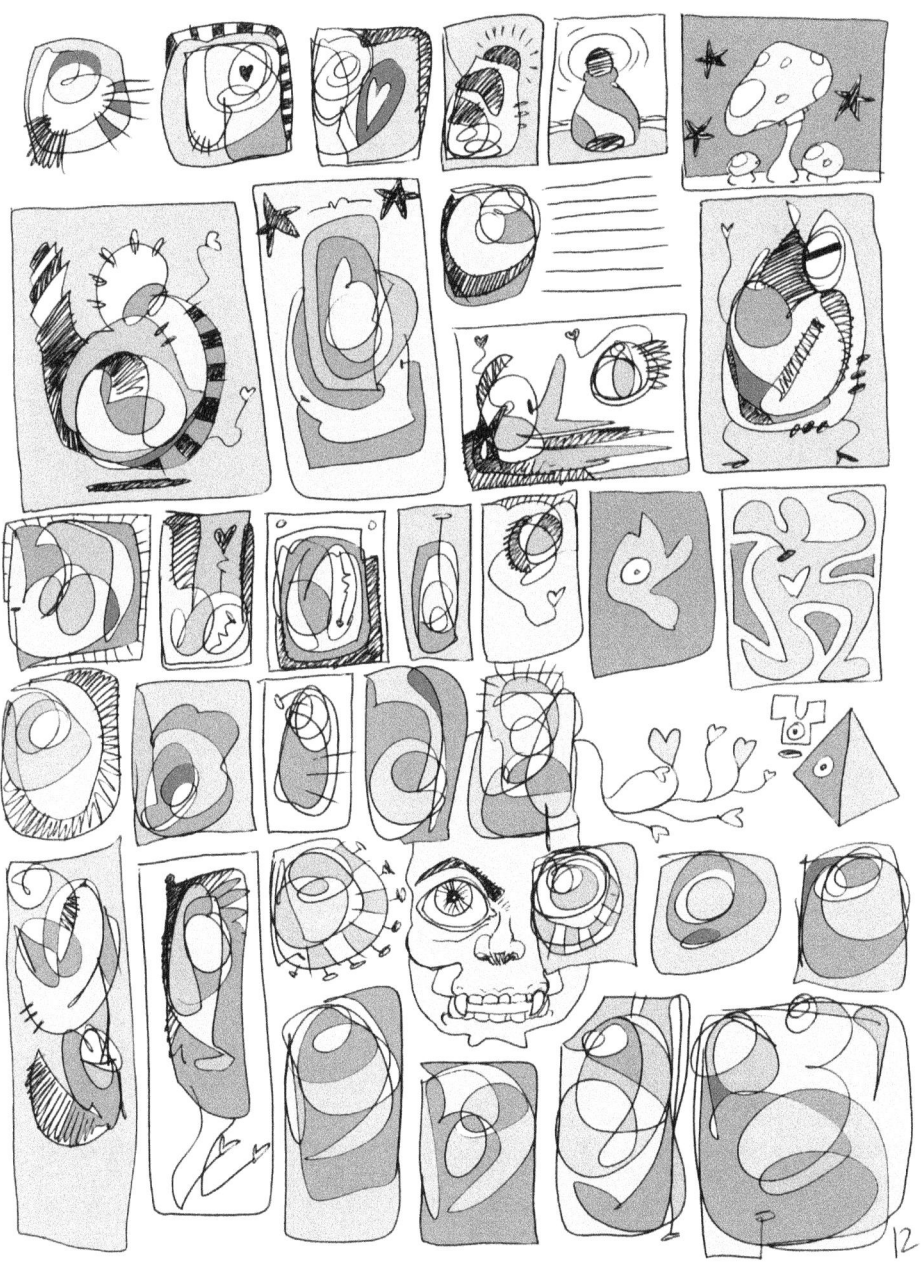

119

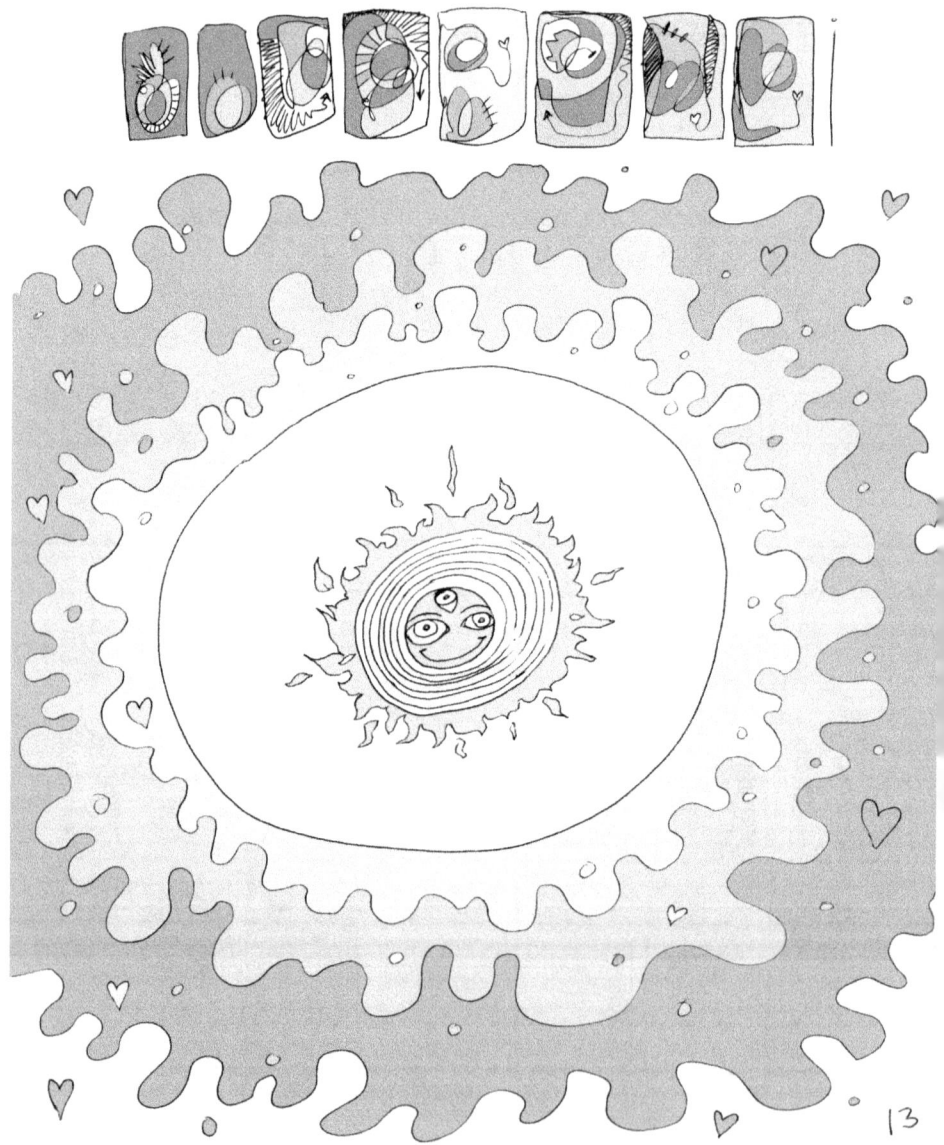

13

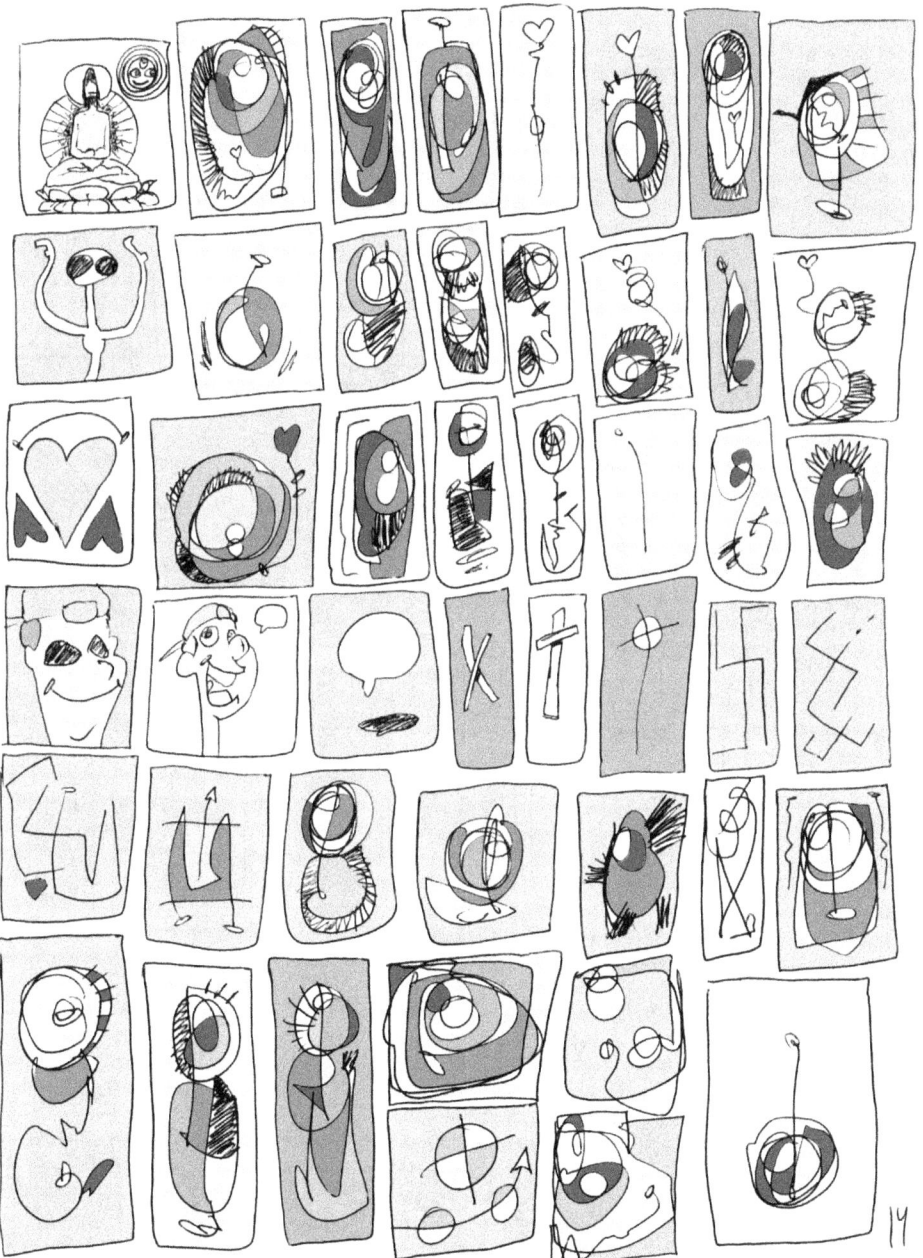

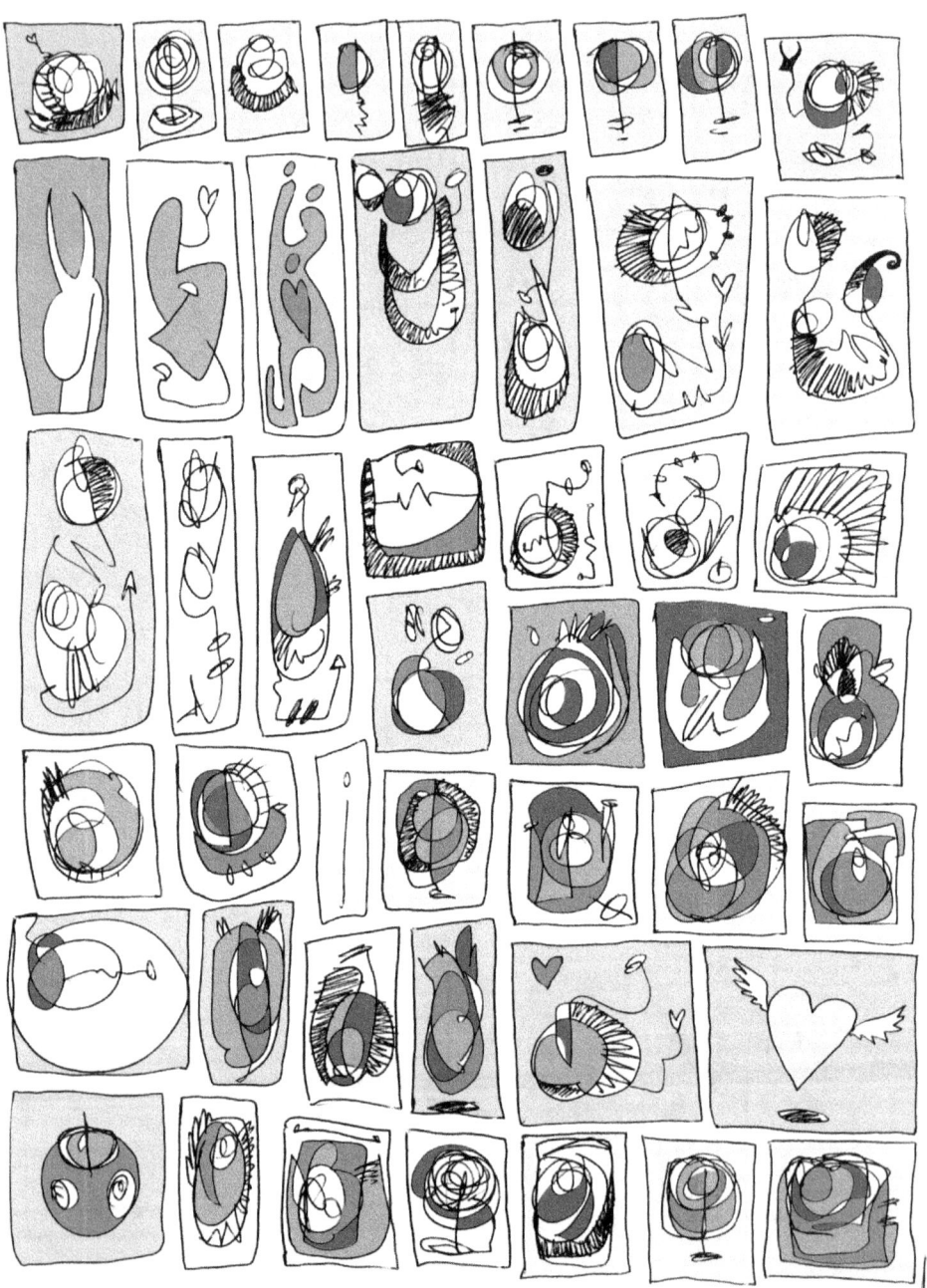

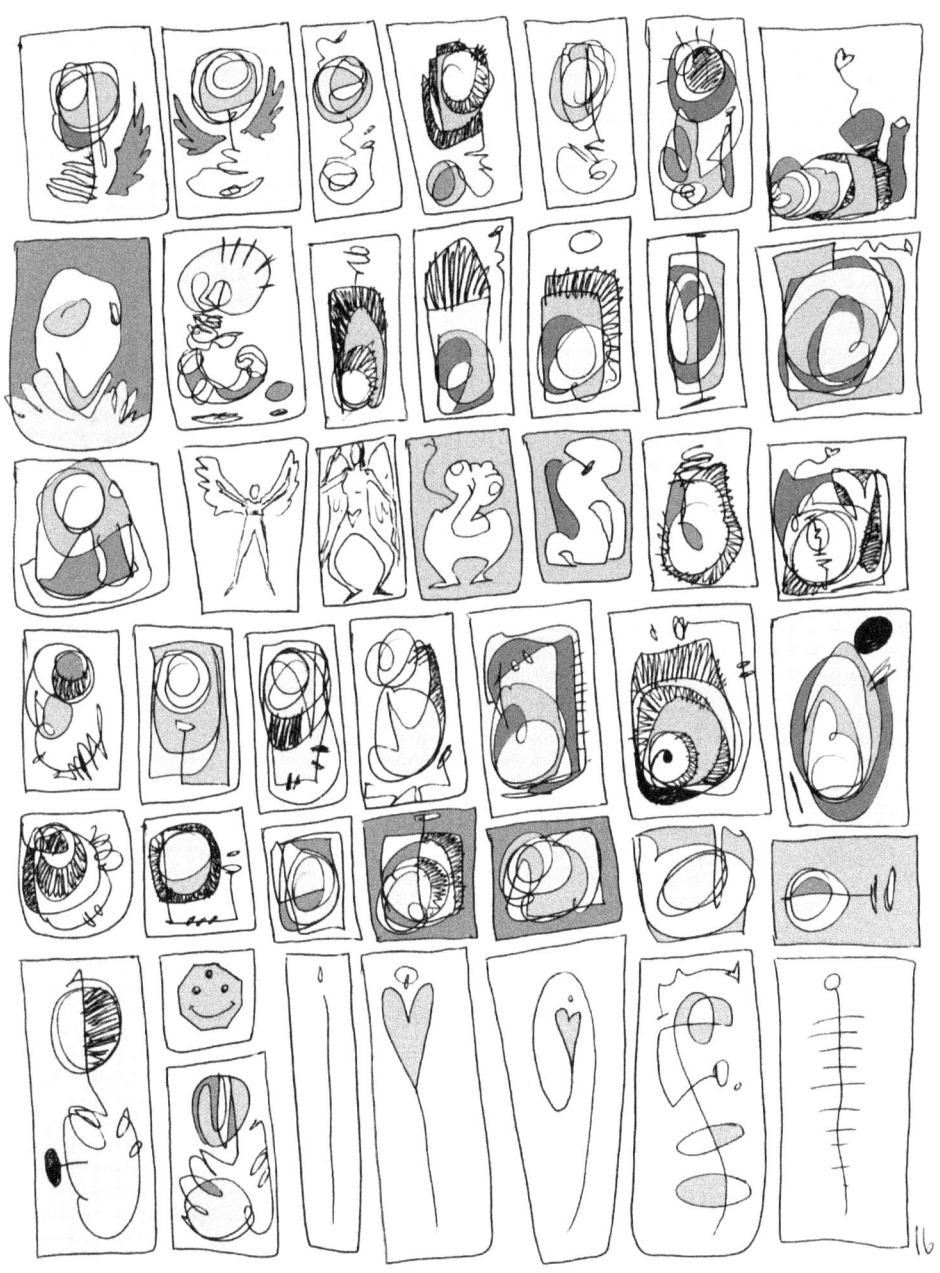

123

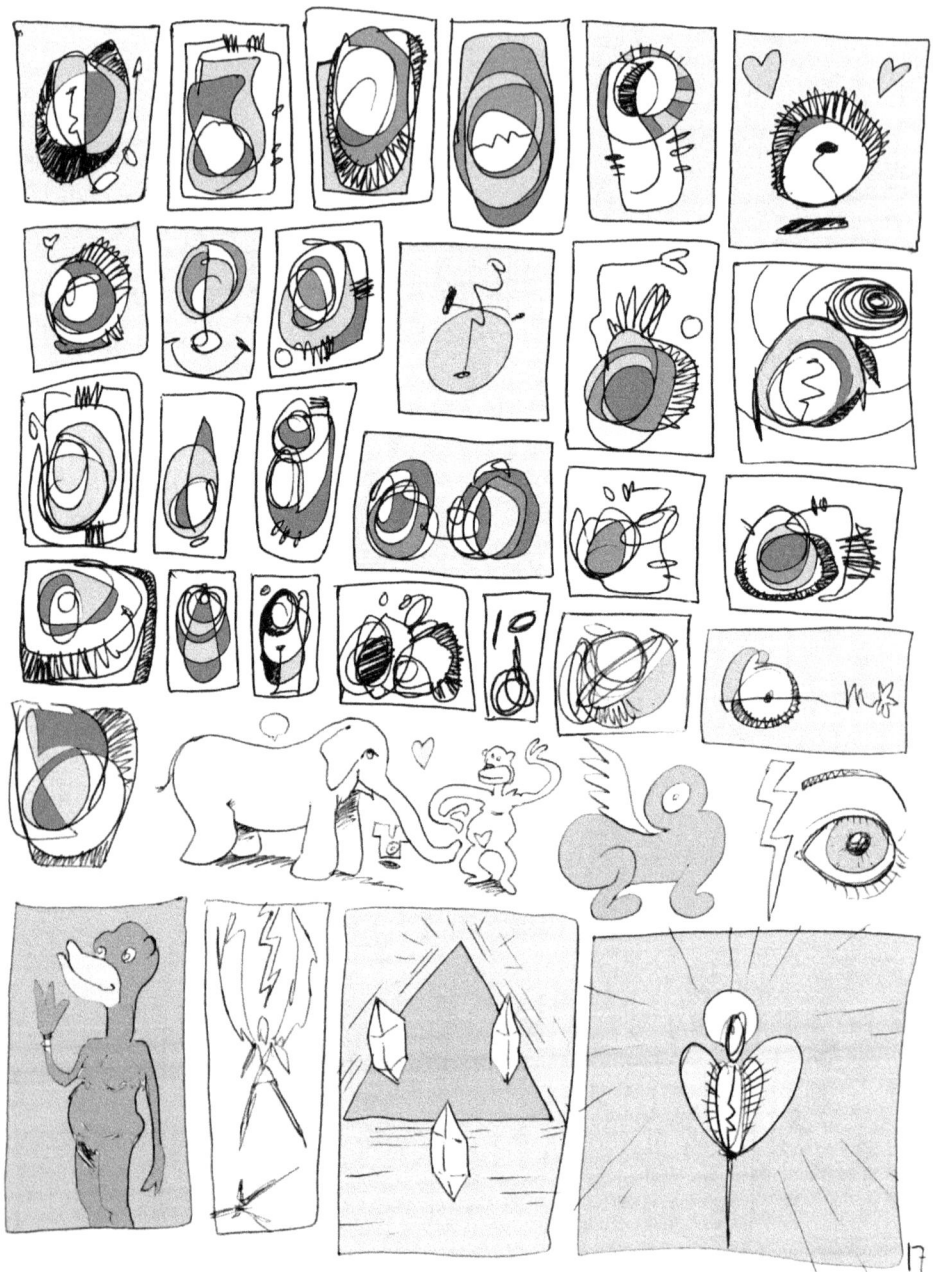

124

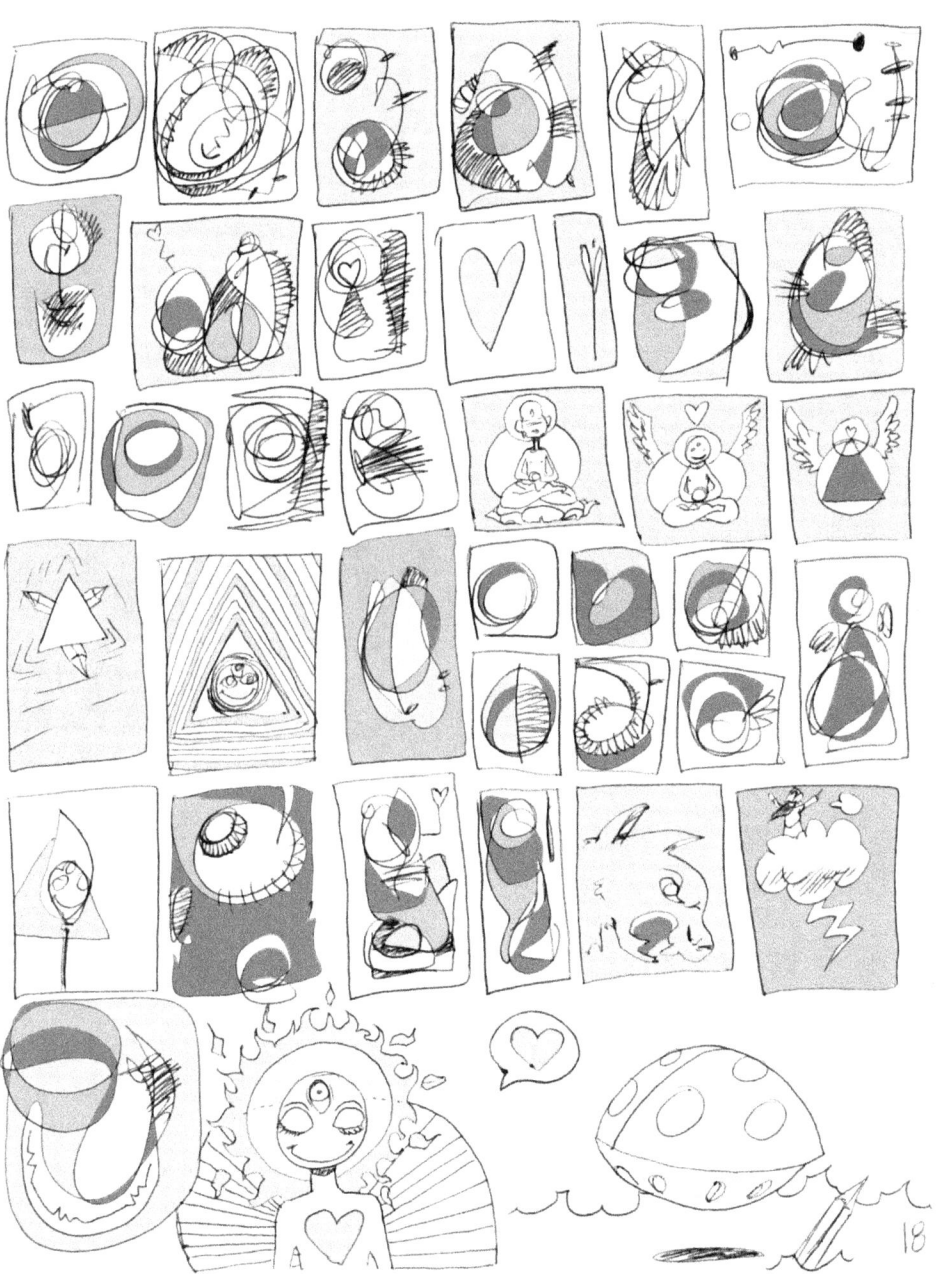

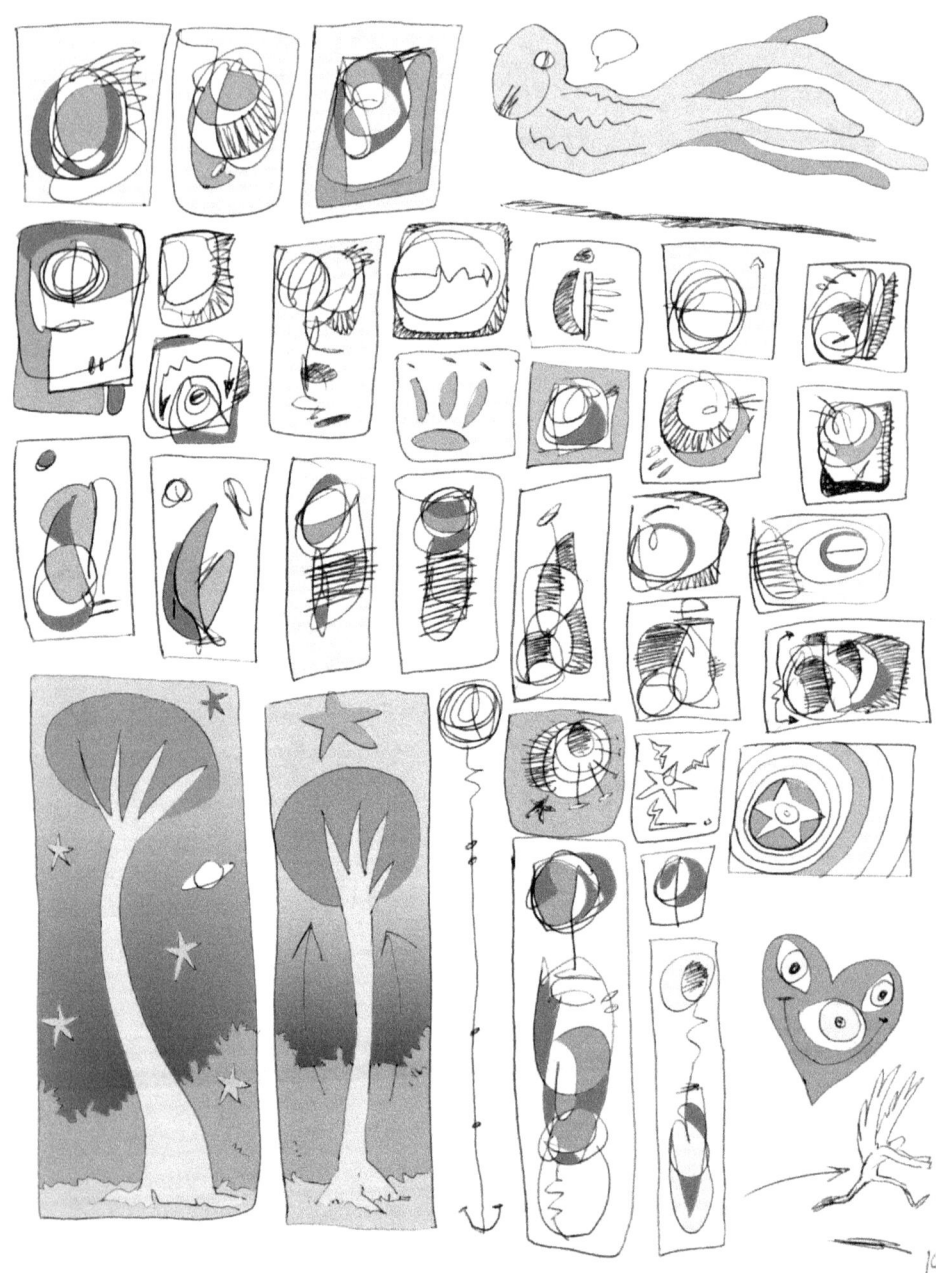

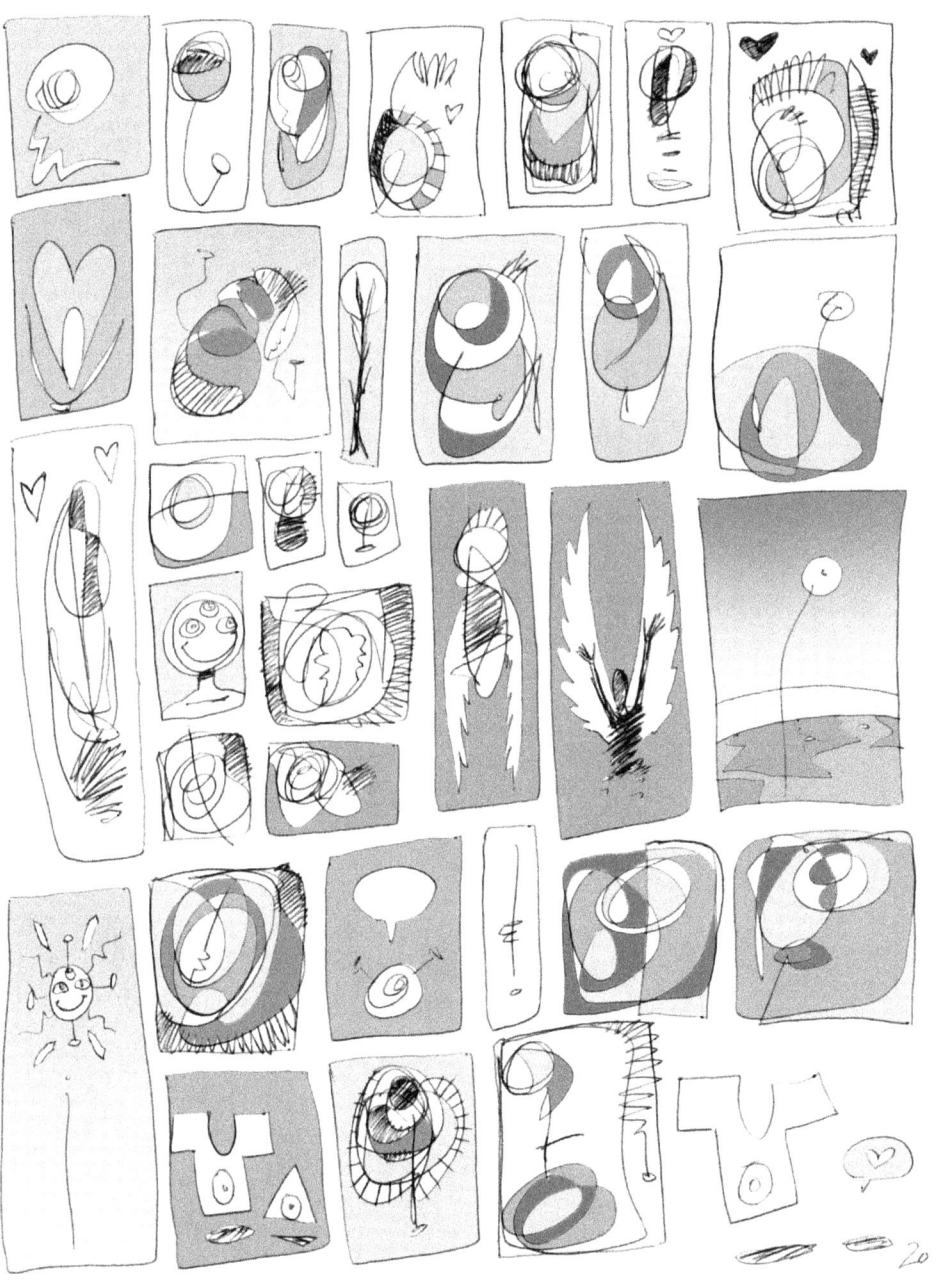

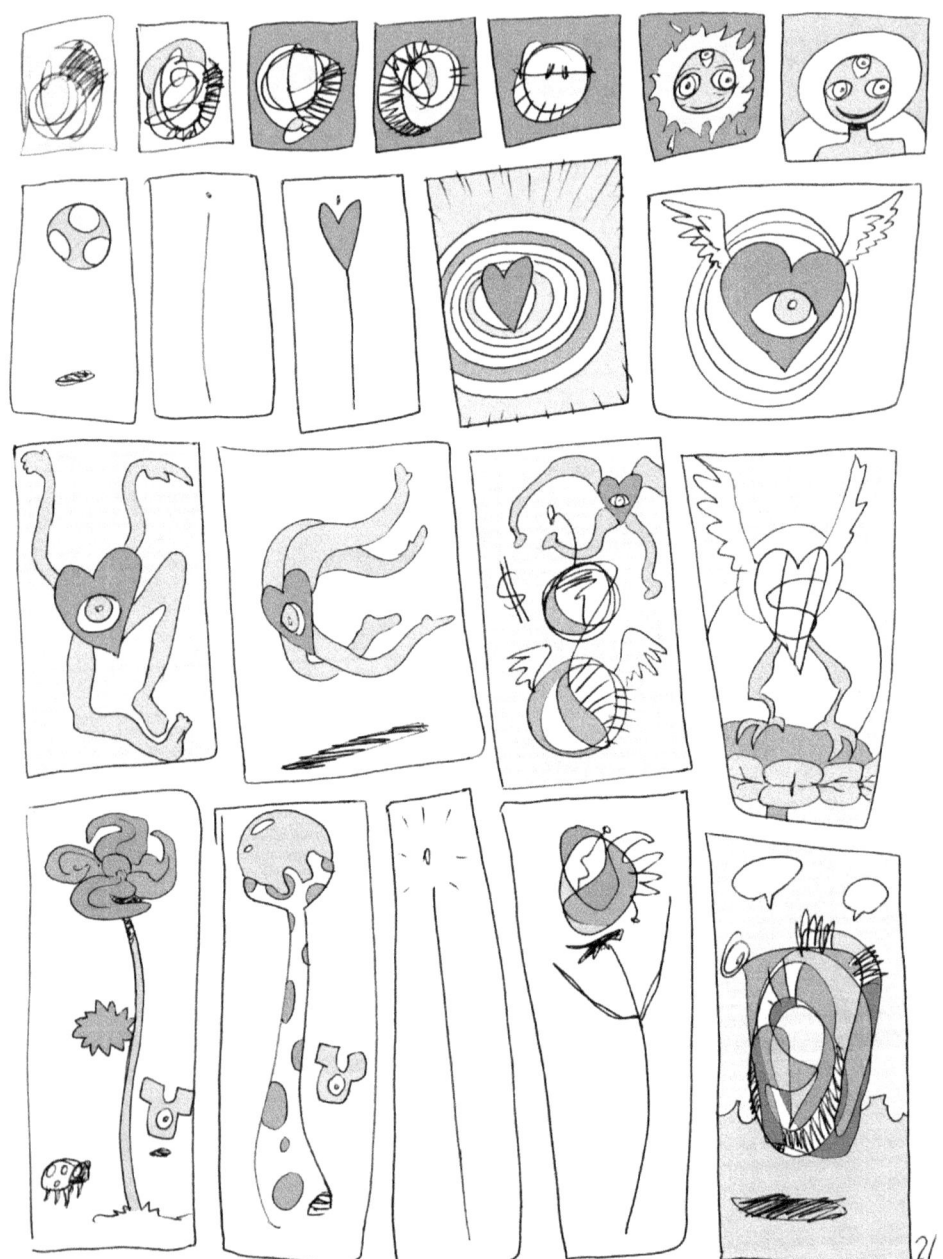

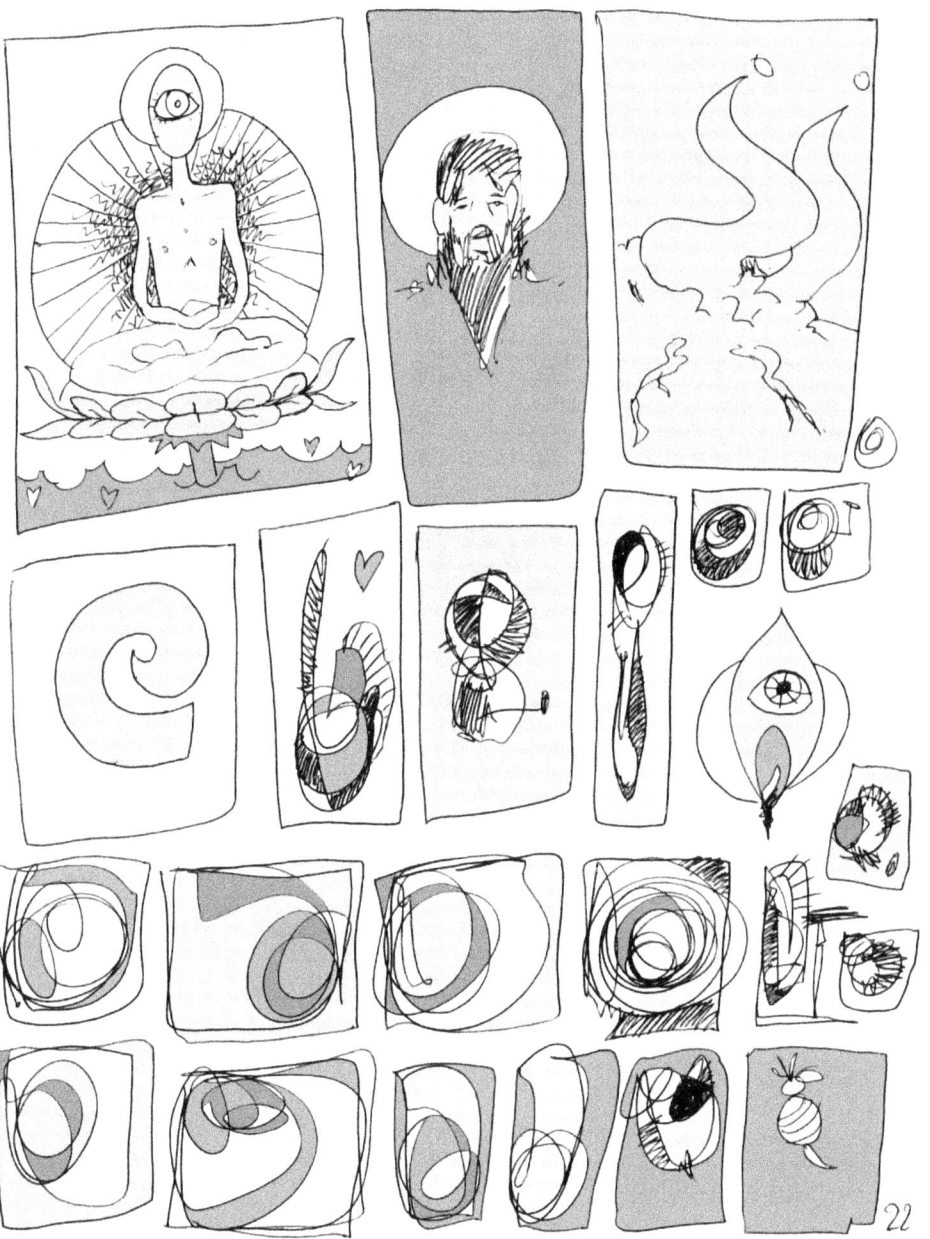

22

129

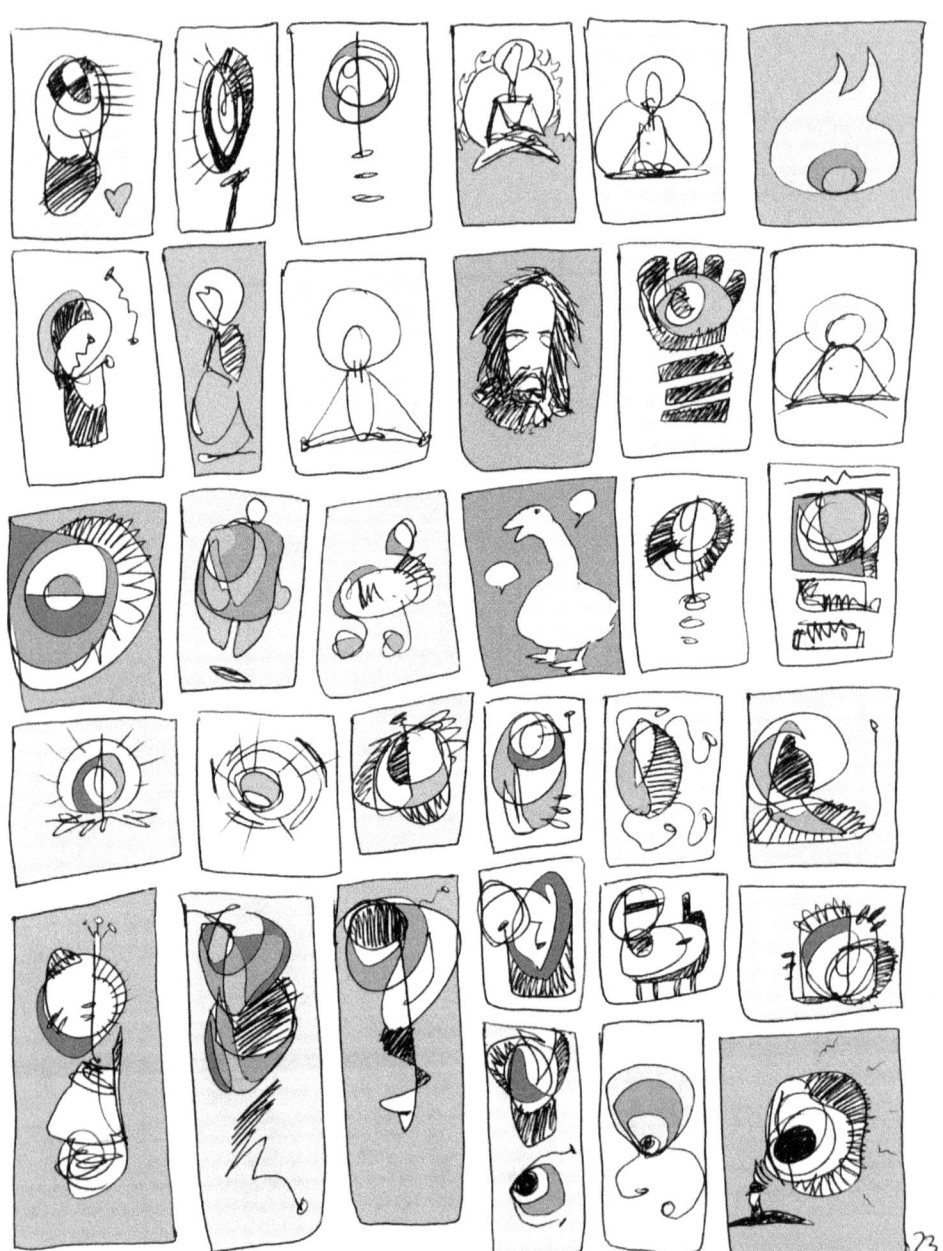

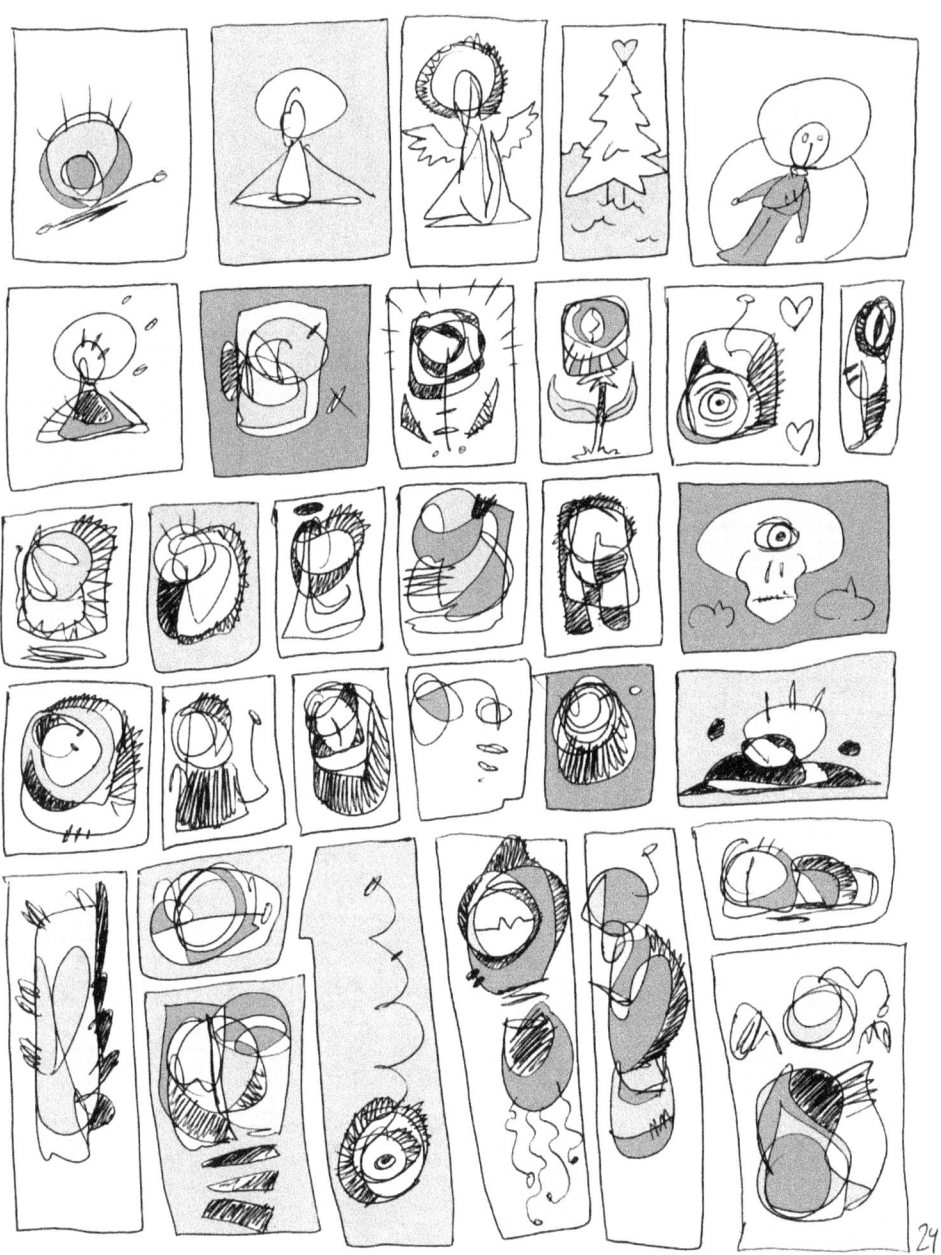

131

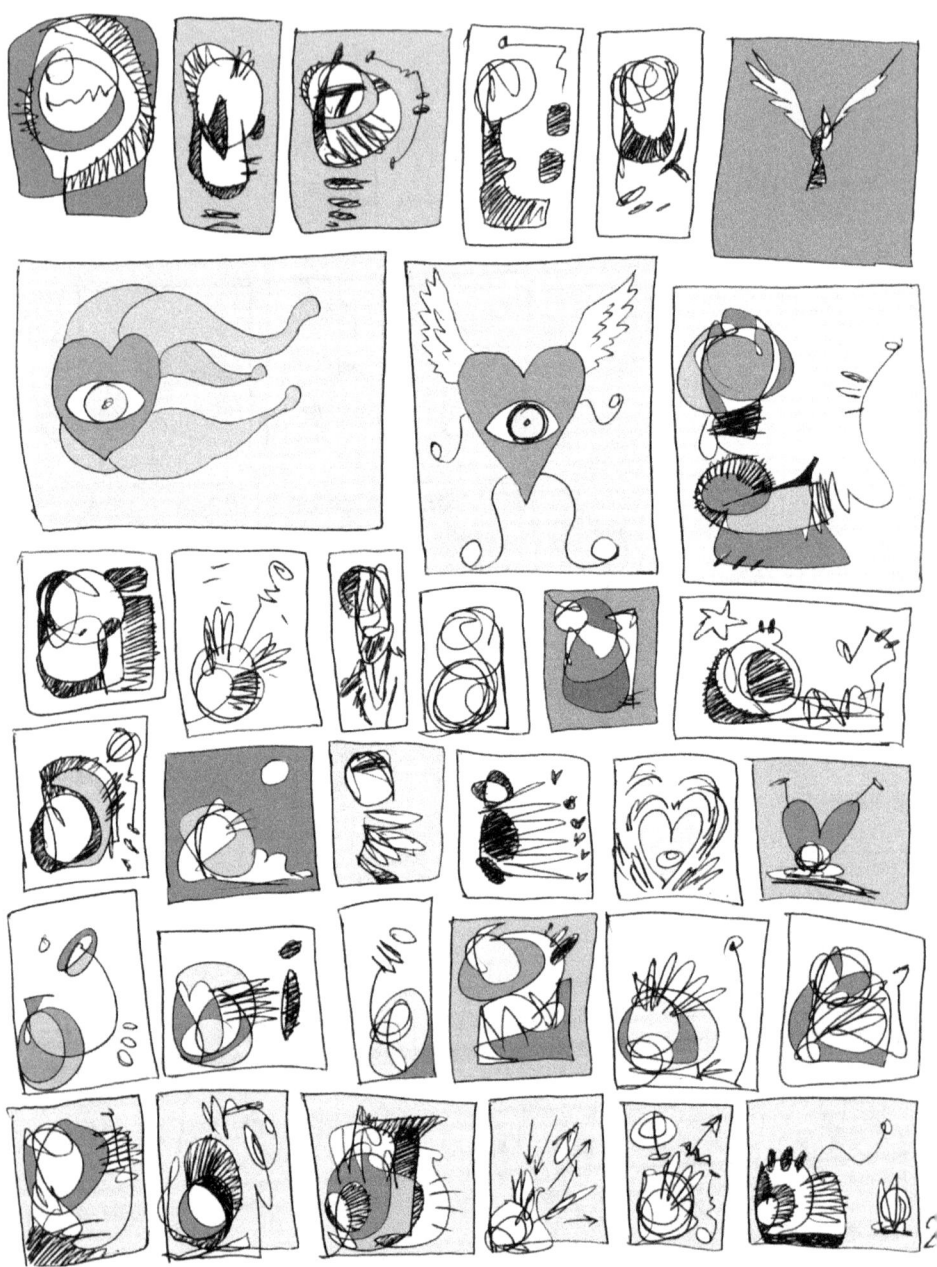

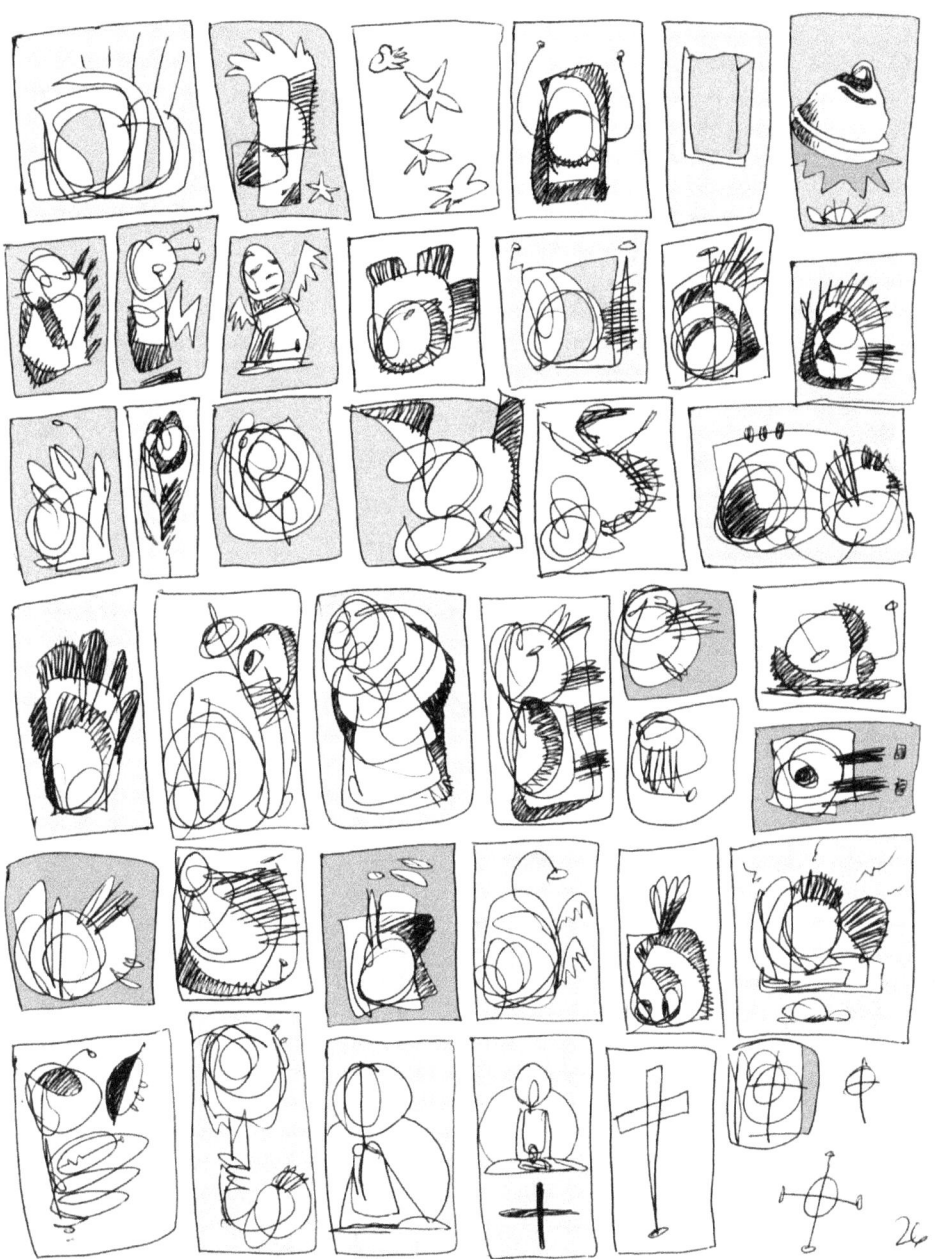

26

133

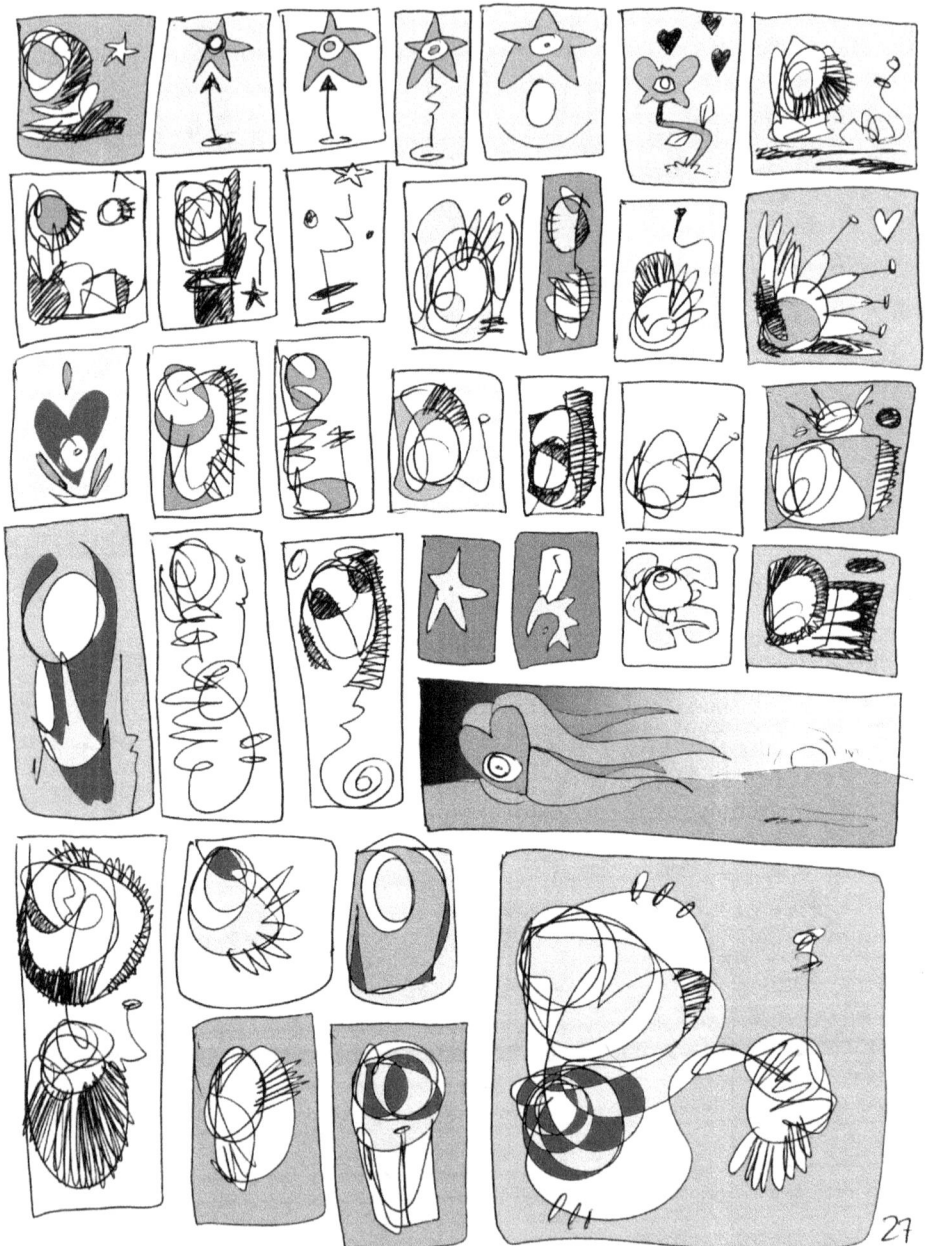

27

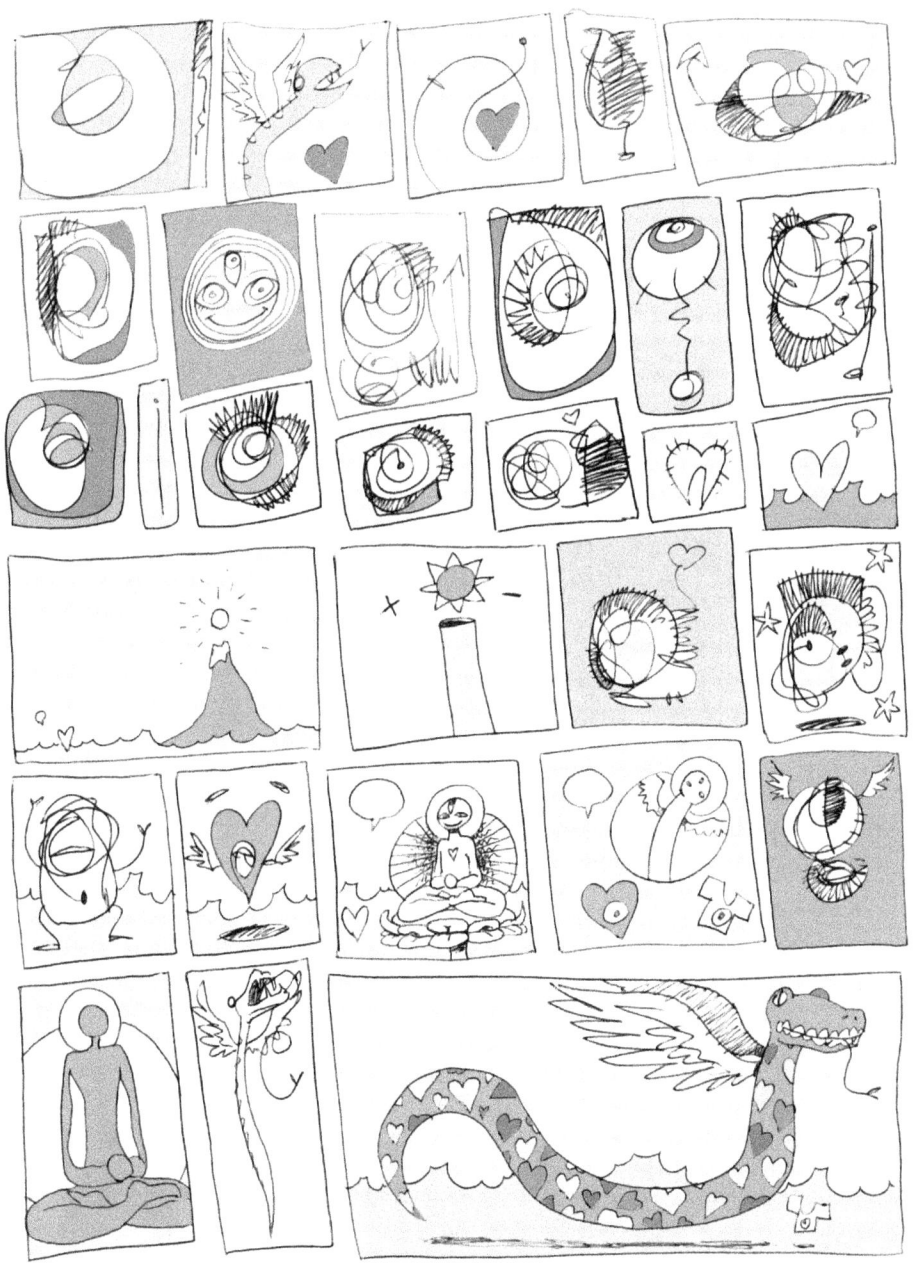

135

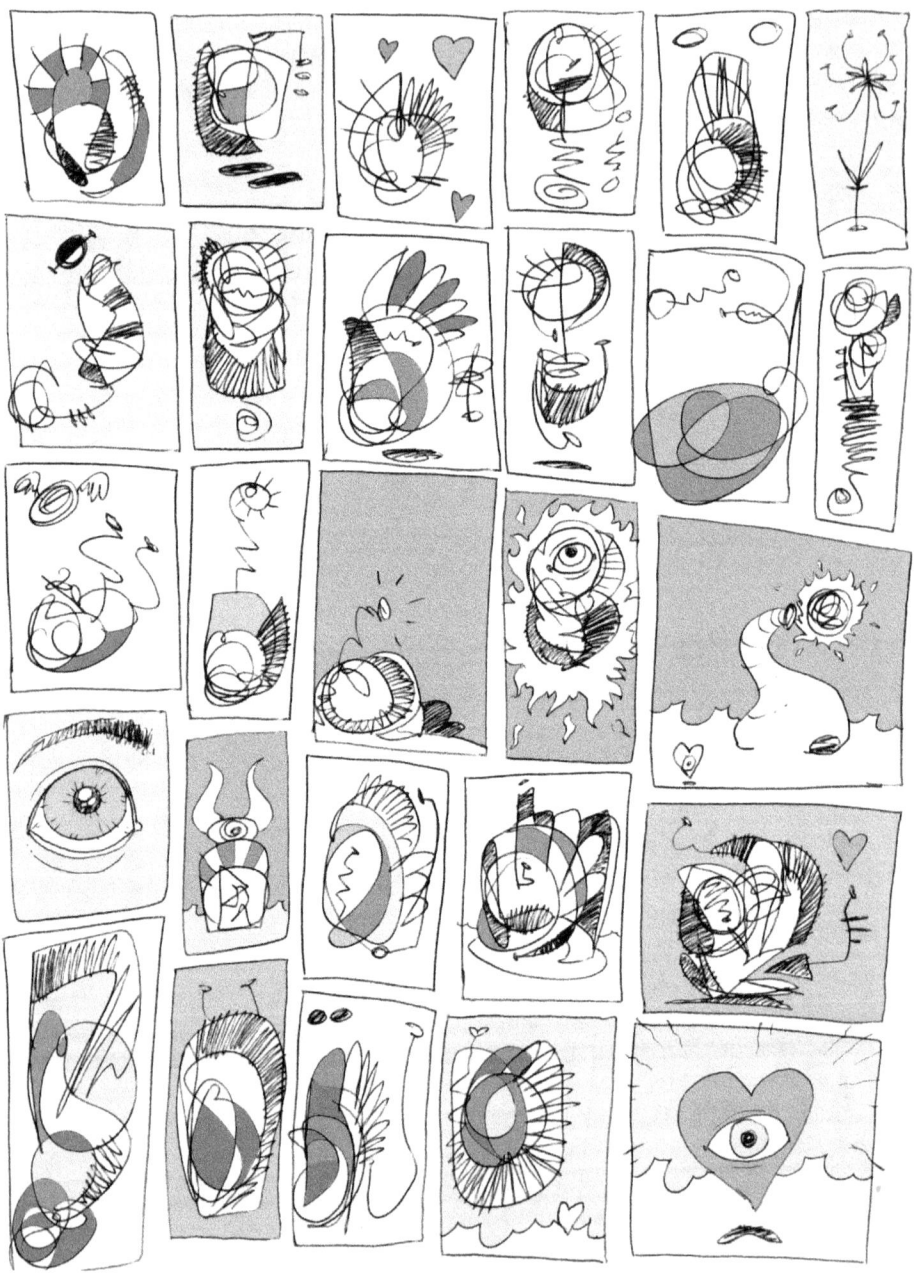

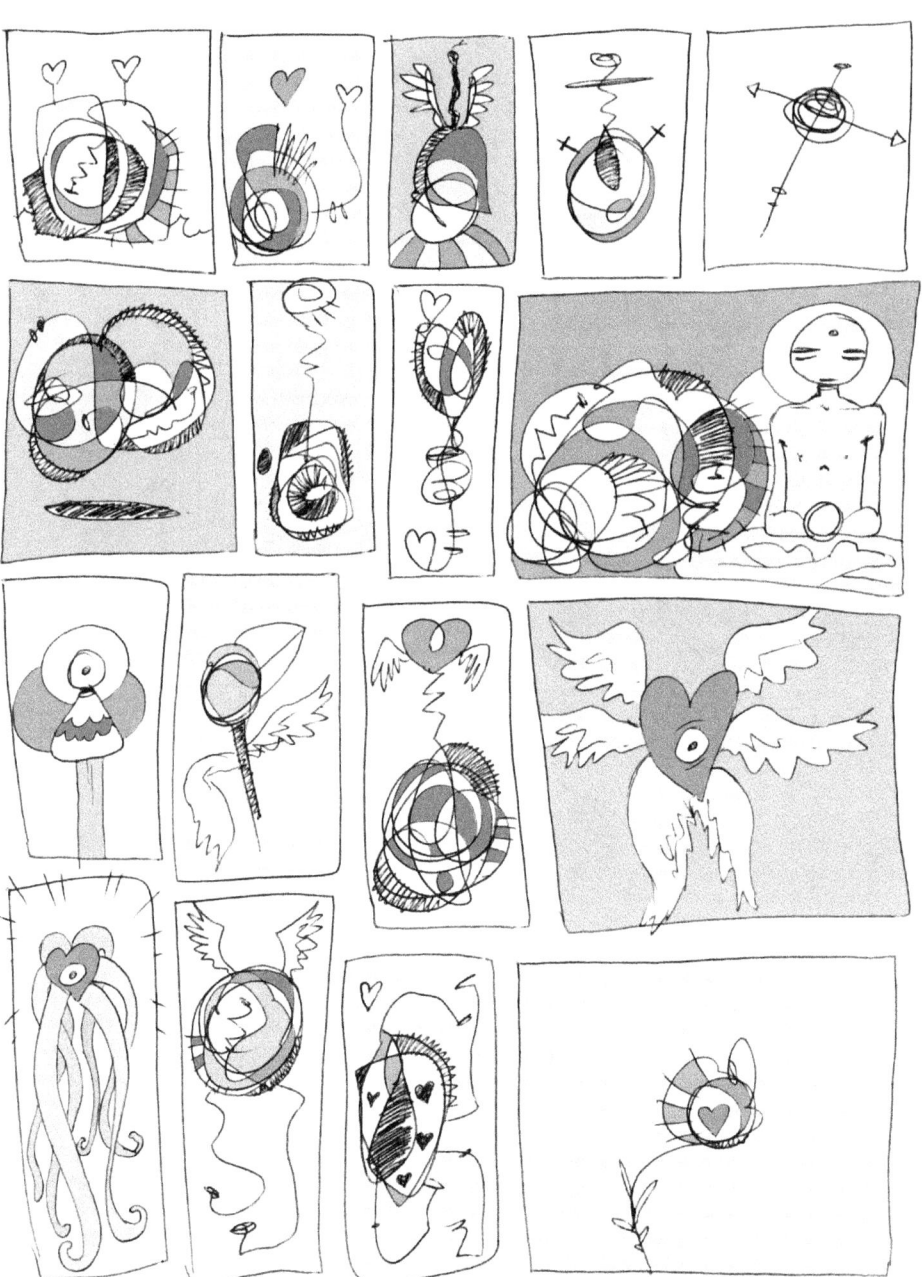

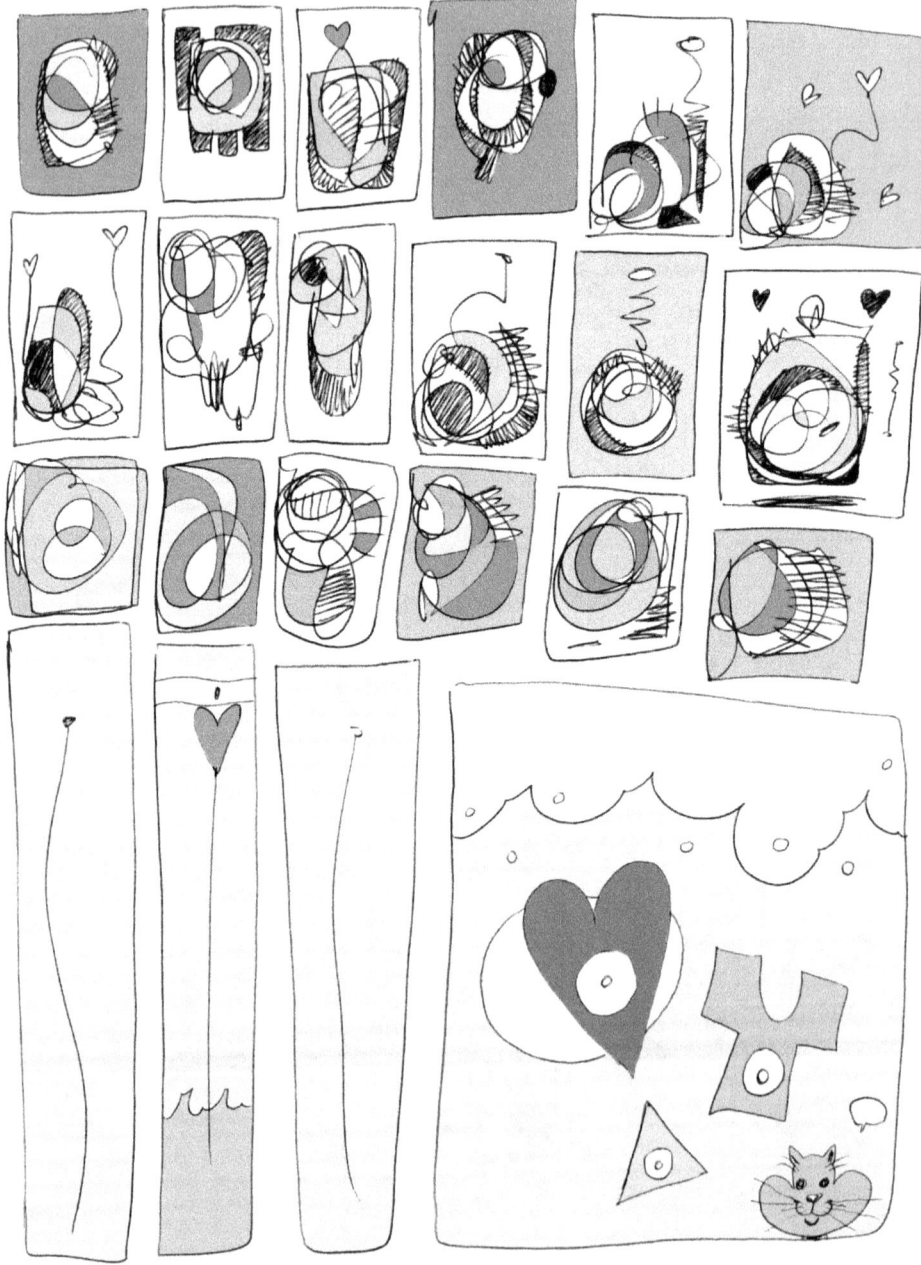

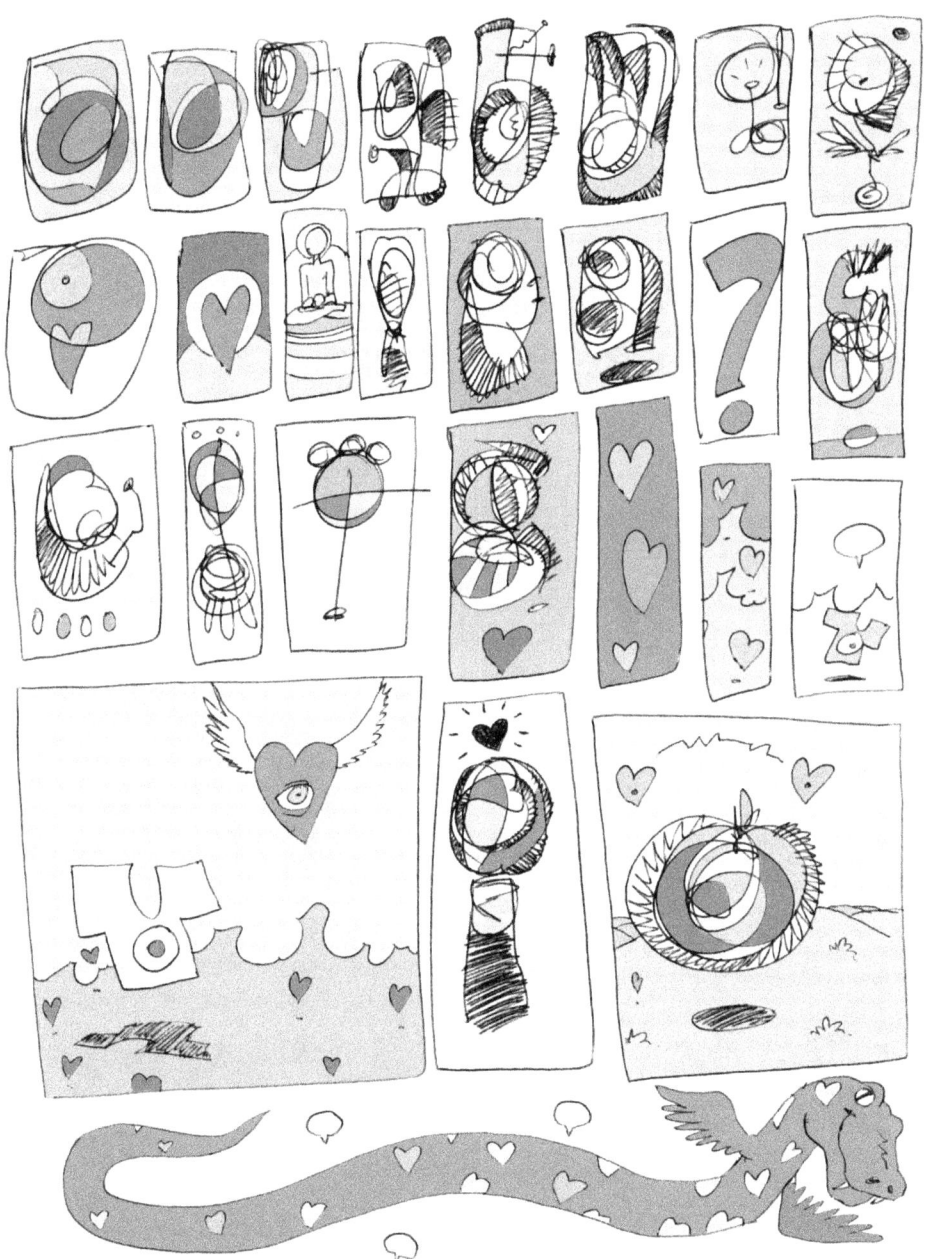

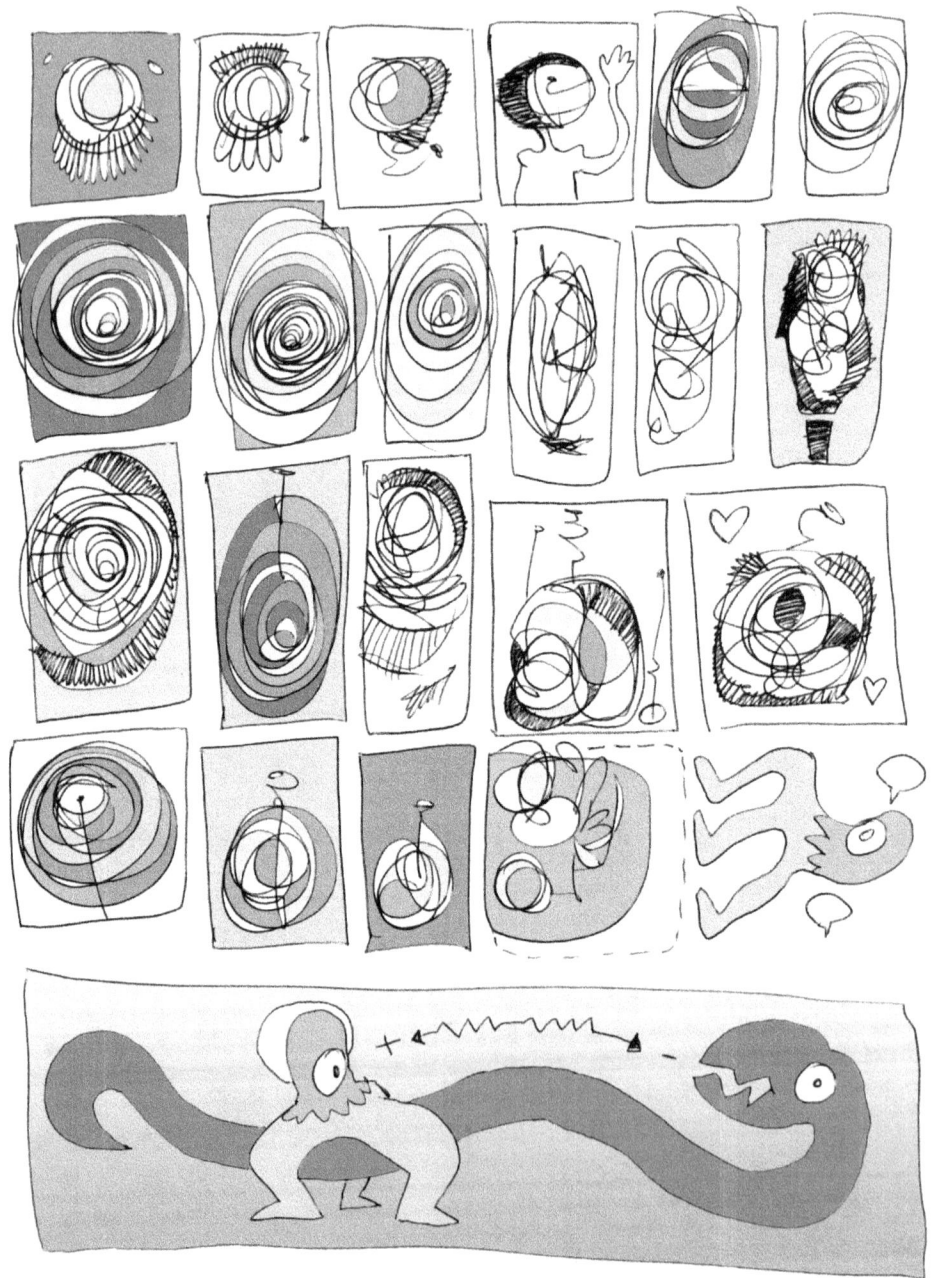

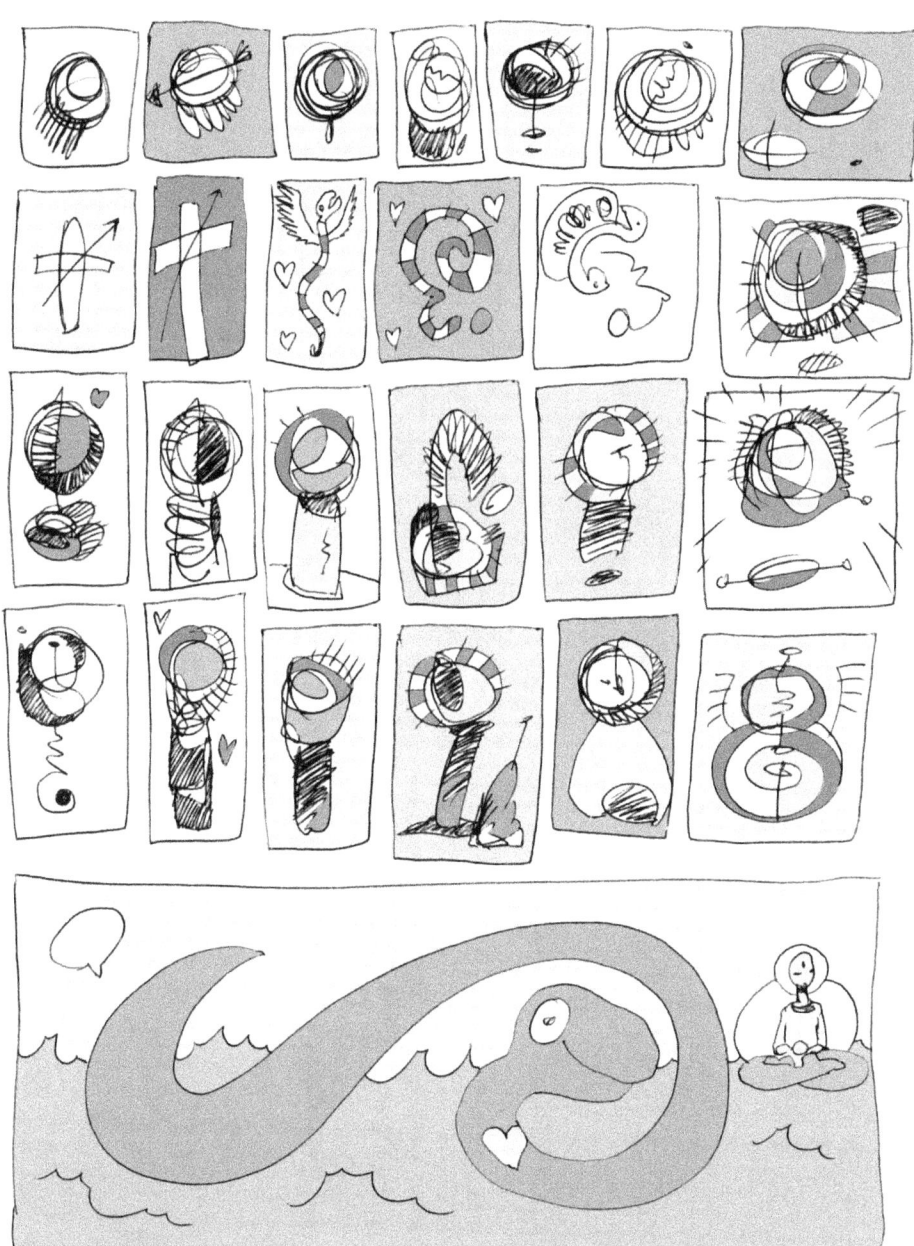

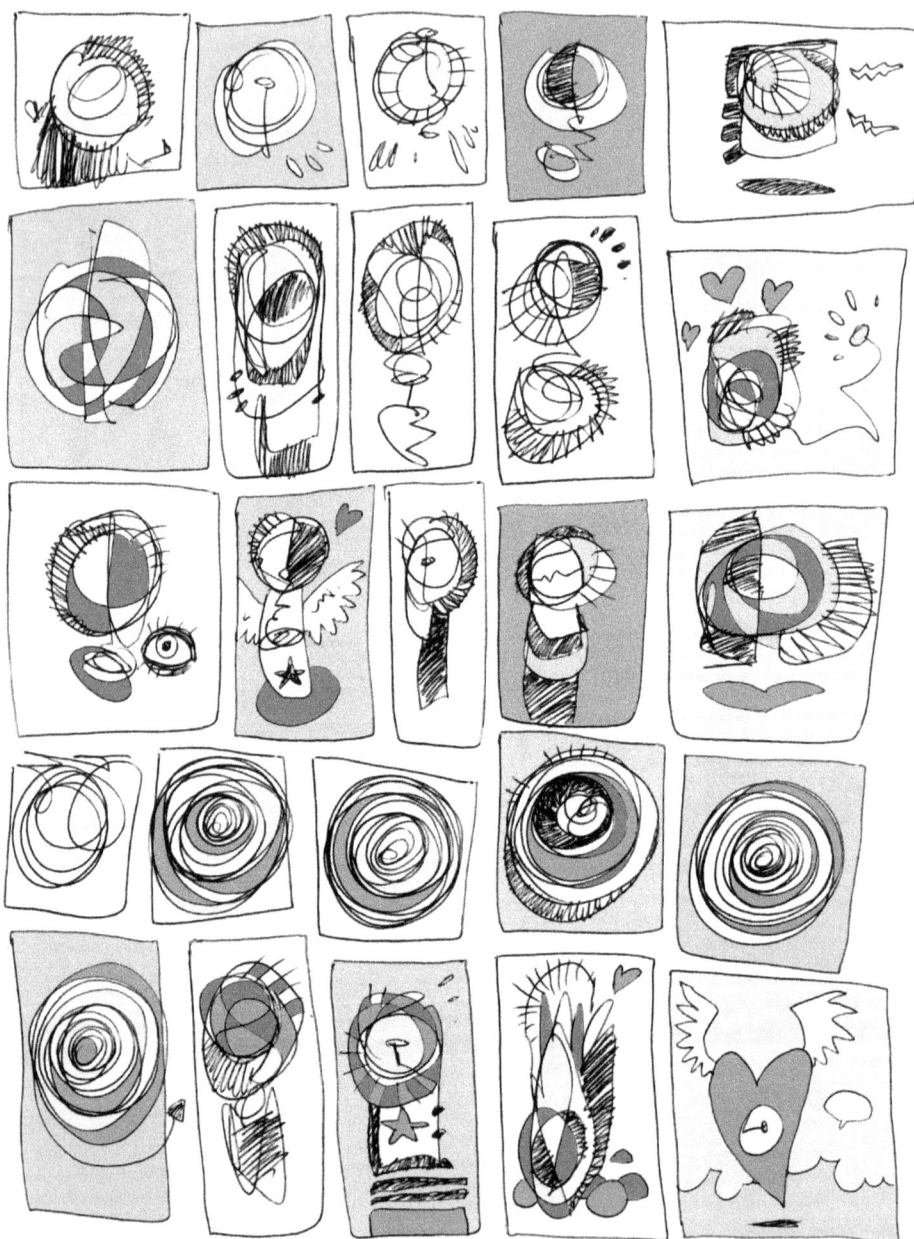

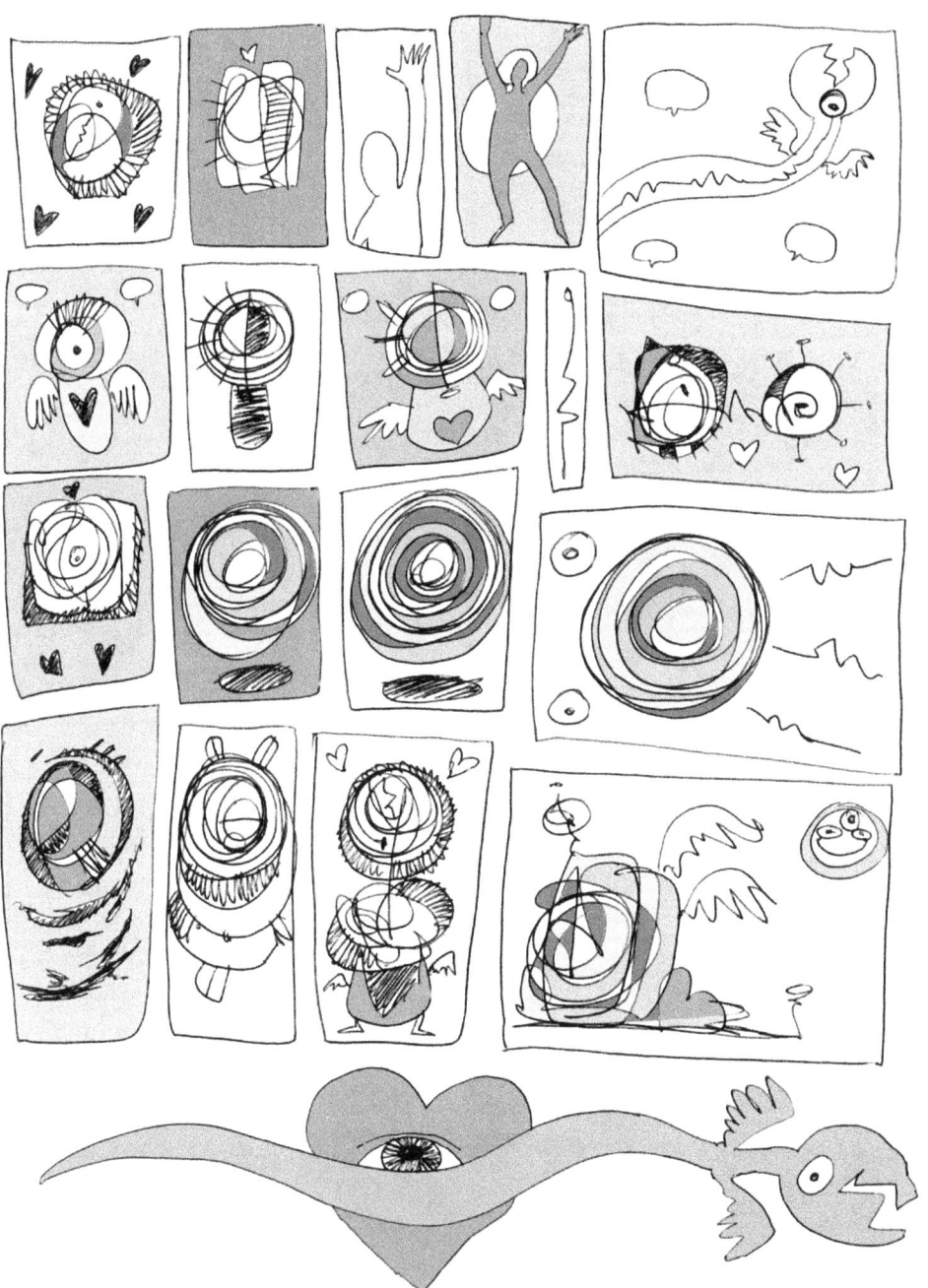

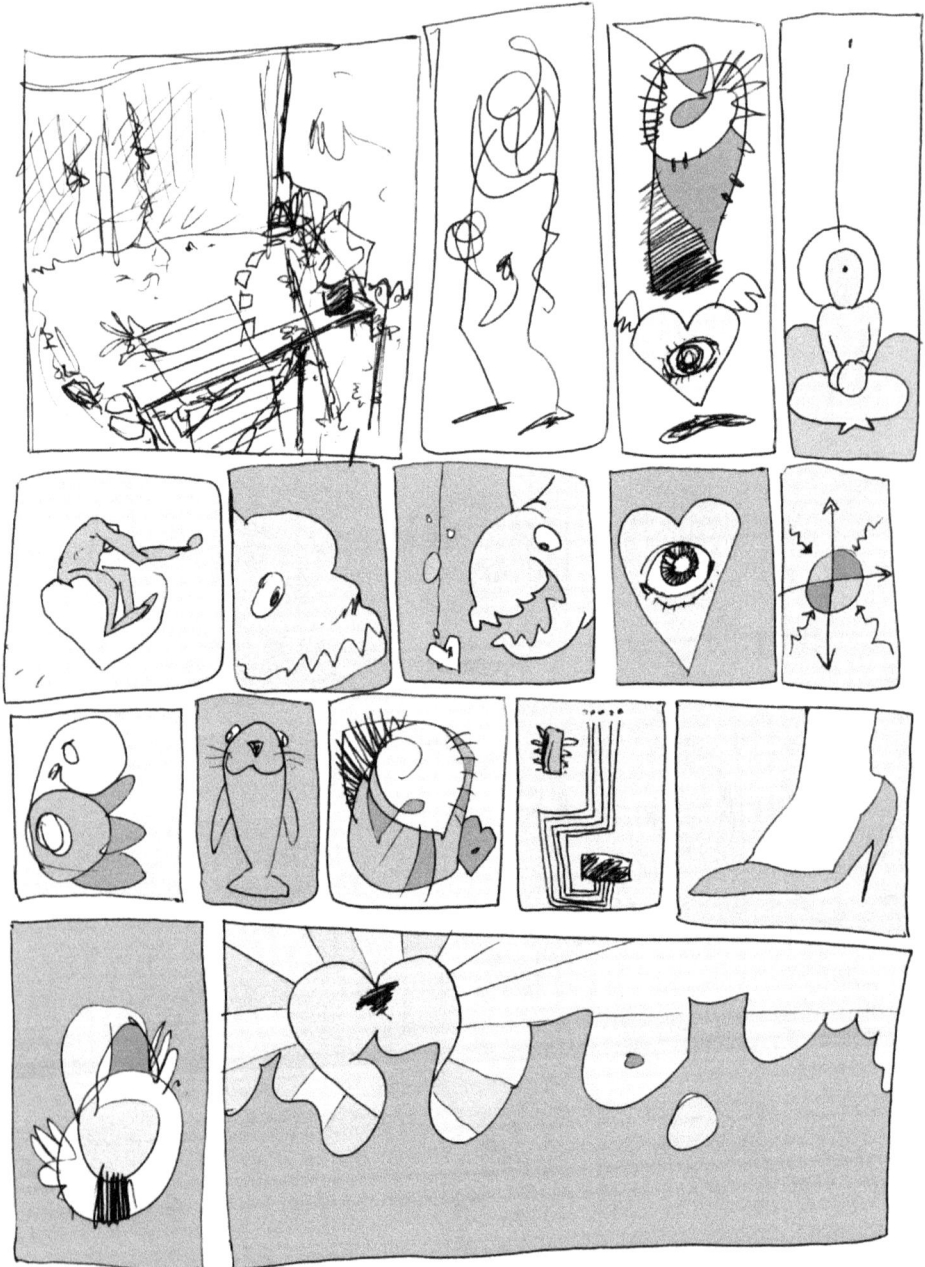

144

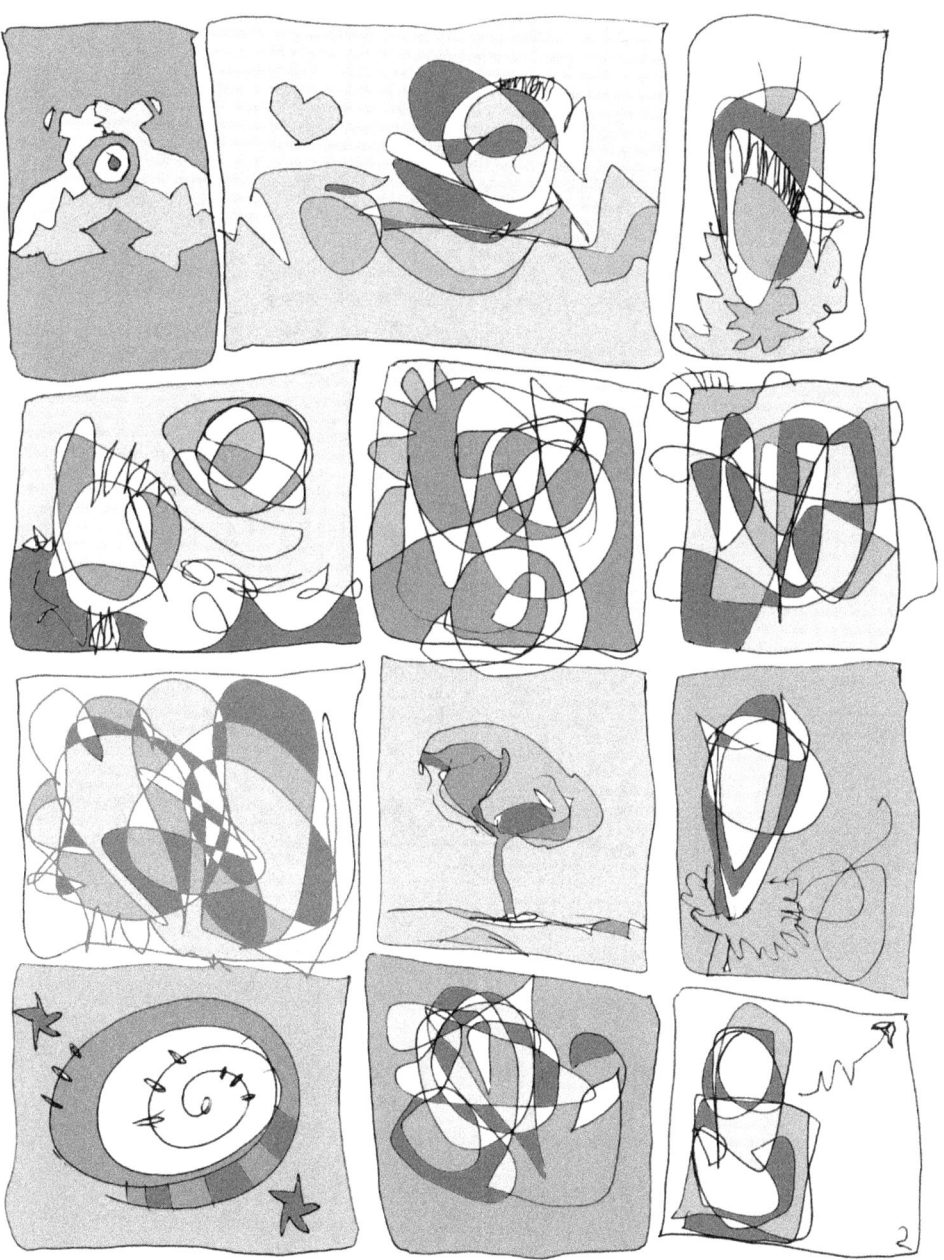

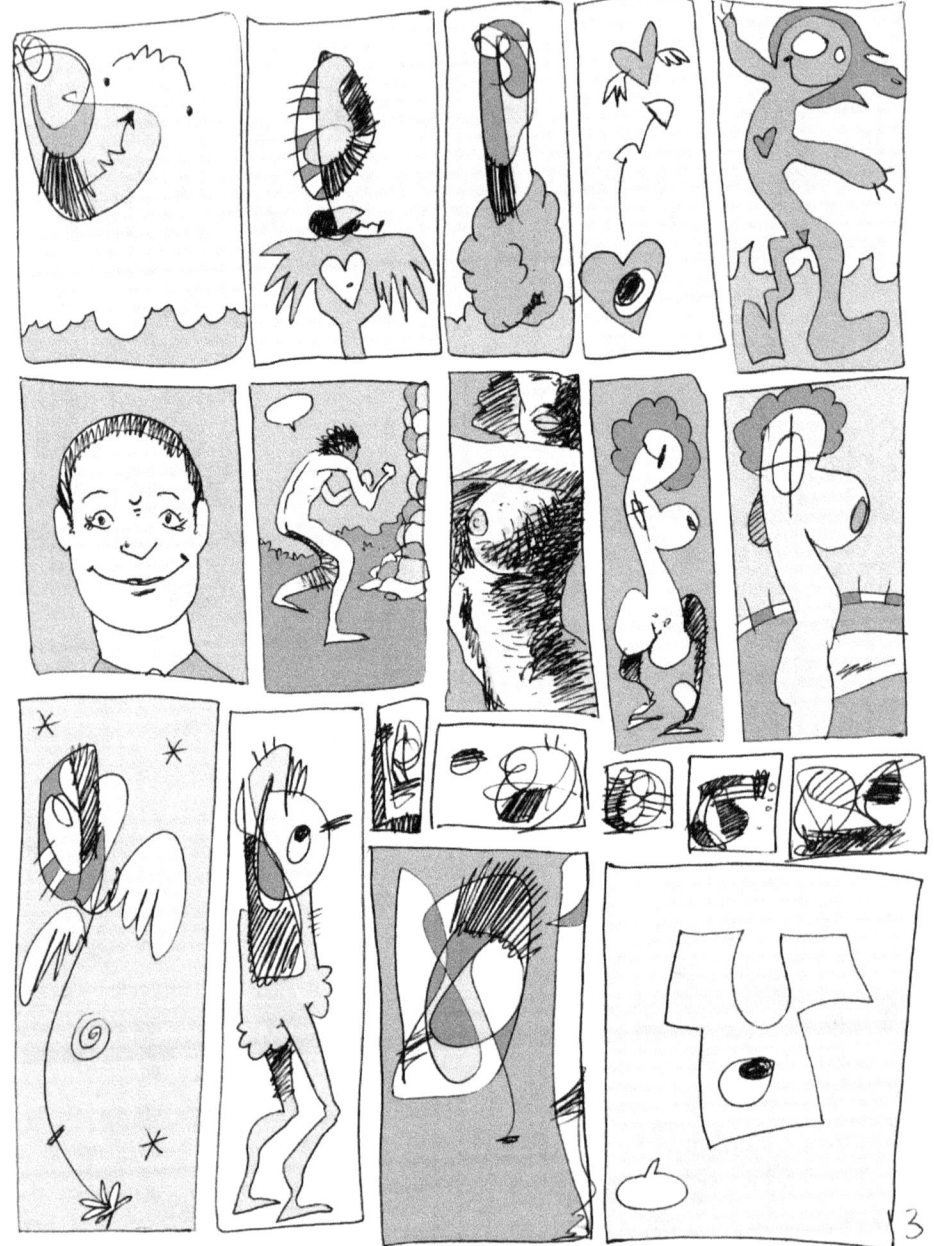

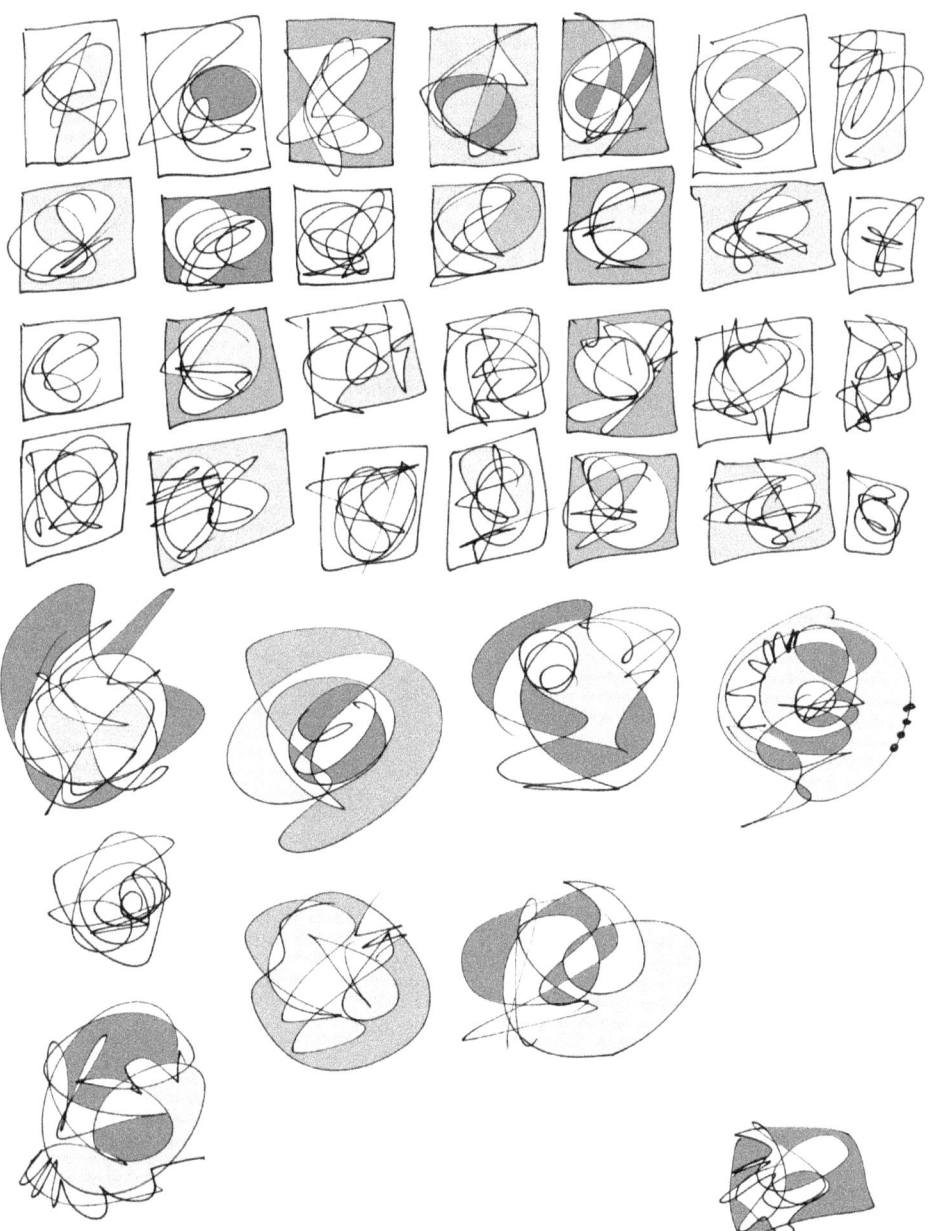

147

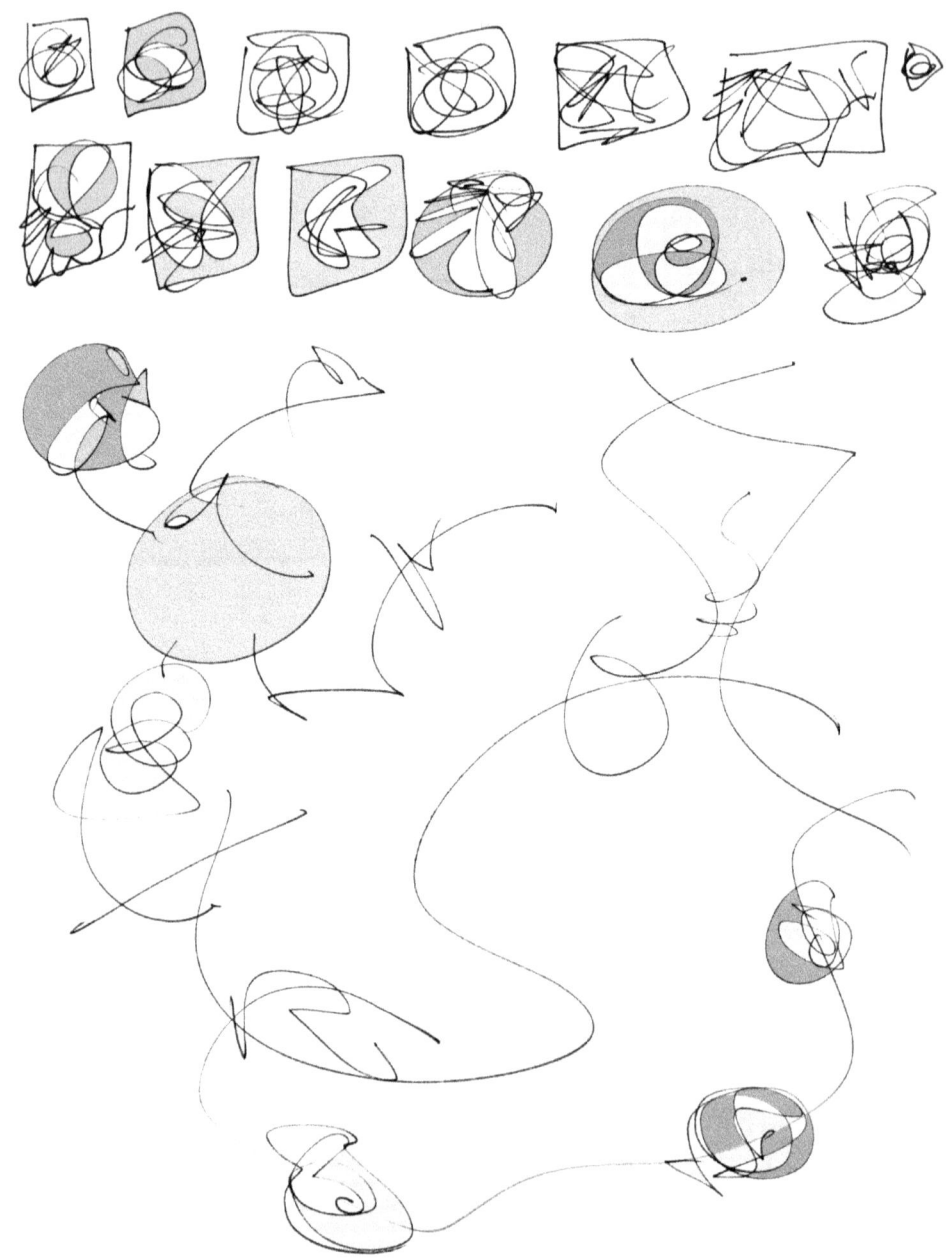

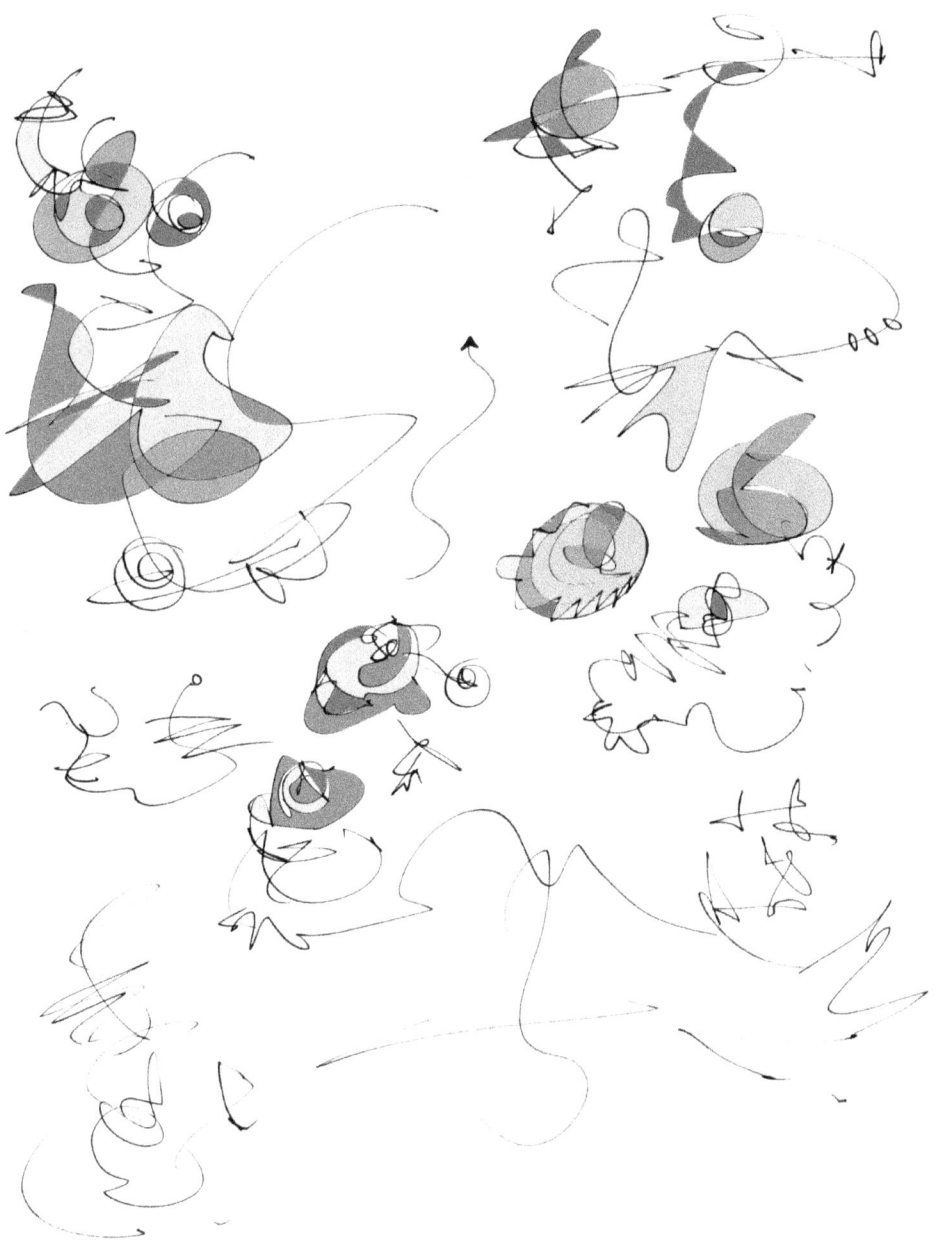

149

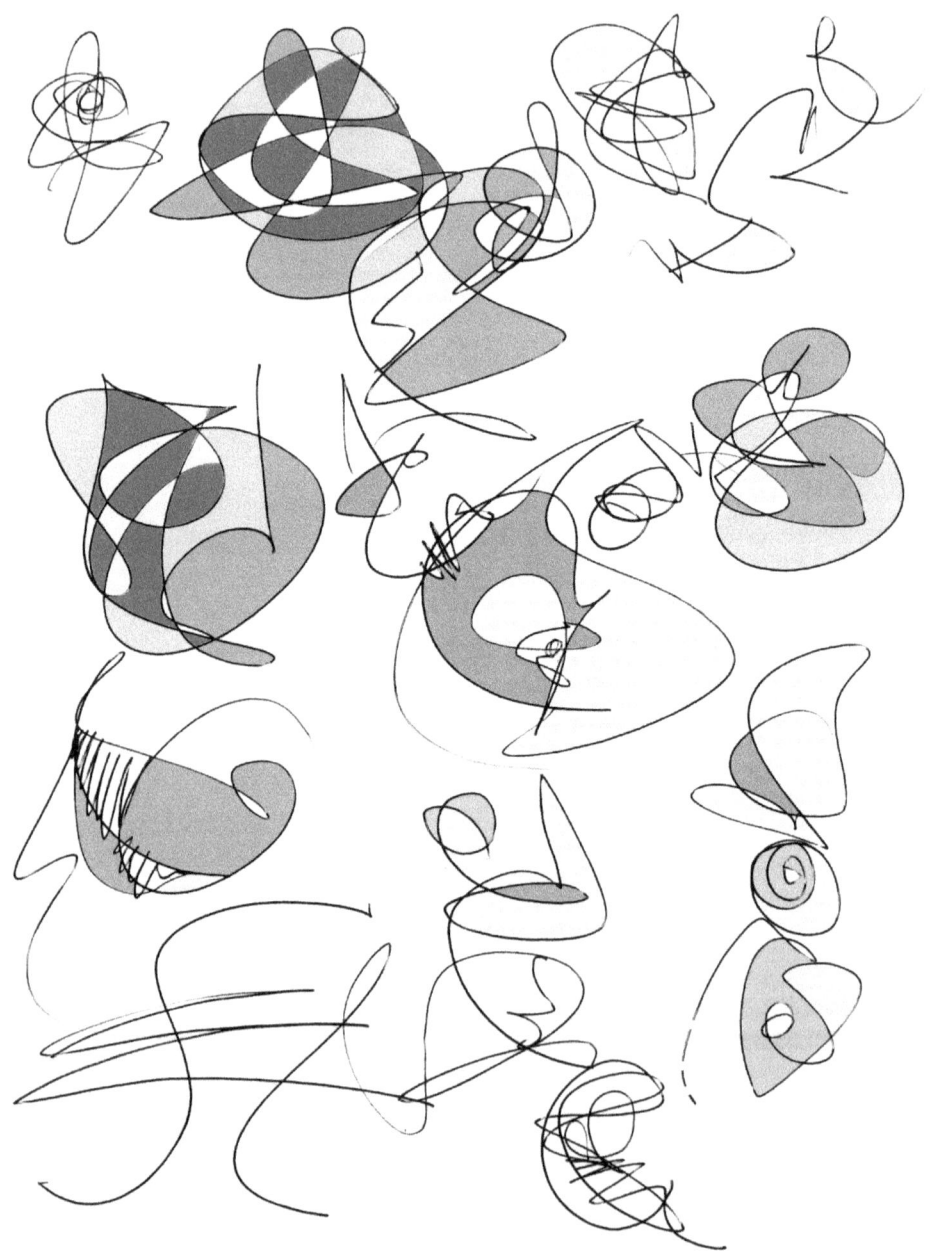

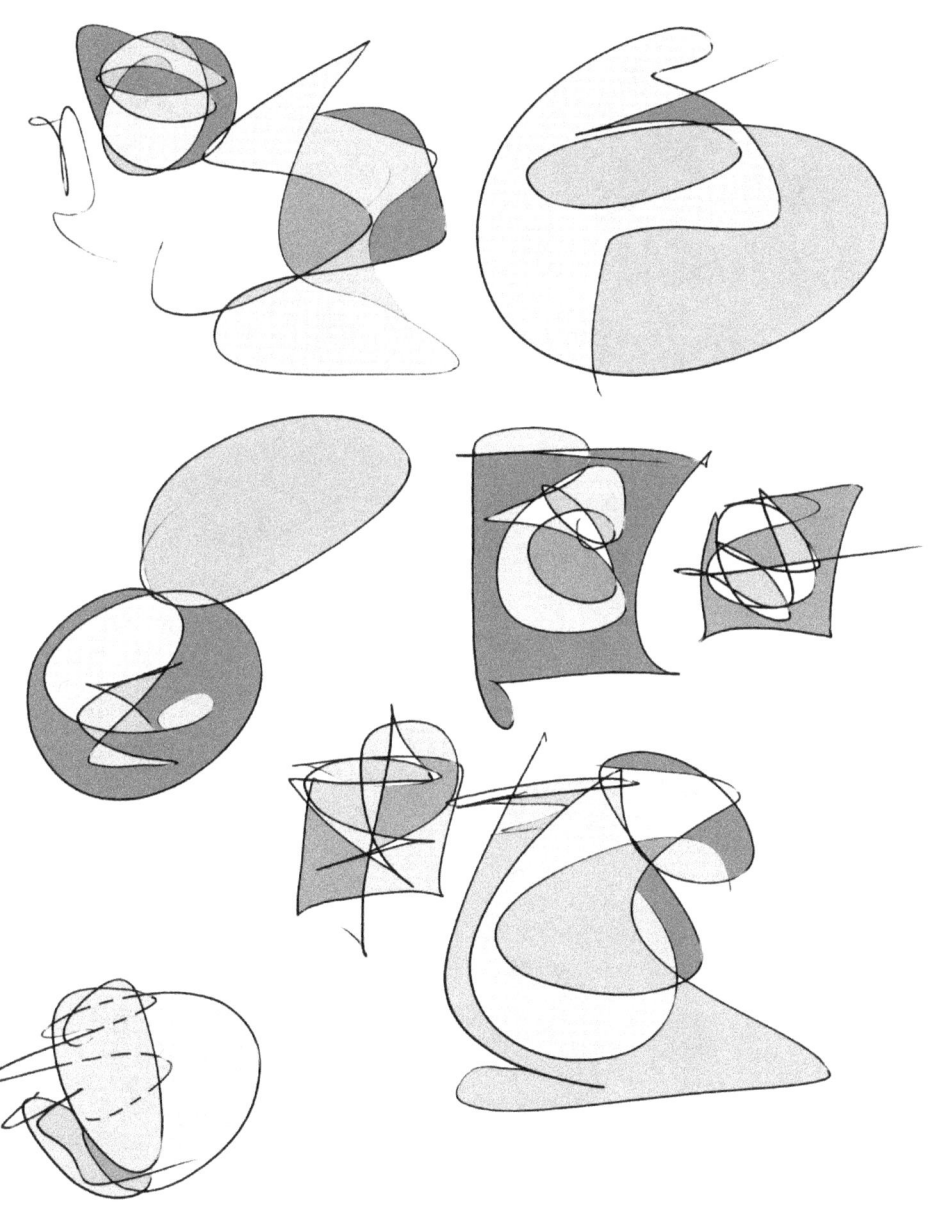

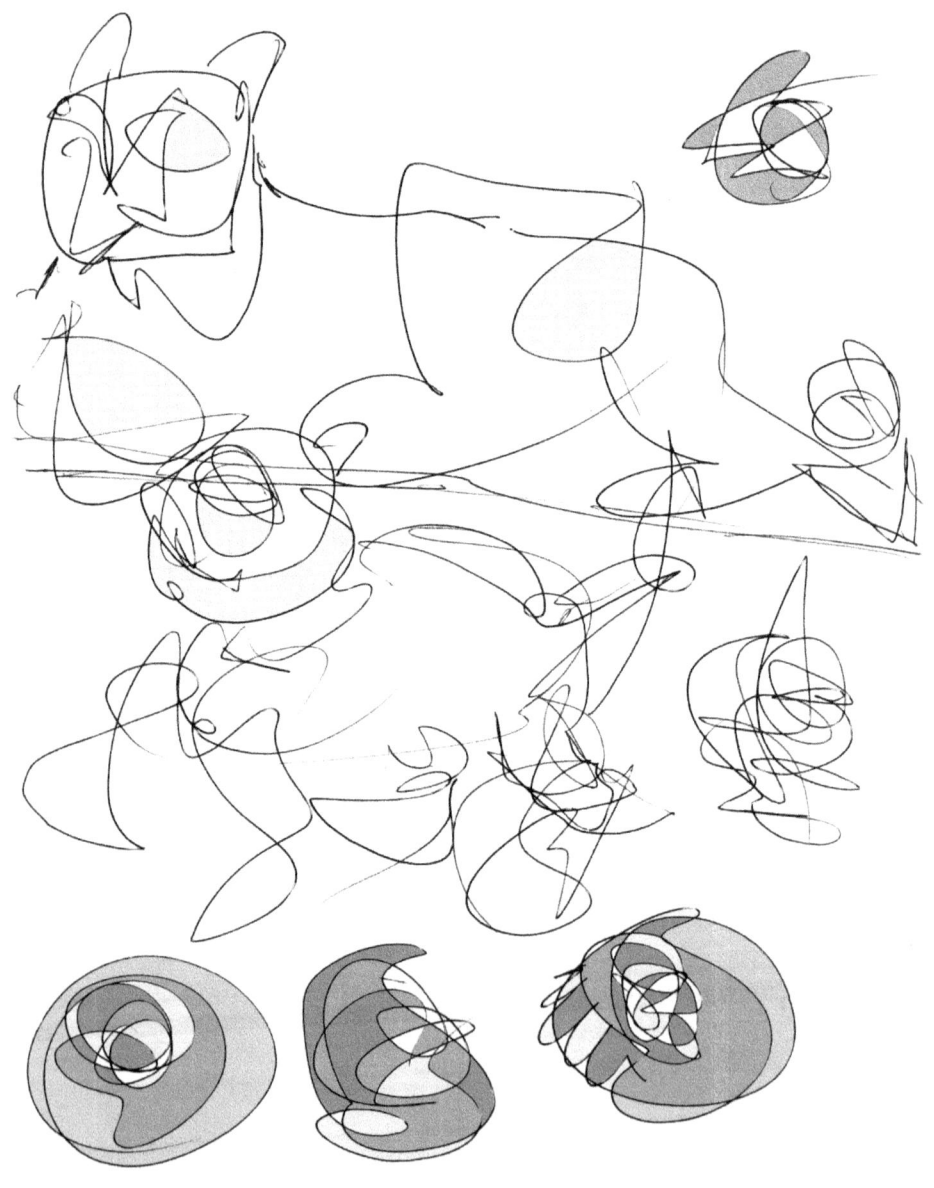

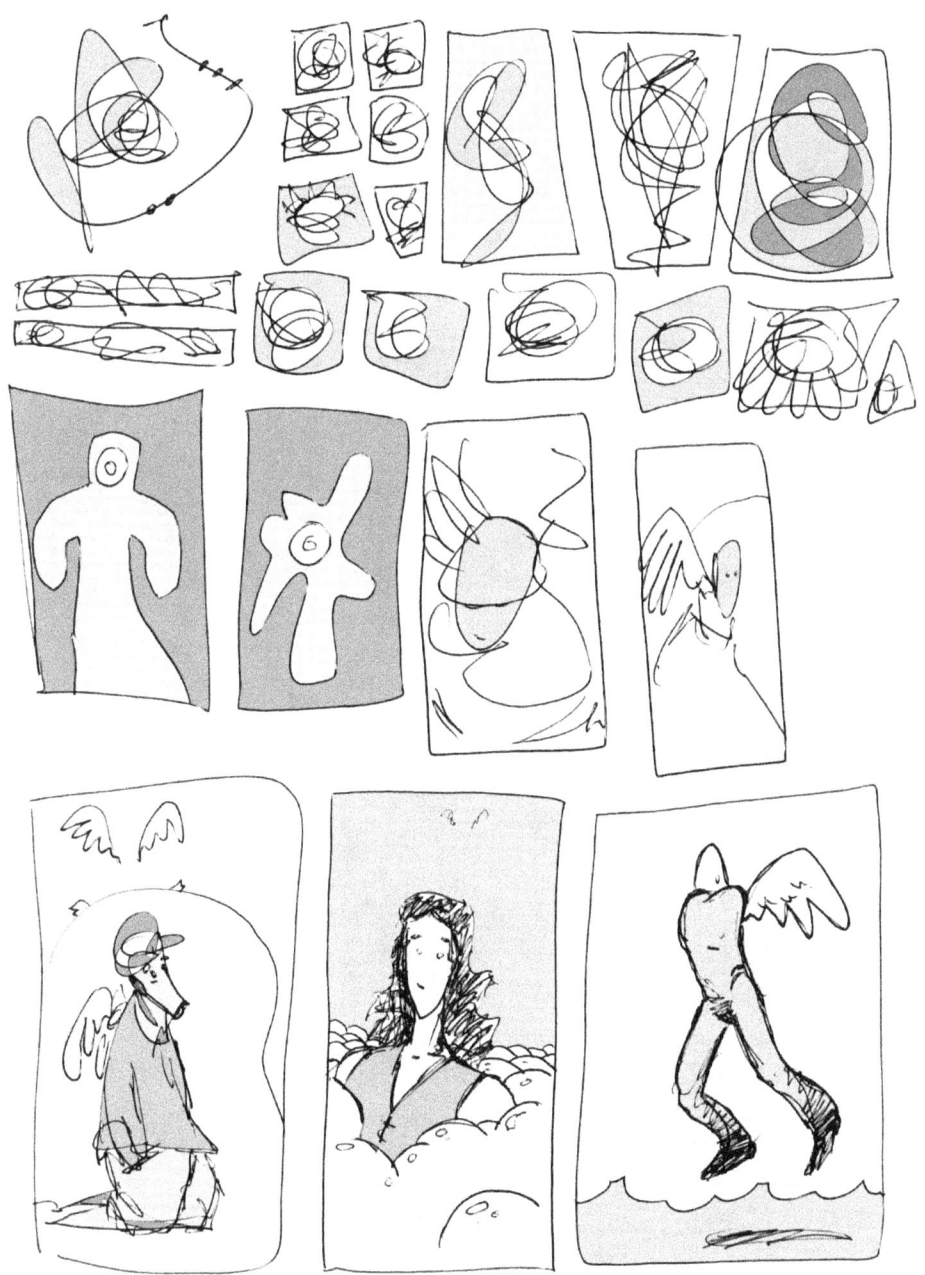

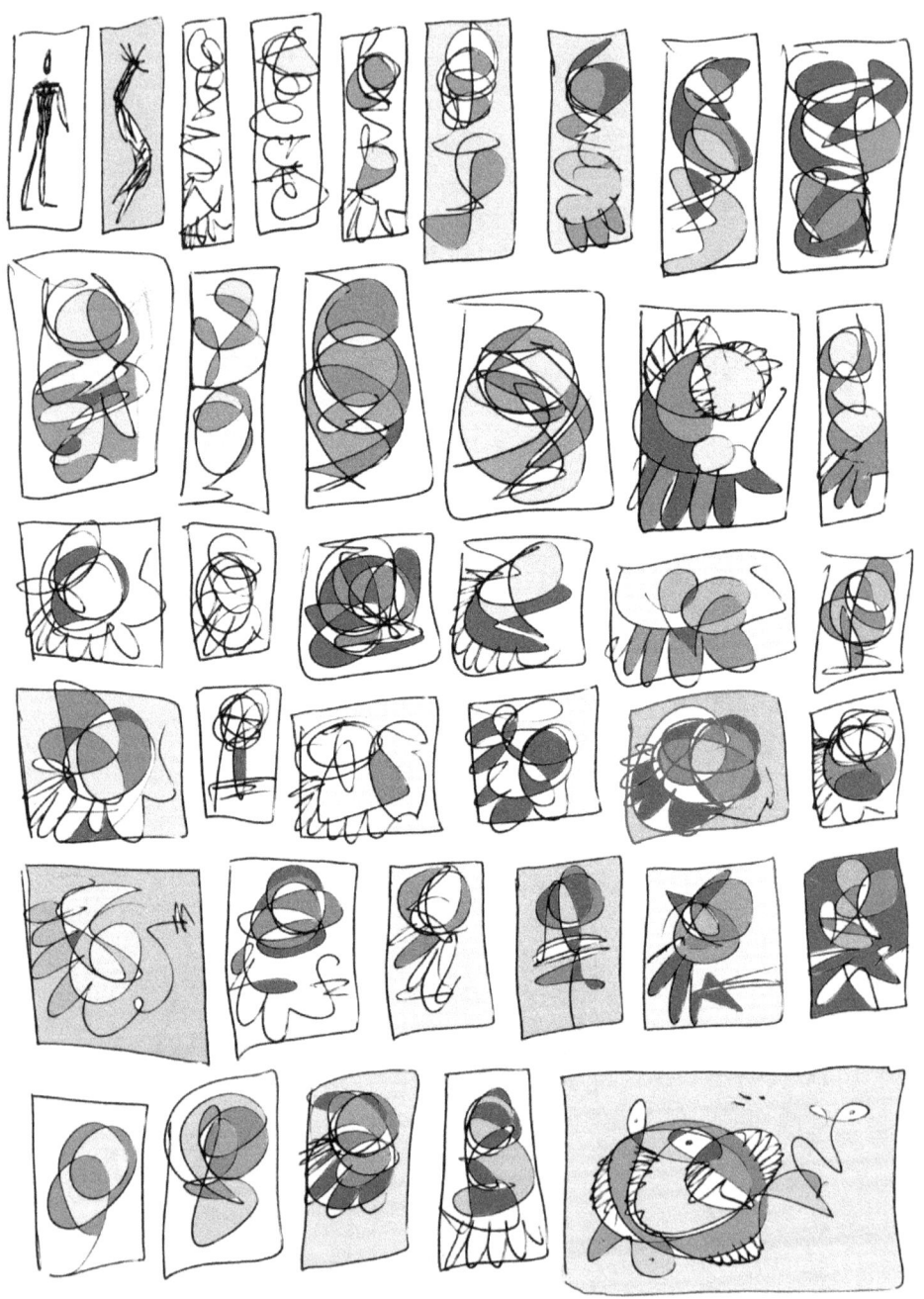

154

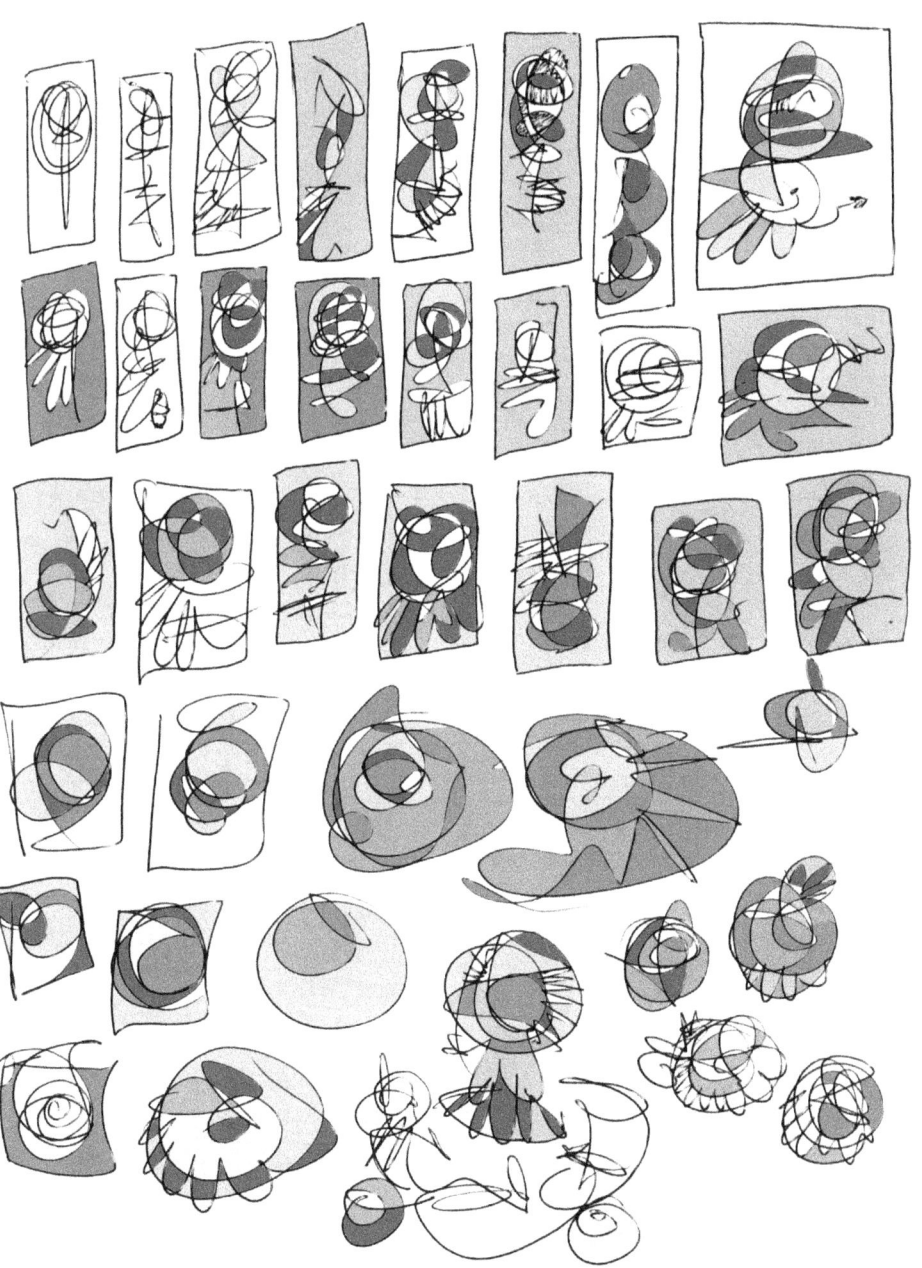

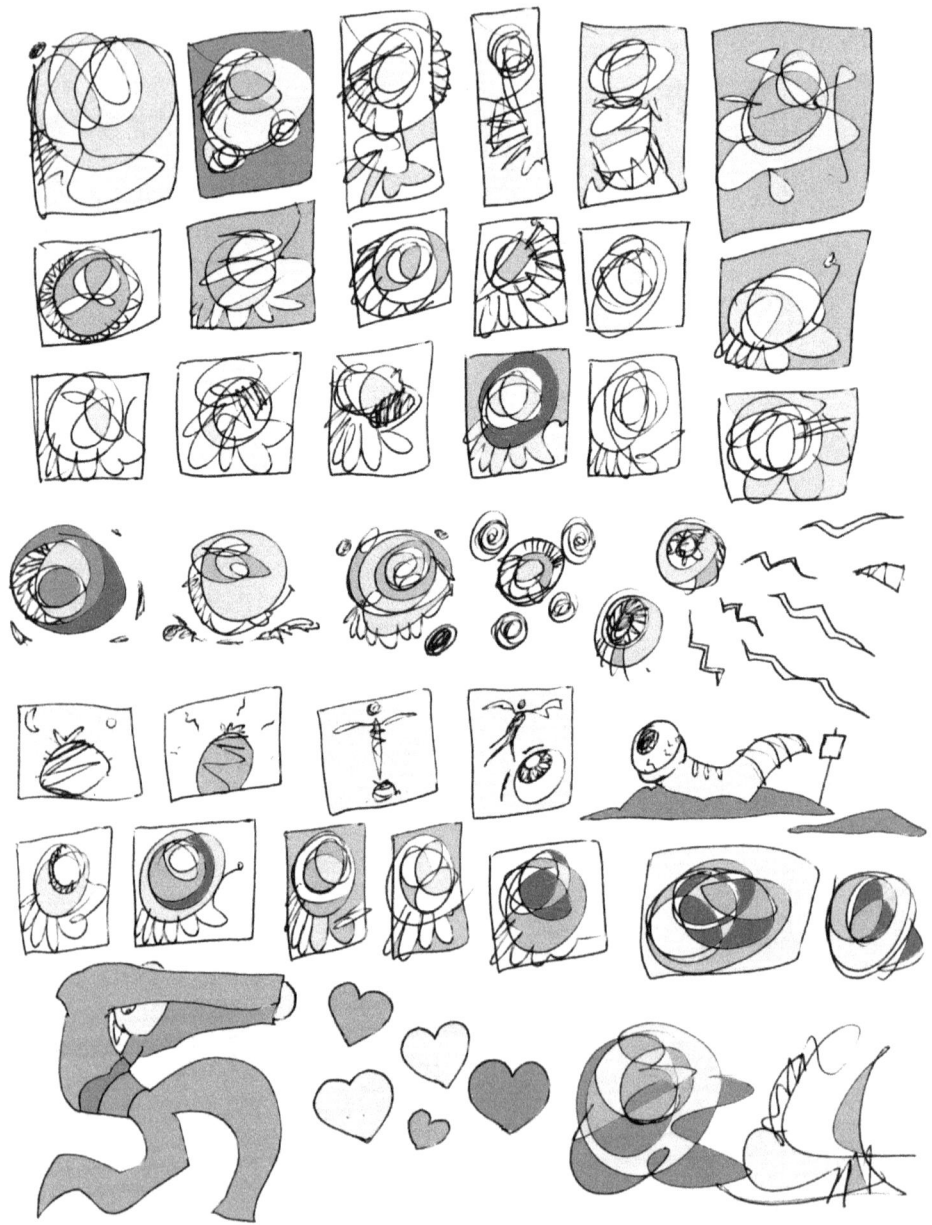

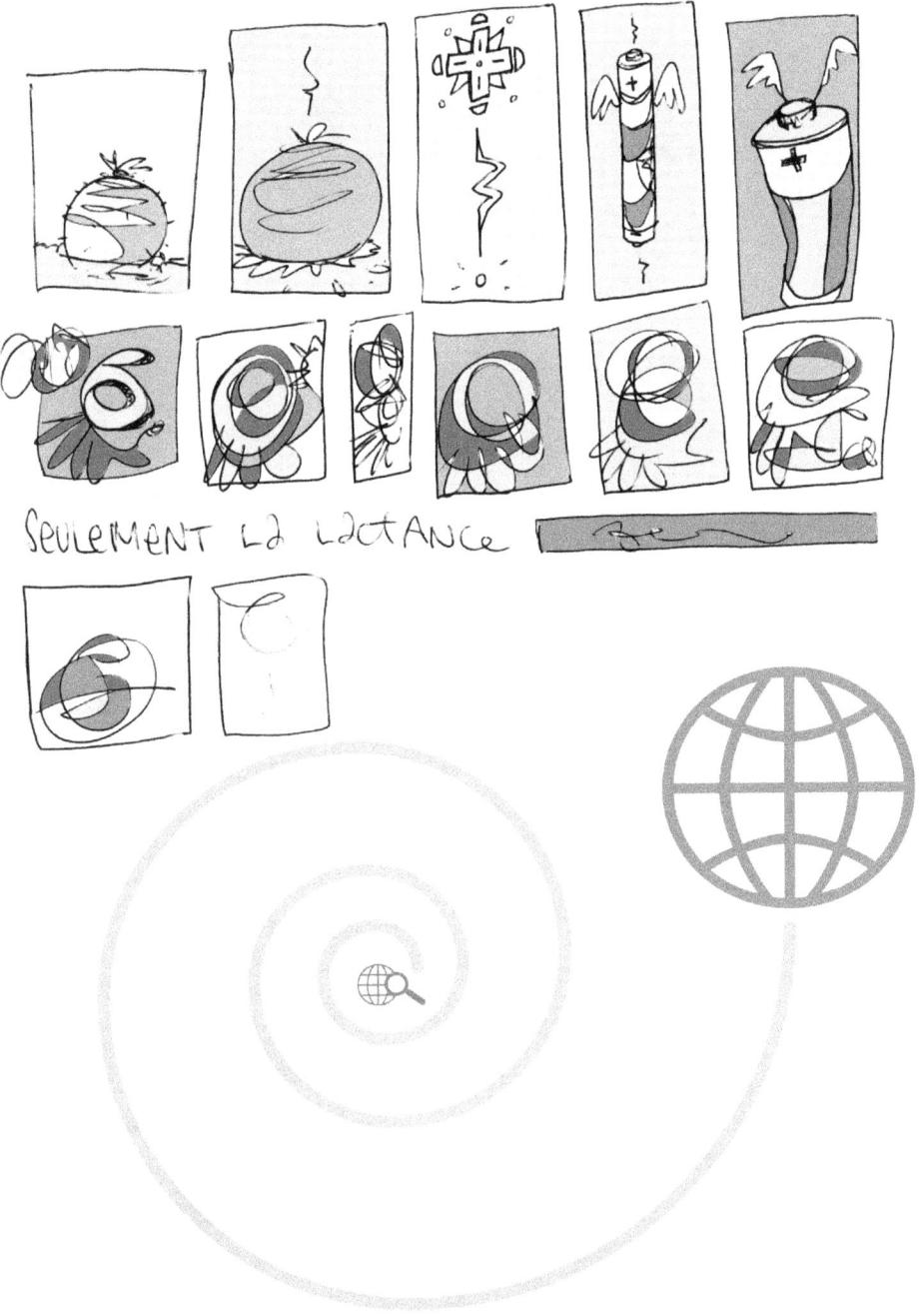

SEULEMENT L∂ L∂CT∂NCE

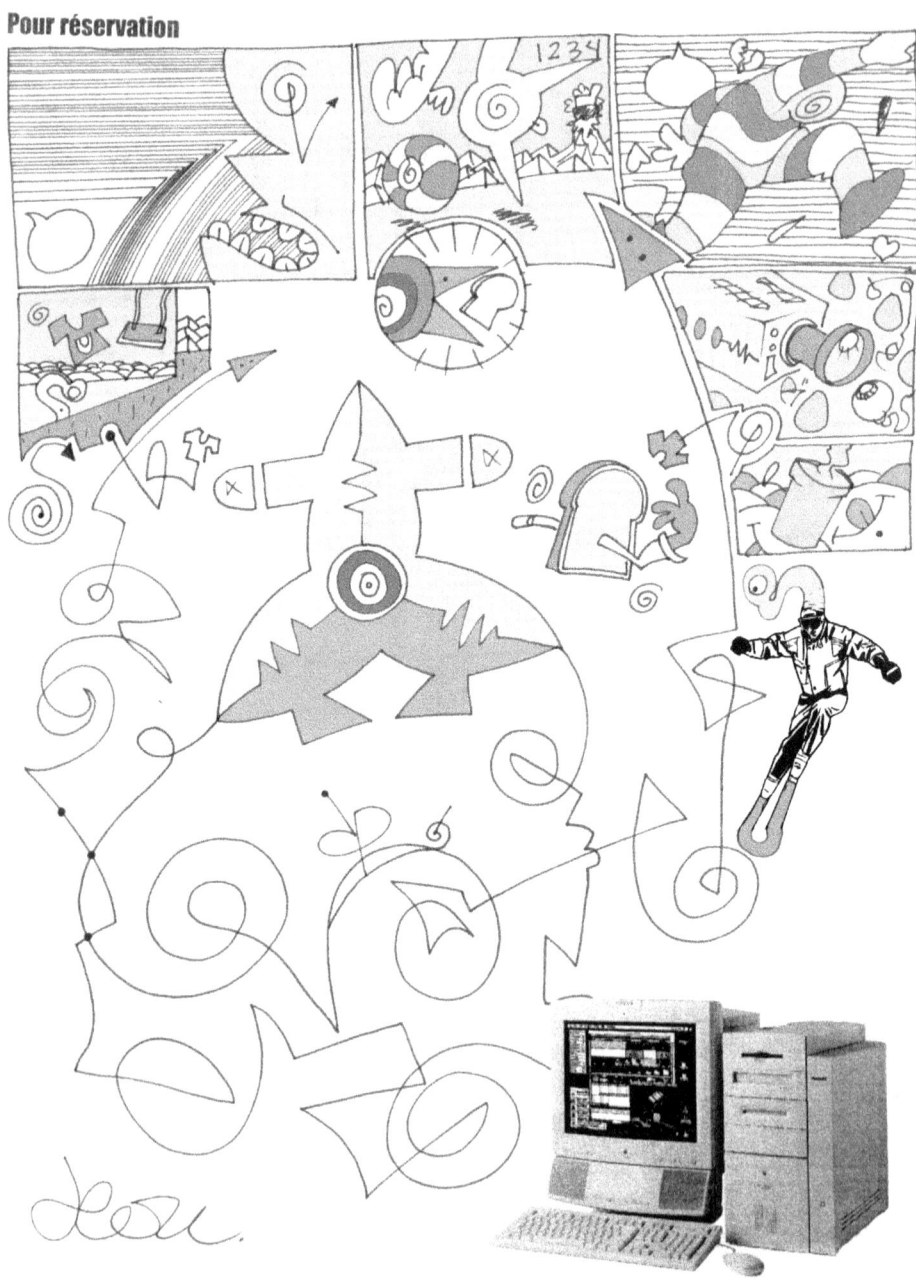

www.ingramcontent.com/pod-product-compliance
Lightning Source LLC
Chambersburg PA
CBHW072140170526
45158CB00004BA/1444